About Island Press

Since 1984, the nonprofit Island Press has been stimulating, shaping, and communicating the ideas that are essential for solving environmental problems worldwide. With more than 800 titles in print and some 40 new releases each year, we are the nation's leading publisher on environmental issues. We identify innovative thinkers and emerging trends in the environmental field. We work with world-renowned experts and authors to develop cross-disciplinary solutions to environmental challenges.

Island Press designs and implements coordinated book publication campaigns in order to communicate our critical messages in print, in person, and online using the latest technologies, programs, and the media. Our goal: to reach targeted audiences—scientists, policymakers, environmental advocates, the media, and concerned citizens—who can and will take action to protect the plants and animals that enrich our world, the ecosystems we need to survive, the water we drink, and the air we breathe.

Island Press gratefully acknowledges the support of its work by the Agua Fund, Inc., The Margaret A. Cargill Foundation, Betsy and Jesse Fink Foundation, The William and Flora Hewlett Foundation, The Kresge Foundation, The Forrest and Frances Lattner Foundation, The Andrew W. Mellon Foundation, The Curtis and Edith Munson Foundation, The Overbrook Foundation, The David and Lucile Packard Foundation, The Summit Foundation, Trust for Architectural Easements, The Winslow Foundation, and other generous donors.

The opinions expressed in this book are those of the author(s) and do not necessarily reflect the views of our donors.

The Hidden Potential of Sustainable Neighborhoods

The Hidden Potential of Sustainable Neighborhoods

Lessons from Low-Carbon Communities

By Harrison Fraker

● ISLANDPRESS Washington | Covelo | London

Library of Congress Cataloging-in-Publication Data

Fraker, Harrison.
 The hidden potential of sustainable neighborhoods : lessons from low-carbon communities / by Harrison Fraker.
   pages. cm
 Includes bibliographical references and index.
 ISBN 978-1-61091-407-9 (cloth : alk. paper)—ISBN 1-61091-407-4 (cloth : alk. paper)—ISBN 978-1-61091-408-6 (pbk. : alk. paper)—ISBN 1-61091-408-2 (pbk. : alk. paper) 1. City planning—Environmental aspects—Sweden—Case studies. 2. City planning—Environmental aspects—Germany—Case studies. 3. City planning—Environmental aspects—United States—Case studies. 4. Sustainable development—Sweden—Case studies. 5. Sustainable development—Germany—Case studies. 6. Sustainable development—United States—Case studies. I. Title.
 HT243.S8F73 2013
 307.1'216—dc23
                          2013005845

 Printed on recycled, acid-free paper

Manufactured in the United States of America
10 9 8 7 6 5 4 3 2 1

Keywords: Brownfield redevelopment; climate-responsive design; cogeneration; distributed energy system; green building; green infrastructure; infill development; LEED ND; low-carbon community; renewable energy; resilience; stormwater management; urban green space; West Village, Davis, California; whole-systems thinking

This book honors "the presence of absence," the almost daily inspiration of those I have lost: my mother, Marjorie Tomlinson Fraker; my daughter, Alison Gwen Fraker; my sister, Wenda Warren Fraker; and my brother, Howard Hopkins Fraker. It is also dedicated to the presence of those who sustain me: my extended family—sons, daughter, brothers, nephews and nieces and grandchildren, but most especially my wife, Molly, for enabling me to lead my singular and privileged existence. Finally, to my ninety-five-year-old father, who at his age wants to know why it has taken so long.

Contents

Figures

Tables

Acknowledgments

This book grows out of a forty-five-year intellectual and design journey, beginning with a fascination with the way buildings interact with climate and expanding to cities and the urban landscape. It involves teachers, colleagues, students, and friends, too many to name, but important individuals and moments stand out. It begins with my discovery of urban design as a form of critical practice during a visiting fellowship at Cambridge University and inspirational exchanges with my master's thesis professor at Princeton University, Jean Labatut. It extends to the design and teaching encouragement given to me by Dean Robert L. Geddes, who hired me immediately off my thesis boards into his architectural practice and then, two years later, hired me as a teacher at Princeton. It includes my early teaching partner, Lance Brown, with whom a vibrant intellectual discourse continues to this day. On many levels it has been an effort to expand the formalism of my first teachers, Michael Graves and Peter Eisenman, by integrating concepts of climate-responsive building performance and questions of sustainability as part of the inspiration for a building's formal and spatial design performance.

These concerns were developed and honed during my "passive solar pioneer" years with my colleagues, competitors, and, ultimately, closest friends Doug Kelbaugh, Don Prowler, Peter Calthorpe, and David Sellers, along with my team at Princeton Energy Group, especially Lawrence Lindsey and Peter Brock.

It naturally expanded to cities and urban landscapes during my years in Minnesota in close collaboration with William Morrish and Catherine Brown, with whom I started the Design Center for the American Urban Landscape. The Center became a nexus for local communities to explore the potential role of the urban landscape and design in addressing their urban design challenges. The process used case studies and design charettes involving contributions from many faculty members and professionals, most notably Patrick Condon and Ken Greenberg.

Over the past seventeen years at the University of California, Berkeley, my work has evolved into an interdisciplinary, integrated, whole-systems design approach for creating more sustainable, low-carbon cities. It has emerged through seminars, workshops and interdisciplinary "capstone" studios, research, and teaching with Dan Solomon, Donlyn Lyndon, Robert Cervero, Elizabeth Deakin, Louise Mozingo, and Gail Brager. Their ideas, imagination, support, and inspiration have been essential in the process.

The idea that a neighborhood could become 100 percent renewable and low- to no-carbon in its energy operation by using a combination of energy efficiency to lower demand and energy supply from local solar, wind, and waste-to-energy systems first emerged in a capstone studio titled "Principles and Prototypes for Transit-Oriented Development," held in Tianjin, China. It evolved into the EcoBlock concept for Qingdao, China, with funding from the Gordon and Betty Moore Foundation enabling a cost and engineering feasibility study with Jean Rogers of ARUP, who became an incomparable collaborator and supporter. It is now being applied to the design of a new zero-carbon campus for Tianjin University with the campus master planner, Leon Huang of Hua Hui Design, who is one of the original collaborators on the EcoBlock concept.

Delays in developing the EcoBlock in China led to the idea for this book, which has evolved over the past four years with the involvement of many Berkeley students in the process of drawing, graphics, research, and analysis. I would like to acknowledge the valuable contributions of Natalia Echeverri, Hazel Onsrud, Jessica Yang, Nancy Nam, Deepak Sohane, Mahammad Momin, Brian Chambers, Ariel Utz, and Mael Castellan. Assistance in overcoming my typing shortcomings has come from family friends Amelia and Susanna Starr, with help from my son Will.

Finally, Heather Boyer at Island Press deserves much credit for her patience, wisdom, and insights and her perseverance in seeing me through the process and helping me overcome the inevitable conflicts in trying to reconcile my writing and design imaginations.

1. Introduction

In our media-saturated culture it can be argued that, until recently, the threat of climate change seems to have been overexposed. People have been numbed by the repetition of potential threats that seem complex, distant, and hard to personalize. All of this is changing as people experience the devastation of extreme weather events, especially with the impacts of Hurricane Sandy and the hundred-year droughts in the Midwest. Climate change is no longer about reports of the Intergovernmental Panel on Climate Change or the efficacy of climate science. Its consequences are real and palpable. As a result, there is a renewed sense of urgency about how to respond and an opportunity, however brief, to ask fundamental questions about business as usual in the way we build, operate, and maintain our cities. How well can cities defend against and recover from severe climate disruptions?

Figure 1.1. Lower Manhattan blackout caused by Hurricane Sandy. *(Photograph by Reeve Jolliffe / Gas Tower Studio.)*

There is a general agreement that mitigation—reduction of our carbon dioxide (CO_2) emissions—alone will not solve the problem, that we will have to pursue a dual strategy of both mitigation and adaptation. We will have to defend our cities against both sea level rise and the consequences of more frequent and severe storms, droughts, and heat waves. This raises fundamental questions about the basic principles and assumptions of our current aging infrastructure. It raises broad, complex, and daunting questions about how we can create more resilient communities that encompass all the dimensions of city building. Given this moment of opportunity, the problem demands that we act with greater urgency, that we question our current modes of thinking and development practices. There have been many ideas for creating greater resilience in the post–Hurricane Sandy New York region—from floodgates to more pervious infrastructure. Robert Yaro, president of the Regional Plan Association, states:

> There are many steps that the region should consider to help reduce damage from the inevitable storms in our future, from physically protecting urban shorelines to rethinking our transit and power networks so that localized outages don't cripple an entire city or region. In all likelihood, we will need to adopt both "hard" infrastructure changes and "soft" solutions that rely on better land-use decisions and tap ecological systems to limit damage.[1]

In the past, efforts at climate mitigation have focused primarily on the building scale (low- to zero-energy buildings) and the large utility scale (solar and wind farms in remote locations). While there has been great progress in the energy efficiency of buildings over the past forty years, buildings alone do not include the transportation and infrastructure systems (energy, water, and waste) as part of the design process, and large renewables in remote locations rely on long, inefficient, and vulnerable power lines. Increasingly, the neighborhood scale (from city block to district) is being recognized as an opportunity because it aggregates all the systems and flows. It has the potential to integrate the design of transportation, buildings, and infrastructure while engaging the design of the public realm as part of the system. It also has the potential to become its own micro-utility. These potentials have been recognized in part by the creation of the Leadership in Energy and Environmental Design for Neighborhood Development (LEED-ND) rating system. The whole-systems opportunities are part of architect Peter Calthorpe's argument that "responding to climate change and our coming energy challenge without a more sustainable form of urbanism will be impossible."[2]

If neighborhoods can become their own micro-utilities, supplying most if not all of their energy while recycling their water and waste, this represents a whole-systems approach, which is much more resilient. As a micro-utility, each neighborhood can continue to operate if the central infrastructure goes down. As an added benefit, development can take place incrementally without adding significantly to existing infrastructure loads. The case studies presented in this book are the first efforts at this kind of whole-systems thinking, and the lessons learned point to a new way of doing business.

The case studies also show that to truly drive change, resilient communities need to be places where people want to live and places that are accessible to all. At various scales, a compelling design that makes the environmental benefits clear has been proven to be critical in gaining support and investment. Paradoxically, who would imagine that this point would be made clear in a car advertisement? Yet consider the opening lines of this advertisement for the Chrysler 300: "If you want to make a fuel-efficient car, the first thing you have to do is design a car that is worth making."

The message is clear. Fuel efficiency alone is not enough. You have to provide the "styling," quality, luxury, and identity that people want, with fuel efficiency an expected side benefit. The advertisement ends with the Chrysler 300 pulling into the driveway of Frank Lloyd Wright's beautifully restored Gregor S. and Elizabeth B. Affleck House, reinforcing the message that design matters. Americans can now have it both ways—fuel efficiency with hip design, "imported from Detroit"!

The advertisement is Detroit's response to the Toyota Prius, arguably one of the most innovative and energy-efficient ventures into the car market— and, for many, one of the ugly ducklings. Beyond the technological wizardry of its hybrid gas and electric power drive and the energy recovery of its flywheel braking system, the more profound innovation is its real-time feedback on the energy performance (in miles per gallon) of driver behavior. The real-time feedback allows us to play the game (*Homo ludens*)[3] "How efficient can we get?," and we love to beat the system. Surprisingly, in designing hip neighborhoods with low- to no-carbon performance, both technical wizardry and user engagement in the process—"the game"—are essential.

This book explores the best practices of first-generation efforts to create low-carbon neighborhoods. It demonstrates the value of system design at the neighborhood scale. Most important, it points to how to achieve a more distributed and resilient infrastructure. It also shows that "human agency," the involvement of the residents in the process, is essential in achieving the goals. All of the systems and benefits are not just technological. In fact, many of the "green," sustainable strategies are out in the open, enhancing the richness and experience of people's everyday lives. It is these cobenefits, many related to health and well-being, that help to create the distinguishing design identity of the neighborhoods that residents desire. The strategies point to a greatly expanded role of the public space in cities—not only to provide the space for public activities but also to play a part in the whole-systems design of infrastructure. The book focuses on a select group of existing first-generation neighborhoods that have attempted to make this final step to sustainability: in Sweden, Bo01 in Malmö and Hammarby Sjöstad in Stockholm, and in Germany, Kronsberg in Hannover and Vauban in Freiberg. Each case-study chapter looks at the planning process, transport, urban form, green space, energy (consumption, generation, and distribution), water, waste, and social issues. The case studies are followed by a chapter that compares the four neighborhoods, and then a significant chapter looks at the lessons learned for the United States, focusing on opportunities for infilling or retrofitting existing areas. The paradox of the US city-building process, especially as it relates to suburban sprawl, is that the resulting pockets of abandonment and underdevelopment are now potential opportunities for sustainable neighborhood development, both within the core cities and in the multiple phases of suburban sprawl. Three of the four case studies seized this opportunity (Bo01, abandoned shipbuilding and manufacturing; Hammarby Sjöstad, obsolete industrial manufacturing site; Vauban, former military barracks), and similar conditions exist throughout the United States.

Why Bo01 and Hammarby Sjöstad (Sweden), Kronsberg and Vauban (Germany)

The case for studying low-carbon neighborhoods first emerged for me in 2006 while I was conducting a graduate interdisciplinary studio at the University of California, Berkeley, on transit-oriented neighborhoods for Tianjin, China.[4] We discovered not only that compact, high-density, mixed-use, walkable neighborhoods around transit stops could dramatically reduce the need for and use of the car but also that they could become zero carbon in operation through the application of energy-efficient design strategies to reduce demand combined with renewable energy supply from local wind, solar photovoltaics, and, surprisingly, capture of energy from the waste streams. This discovery led to the development of the EcoBlock concept in collaboration with the San Francisco engineering firm ARUP.[5] Its principles and strategies are currently being applied in the development of a new zero-carbon green campus design for Tianjin University, the first in the world. During the evolution of the EcoBlock concept, the question occurred as to whether a similar kind of integrated, whole-systems approach to neighborhood design had been attempted elsewhere in the world, and if so, whether there were any performance data. Fortunately, during this same period I was able to take a yearlong sabbatical and decided to conduct a global search to discover any precedents and best practices of whole-systems thinking at the neighborhood scale similar to the EcoBlock concept. Not surprisingly, very few have been built and performance data have been collected for even fewer; nonetheless, there have been enough to inspire a comparative analysis of the four case studies chosen.

In conducting my search, I established a simple set of criteria related to sustainability. It seemed that each neighborhood should be large enough, at least 1,000 units, to generate sufficient flows of energy, water, and waste to enable potential borrowing, balancing, and stealing among systems; that each should be mixed-use with at least a 30 percent jobs-to-housing balance within a reasonable walking or biking distance; that each should have a convenient public transit system with good and frequent connections to jobs and services; and that each should have set aggressive goals for energy and water conservation with equally aggressive goals for recycling and waste treatment. In addition, I was looking for neighborhoods that integrated into their planning process goals for generating most or part of their energy from local renewables. But most important, I was looking for neighborhoods that had been in existence (in whole or part) long enough for performance data to have been collected.

While specific criteria related to sustainability were critical, I was searching equally for projects with clear ambitions about a high-quality built environment for the residents—where the urban design, the architecture, the landscape, and the design of the public realm were as important as the goals for sustainability. In other words, I was looking for projects that demonstrated an integrated approach to urban design and sustainability, ones in which sustainability was not the only goal. I was curious whether there were any conflicts between the two, and if so, what trade-offs were made and whether they affected performance.

These criteria quickly eliminated several smaller iconic projects, such as London's one-hundred-unit Beddington Zero Energy Development (BedZED), even though it has one of the most innovative whole-systems approaches in both urban design and sustainable systems. The criteria also eliminated some of the newer projects, such as the Greenwich Millennium Village, in London, and Sarriguren, outside of Pamplona, Spain, for lack of performance data. Ørestad, on the southwest edge of Copenhagen, has excellent subway and rail access to both the downtown and the international airport, but so far it is composed of large "object" buildings on big blocks with limited entrances and street access. The result is high-style signature buildings with a bland and sterile pedestrian environment, in surprising contrast to the vibrant pedestrian environment of Copenhagen. Furthermore, beyond its medium-density, transit-oriented development, no other integrated energy, water, or waste strategies for sustainability are evident at the neighborhood scale.

In looking carefully at all five continents, I discovered that there were dozens of projects in the planning and development phases (witness the sixteen founding projects chosen for the William J. Clinton Foundation's Climate Positive Development Program),[6] but only a handful had been built and occupied long enough to have performance data. The lack of models that accomplish this was highlighted by Lord Nicholas Stern at the closing of the Copenhagen Climate Change Conference in 2009. In response to a question about the impediments to achieving a lower-carbon future, Lord Stern commented that beyond the economic, legal, and social inertia in our current development practices, we just do not have good alternative models with known performance.[7]

At first, I thought a survey of all eight projects—BedZED, Greenwich Millennium Village, Sarriguren, Ørestad, Bo01, Hammarby Sjöstad, Kronsberg, and Vauban—would be the most useful, but after further investigation I decided that a detailed comparison of the best four would be even more instructive and would provide a more precise set of lessons learned. Using my selection criteria and the desire to choose only the best practices, I quickly zeroed in on the latter four projects, which are covered on the following pages.

Beyond meeting the basic selection criteria, Bo01, Hammarby Sjöstad, Kronsberg, and Vauban together demonstrate the four possible strategies for generating energy from local renewables—wind, solar, geothermal, and waste—each with a different emphasis and combination. They represent the first integrated "wizardry under the hood." Bo01 uses local wind generation to power a geothermal ground- and ocean water heat pump for heating and cooling. Hammarby Sjöstad has three different waste-to-energy systems: the first burns combustible garbage to power a local district heating and electric cogeneration plant, the second recovers heat from the sewage treatment system, and the third converts sludge to biogas for cooking (1,000 units) and to power local buses. Kronsberg has two large-scale wind machines (3.2 megawatts) that generate 50 percent of its electricity; a gas-fired heating and electric cogeneration plant provides the other 50 percent. Vauban has a local heating and electric cogeneration plant powered by waste wood chips from the city. It also has a section that demonstrates the most successful solar strategies, combining a model passive solar direct gain system for heating and a rooftop photovoltaic array for electricity, delivering an additional 15 percent energy back to the city.

All four neighborhoods demonstrate good energy conservation standards, with Kronsberg and Vauban having sections that meet the very aggressive "passive house" standard of 15 kilowatt-hours per square meter per year ($kWh/m^2/y$) for heating. Together, the neighborhoods have employed all types of solar collection. Bo01 uses evacuated tube collectors to assist the district heating system. Hammarby Sjöstad uses flat-plate panels and evacuated tubes to preheat water for domestic use. As a test case, Kronsberg combines a large solar hot-water array with a large seasonal storage tank in order to capture summer solar energy to augment winter solar heating. All four neighborhoods have applied photovoltaic arrays to buildings. Hammarby Sjöstad has vertical arrays on south-facing walls and Kronsberg has them on rooftops, primarily for demonstration purposes. Boo1 also has photovoltaics for demonstration, while Vauban has a more aggressive deployment of photovoltaics on the roofs of residential units and on large parking structures. All four neighborhoods have well-developed systems for solid waste collection, with Boo1 and Hammarby Sjöstad using evacuated tube systems. In addition, all four have developed on-site storm-water management systems that create significant landscape design features. On the other hand, none has employed a local sewage treatment system or recycling; each relies entirely on the city's central facilities for sewage treatment and on the city's supply of potable water.

The full array of sustainability strategies outlined in this book provide rich dimensions for comparison. A comparison of the different principles and strategies using real performance data can reveal which strategies are the most critical in achieving low-carbon and low-energy goals. It also allows us to assess which strategies might contribute to the greatest resilience. The various reports on each of the neighborhoods prepared by multiple agencies provide some performance data, but many gaps and inconsistencies exist. Not surprisingly, collection of performance data has been extremely difficult because of the complexity of the neighborhood systems, the multiple agencies involved, and the lack of carefully developed monitoring plans to begin with. The power companies, utilities, and agencies have had to rely on normal metering systems that would be installed on any project to collect gross data. Without additional meters and sensors, it has been impossible to break down the performance of individual systems. Nonetheless, by cross-referencing the multiple reports from different agencies and interviewing some of the key people involved, my students and I have been able to piece together a reasonable set of data. One goal of this book is to provide a set of measures, a framework by which to compare these dimensions of sustainability. The hope is to create a baseline of performance not only to determine what these first-generation whole-systems strategies can achieve but also to establish a benchmark for comparing future performance of the dozens of sustainable (zero-carbon to plus-energy) neighborhoods that are on the drawing boards or in the approval process.

Of course, innovative strategies for sustainable neighborhoods do not occur on their own. By necessity, they are the result of a development process. In case after case, the development process has been shown to be as important in achieving the goals of sustainability as are the logic, elegance, and cost-effectiveness of any technical system. All four projects offer important lessons about the steps and dimensions of the development process that enabled the projects to achieve most of their sustainability goals.

These neighborhoods illustrate convincingly that sustainability at the neighborhood scale is not just a matter of finding and applying the "right" technical systems and following the "right" development process, as important as these may be. It involves thinking of technical strategies and urban design as one and creating a high-quality built environment, one that fosters a rich experience and sense of community. After all, no one wants to live inside a sustainability diagram. Such a system would reduce life to counting kilowatt-hours. The challenge for designers is to learn how sustainability strategies can enhance the quality of the built environment and deepen the experience of people's everyday lives. How do concepts of urban design—the design of the streets, blocks, parks, and urban landscape—interact with strategies for sustainability? Are there conflicts? What, if any, trade-offs have been made?

On one level, the urban design—the principles of urban form—for all four neighborhoods is similar. They all assume a conventional plan of streets and blocks. Each plan is then modified to take advantage of the particular conditions of the site and landscape, including such features as lakes, shorelines, and hills; orientation for sun and wind; and views. Different open space strategies for parks, recreation areas, courtyards, plazas, and urban landscape functions further enrich the form of each neighborhood. While the plan is quite conventional as an urban design framework, the subtle responses in design of the blocks, the architecture, the streets, and the urban landscape are what merit examination and attention. This is where the integration of sustainability and urban design comes alive. In order to illustrate these subtle responses, a further goal of this book is to present a careful graphic comparison of the physical and spatial dimensions of the urban design ideas and components in order to give an accurate empirical comparison of their qualities.

The case studies offer a set of lessons learned for delivering a more rewarding, healthy, and environmentally enriched lifestyle in which low- to no-carbon operation is just another dimension of experience. Even though the case studies are in a European context, the lessons learned form the basis of a road map for achieving sustainable neighborhoods around the world. Using a tool-kit approach, the book highlights the principles, policies, practices, and whole-systems wizardry that support the creation of these neighborhoods to suit particular national and local circumstances. Surprisingly, the lessons learned do not apply only to the development of new neighborhoods; much of the integrated thinking and whole-systems design is applicable to existing neighborhoods, districts, and cities as retrofit strategies. Since much of the US urban infrastructure will have to be restored, renovated, or rebuilt over the next fifty years, the road map and tool kit of strategies will be a useful alternative guide to business as usual.

Ultimately, wrote Adam Ritchie, "sustainability is about poetry, optimism and delight. Energy, CO_2, water and wastes [while extremely important] are secondary. The unquantifiable is at least as important as the quantifiable; according to Louis Kahn, 'the measurable is only a servant of the unmeasurable' and ideally the two would be developed together."[8]

Too often, however, urban design imperatives have been an excuse to ignore the empirical dimensions of sustainability. On the other hand, given the threat of climate change, the empirical demands of sustainability can become ends in themselves; they can become a moral imperative at the expense of other design imperatives. For "sustainability" to be sustainable, urban design must find a way to bring these two ways of thinking and making together into a compelling whole. The ultimate purpose of this book is to show how these four neighborhoods and a recent US example have attempted to achieve such a whole, to illustrate their urban design qualities together with their sustainability performance. It is hoped that these five examples of the best first-generation practices will provide a baseline that stimulates new forms of design thinking and design innovation. Together their strategies and hidden dimensions represent a new model, the beginning efforts to create an integrated whole-systems approach to sustainability that closes the circle, leading not only to a low-carbon future but also to an enriched form of urban living, to sustainable delight, which promises much greater resilience. As Buckminster Fuller said, "You never change things by fighting the existing reality. To change something, build a new model that makes the existing model obsolete."

2. Boo1, Malmö, Sweden

Boo1 was planned and built on a spectacular site overlooking the Öresund Strait between Copenhagen, Denmark, and Malmö, Sweden, as the European Millennium Housing Exposition, opening a year late in 2001. It is the first phase of a larger revitalization project called Västra Hamnen (Western Harbor), nicknamed the City of Tomorrow.

Figure 2.1. Aerial view of Boo1, Malmö, Sweden, looking southwest. *(Photograph by Joakim Lloyd Raboff.)*

Three hundred fifty of the 1,303 units planned for the Boo1 area were completed by the exposition's opening. The remaining 953 units of Boo1 have since been completed, along with units in Dockan and Flagghusen, neighborhoods within the larger Västra Hamnen development area, for a total of 2,822 units. Development continues, and Västra Hamnen is planned to be completed by 2016. When fully developed it will consist of approximately 8,000 dwellings, commercial and service space for 20,000 workers and students (Malmö University), three schools and seven elementary schools, and parks and recreation facilities. As one of the first attempts to create "a national example of sustainable urban development," the Boo1 exposition and the ongoing development in the Western Harbor have become among the most visited, toured, published, and cited examples of sustainable development in the world. This

is the first neighborhood in the world to claim that its energy is 100 percent renewable. Even ten years after the exposition's opening, the story of the project, the approach, the process, the design concepts, and the systems installed and evaluated hold important secrets about the potential for sustainable development at the scale of the neighborhood or urban district.

Figure 2.2. View of Öresund Bridge from Boo1. *(Photograph by Joakim Lloyd Raboff.)*

Process and Plan

The development of Boo1 began in 1995 as the result of a comprehensive visioning process undertaken by the City of Malmö. The process was prompted by the closing of the Saab factory in 1990 on the original site of the Kockums shipyard, which freed up 140 hectares of prime land on the Öresund Strait. In addition, construction of the dramatic bridge and tunnel connection over the Öresund between Malmö and Copenhagen created a thirty-minute transit link to downtown Copenhagen and its international airport and thus to new development opportunities for the city. The visioning exercise generated two strategic projects: (1) establishment of the independent Malmö University and (2) Malmö's application for one of Sweden's housing expositions sponsored by SVEBO (Svenska Bostäder, an organization formed by BOVERKET, the Swedish National Board of Housing, Building and Planning).[1]

Sweden has a long tradition, going back to the 1930s, of sponsoring housing expositions in order to promote innovation and change in housing con-

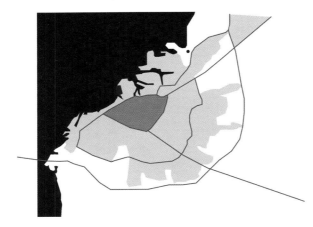

Figure 2.3. Location of Bo01 within Malmö. *(Drawing by Jessica Yang.)*

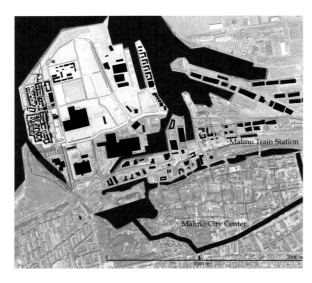

Figure 2.4. Context plan of Bo01. *(Drawing by Jessica Yang.)*

struction over conventional everyday practices. With the support of SVEBO and strong personalities within the government and national administration, the idea emerged for a "Housing Exposition as an innovative project with the most farsighted solutions for sustainable building and city development in every respect being applied concertedly for the first time in Sweden."[2] In 1996, Bo01 in Malmö was chosen over a number of other Swedish municipalities to become the first European Millennium Housing Exposition. With Malmö's selection, the city purchased the site and buildings and work began in earnest. Following SVEBO's appointment of an organization of planners and architects, including Professor Klas Tham as principal exhibition architect, planning commenced in a collaborative partnership with the City Planning Office and input from prospective developers. In 1999, the process produced the Quality Program, which established the principles and standards to guide project development.[3] The City of Malmö and SVEBO exposition architects prepared a concept plan for creating a compact, lively, sustainable city district with conditions for a high quality of life using the Quality Program, which "endeavored to exemplify a holistic approach but also gave criteria, detailed objectives and directions for more sustainable solutions, e.g. concerning energy efficiency, source separation of waste, greenery, biodiversity, and also for the more elusive quality of human sustainability."[4]

As the primary landowner, the City of Malmö became the "horizontal developer," responsible for planning and construction of all the public spaces and infrastructure, while the private developers were responsible for all construction inside the individual plot boundaries.[5] The Estates Department and the Parks and Highways Department appointed organizations to begin the planning and construction of technical infrastructure and public areas.

Although the City of Malmö and the SVEBO-appointed Expo Architect Committee were the primary authors of the Quality Program, because of their participation in the process, interested developers willing to meet the more stringent requirements were already on board. The City of Malmö and SVEBO set up a joint housing exposition company to take charge of planning all expo activities. Sixteen architect-developer teams from around the world devised projects for the opening of the expo. They were approved by the city architect and the housing expo architect together. The sixteen teams then signed land allocation agreements with the City of Malmö pledging to comply with the Quality Program. Further agreements for development were drawn up between the Housing Expo Company and the developers concerning the conduct of the expo and between the City of Malmö and SVEBO concerning the temporary parts of the expo.

Basic funding for the housing expo planning was provided by SVEBO, but additional government funding was sought from Sweden's Local Investment Program (LIP) to cover the add-on costs of planning and designing the sustainable systems. The LIP, in operation from 1998 to 2003, was established by the Ministry of the Environment to accelerate Sweden's conversion to an ecologically sustainable society. Projects receiving funding were intended to achieve as many as possible of the following aims:[6]

- Reduce environmental impact.
- Enhance energy efficiency.
- Favor the use of renewable raw materials.
- Increase reuse and recycling.
- Preserve and strengthen biodiversity.
- Improve the circulation of plant nutrients.
- Reduce the use of hazardous chemicals.
- Create new jobs.
- Encourage and facilitate people's involvement in the change to sustainable development.

In 1999, B001 received 250 million Swedish krona (27 million euros) from the LIP to help fund sixty-seven projects in the following eight initiative areas:[7]

1. **Urban planning.** The City of Malmö and the SVEBO exposition architects prepared a concept plan based on a creative evolution of the traditional European perimeter block housing model.

2. **Soil decontamination.** The City of Malmö prepared plans for decontaminating the former industrial site. The plan was based on the strategy of "cap and cover" of existing infill soils.

3. **Energy.** Sydkraft, the local utility, devised an integrated systems approach for providing 100 percent of the energy by combining energy efficiency improvements in the buildings with use of local renewables, including wind, geothermal, and solar power.

4. **Eco-cycle.** The City of Malmö, after extensive analysis of alternative waste and sewage systems, devised a plan to minimize material use, reuse materials, and recover energy from waste and residual products wherever possible.

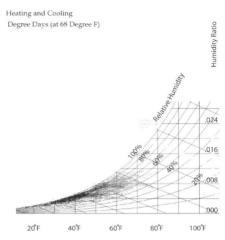

Figure 2.5. Psychrometric chart showing daily temperature ranges per year in B001. The range indicates that passive solar heating is the most effective climate-responsive design strategy. Heating degree days (HDD) at 65°F = 6,241; cooling degree days (CDD) at 72°F = 186. *(Diagram by author. Data source: ISK_E5NEMA2-Weather Station Code, Malmö, Almåsa, Skåne, Sweden [13.13E, 55.57N].)*

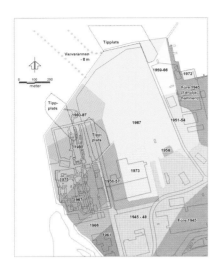

Figure 2.6. Plan showing dates and locations of different infill soils at Bo01. *(Source: Formas [Swedish Research Council for Environment, Agricultural Sciences and Spatial Planning]; City of Malmö.)*

5. ***Traffic.*** The City of Malmö prepared a holistic concept first to reduce the need for transport and then to favor the most environmentally favorable modes, including walking and biking; to make public transit (buses) convenient (within 300 meters) and frequent (every six to seven minutes); and finally to create provisions for "green" vehicles and carpooling options, all supported by a mobility management information system.

6. ***Green structure and water.*** The City of Malmö and SVEBO housing exposition architects prepared a plan to create a habitat-rich city district including an ecologically appropriate storm-water system that demonstrates water retention and acts as an urban amenity, a minimum green space factor that gives green points for greenery on the ground, green roofs, green facades, planting beds, permeable paving, and designated habitat study areas.

7. ***Building and living.*** The City of Malmö and SVEBO architects developed an area development plan and other specific rules concerning green space and color scheme. The framework has been flexible enough to provide a rich variety in the design of individual housing projects.

8. ***Information and knowledge dissemination.*** The City of Malmö and SVEBO, before, during, and after the expo, prepared exhibitions, information, reports, and postoccupancy evaluations and assessments of the project. No fewer than thirteen separate articles by individual researchers; an extensive report published by Formas, the Swedish Research Council for Environment, Agricultural Sciences and Spatial Planning; multiple pamphlets and brochures by the city; thirty or more "fact boxes"; and public educational projects have ensured that Bo01 has been a focus of information, knowledge, and debate about sustainable urban development.

The thinking and innovation associated with the development of Bo01 as one of the first Swedish models for sustainable urban design was made possible by top-down government policy and funding initiatives. The additional resources provided by SVEBO for the European Millennium Housing Exposition, along with funding from the European Union and the LIP to promote Sweden's transition to a more sustainable future, made it possible to explore a new model of sustainability at the scale of an urban district, with Bo01 as the first phase.

The development of Bo01 was influenced greatly by SVEBO's high expectations for creating "a national example of sustainable urban development,"[8] with closed eco-cycles and all energy generated by local renewables. But the vision of the city and the exposition architects for the project encompassed many dimensions beyond a typically narrow definition of sustainability as involving energy, technology, pollution abatement, and green space, requiring a certain level of inconvenience or sacrifice. Their holistic approach was designed to put sustainability in the service of high-quality urban living.

The Quality Program,[9] drawn up between the City of Malmö and the developers, was the steering instrument for achieving these broad goals. It was intended as a "single basic standard" for developers, to secure high quality in the district's environmental profile, technology and services, and architectural concept. Not surprisingly, with such broad and holistic goals, most requirements in the Quality Program were qualitative, not quantitative, in order to allow for innovation and creativity on the part of the sixteen architect-developer teams. Even though the Quality Program was inscribed in the land allocation agreement between the city and the developers, there were no sanctions for not achieving the goals, nor were there any incentives for outstanding performance. Thus, the signing of the agreement can be seen more as a moral commitment on the part of the developers; however, with thousands of expo visitors and the LIP contract to evaluate and report performance, the developers' reputations were clearly on the line.

Transportation

The goals and objectives for traffic in Boo1 were developed by the City of Malmö. During the process, the city located a new Mobility Office in the district. Over the course of development, the concept for Boo1 has emerged as a model for a new way of creating an environmentally adapted traffic system for the whole of Malmö. The plan did not call out specific targets for the split among different transit modes but instead used design, incentives, and an information system to encourage walking, biking, car sharing, and use of public transit and green vehicles over the use of private cars.

Boo1's sustainable transport strategy begins with the concept of reducing dependence on the car. By providing a complete array of services and recreational activities within the development

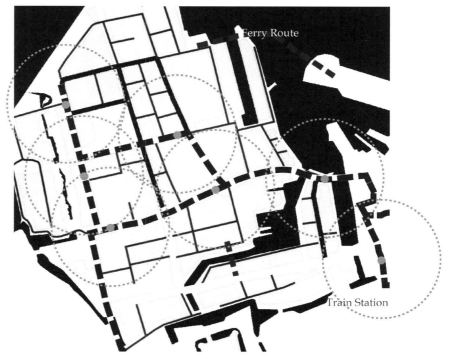

Figure 2.7. Transit plan for Boo1. *(Source: City of Malmö, "Design Principles." Redrawn by Mahammad Momin.)*

area, the demand for trips outside the neighborhood is reduced significantly (see the discussion of urban design later in this chapter).

Next, the bicycle circulation system and pedestrian network may be the most important elements of the green transit strategy because the design gives priority to these completely renewable, carbon-free modes of travel. The bicycle paths are designed to be a complete network, clearly marked and connecting to important routes and destinations in the city. The pedestrian paths and sidewalks are constructed of high-quality materials, including a variety of brick, concrete, granite, and wood pavers. The ground floors of all buildings are designed with higher ceilings to allow for shops and services, activating the pedestrian experience along the streets. Just as important as the interest on the ground level, there are multiple and interesting short-cuts through blocks, allowing a variety of routes. While cars have access to the space in the inner blocks, it is clear that pedestrians and cyclists have priority.

Public transport is an integral part of the strategy, with a comprehensive bus system that has been available from the beginning of the development. Stops are located such that no residence is more than 300 meters from a stop, and buses come at a frequency of every six to seven minutes. The bus lines connect to important destinations in the city, and the vehicles run on environmentally sensitive fuels (electricity and natural gas). All residents and businesses in the area have access to mobility management information indicating bus schedules and arrival times, available on the city's transportation website. The stops themselves display the same information, giving riders vital information to help them plan their public transport use.

Parking is provided in underground structures, with limited on-street parking. The parking ratio for the initial phase of Bo01 was 0.7 space per unit to encourage walking, biking, and use of public transit. However, in later phases it was changed to 1.5 spaces per unit to respond to market demand. In order to encourage ownership, "green" vehicles have been given priority access to parking spaces, with the added provision of slow charging in designated spaces. In addition, the neighborhood features a filling station for natural gas and hookups for quick charging. Residents are also invited to join a car-sharing service made up of green vehicles to reduce the need for private car use.

The LIP funding gave the city the opportunity to develop its sustainable transport strategy for Bo01. The experience has been so positive that the plan has become a model for the whole of Malmö. To encourage education on more sustainable transport behaviors, the city opened a Mobility Office in the district. It advises residents and businesses on more environmentally sensitive transport options, which can be more cost-efficient than exclusive use of private cars.

No comprehensive survey of transport behavior has been conducted yet for the Western Harbor development area. It would be premature to conduct a survey to determine the mode split between walking, bicycling, use of public transit, car sharing, and use of private cars. There are still too many gaps, undeveloped properties, in the development plan to create the necessary continuity in the pedestrian and bike networks for them to be fully operational and be compared with the other modes of transport. Preliminary anecdotal reports, however, suggest that at this stage of development the mode split is similar to the average for Malmö, or 50 percent car use and 50 percent remaining modes. The doubling of the parking ratio, from 0.7 space per unit to 1.5 spaces per unit, for new development properties indicates a higher demand for car ownership (reflective of the district's more affluent demographics), but it does not necessarily indicate a higher ratio of car usage.

Urban Form

One major contributor to the success of Boo1's urban form is the quality and diversity of architectural expression within a modern vocabulary. The project has been achieved by dividing the project into many small development plots and assigning them to leading architects. While each architect-developer team had to conform to the urban design guidelines of height, density, green points, and the like for each plot, the teams were free to develop their own individual architectural responses to site conditions.

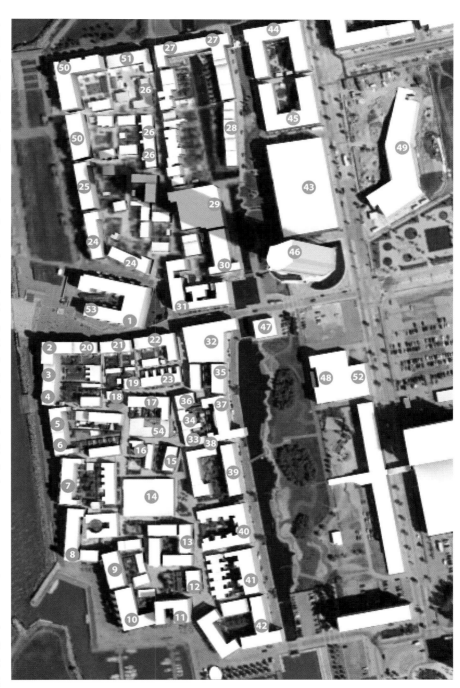

Figure 2.8. Guide to Boo1 architecture showing number and location of different architect-developer teams. *(Source: City of Malmö, 2006.)*

The vision was to create the first phase of "a complete urban quarter comprising work and study facilities, services and housing—an urban area which stimulates the transition to a knowledge city and is a vibrant neighborhood community long after the Expo."[10] The city saw the project as an opportunity to reestablish Malmö's close link to the sea, with direct access from the city center to the Öresund Strait and its sweeping views, and to combine sustainability with "a high level of quality in terms of architecture, public environment and materials." It was to be at least as convenient, attractive, and beautiful as the "unsustainable" city, with no sacrifices, providing for residents' long-term enjoyment and comfort.[11]

On many levels, Boo1 is a remaking of qualities inherent in the historical European city—its compact high density, its complex layering of many different architecture and design strategies, its mixed use, its integration of public parks and plazas with distinct and quiet residential neighborhoods, and its diverse network of streets, boulevards, promenades, paths, and alleys creating rich contrasts between legibility, mystery, and surprise.

The urban form of Boo1 is organized to take advantage of the "magnificence of its site—the sea, the great sky, the horizon, the sunset and the Öresund Bridge." It is carefully designed to temper the microclimate—"the

Figure 2.9. Master plan of Boo1. *(Source: City of Malmö, "Design Principles.")*

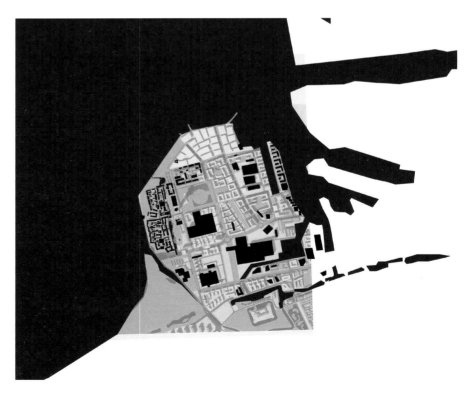

forceful winds from the west."[12] It provides alternative pedestrian routes so that people can choose depending on the weather and their mood.

The plan is structured around what appears to be a traditional pattern of streets and promenades defining large, semipublic blocks. The pattern provides a clear and legible framework, yet each element has been transformed in both bold and subtle ways, creating a richer order of surprise, unique urban rooms, and dramatic contrasts between the magnificent and the intimate.

The design purposely intensifies the contrast between the outside and the inside. A wide public promenade, the Sundspromenaden, is located along the entire west edge of the site, commanding panoramic views of the sea and the Öresund Bridge, with Denmark on the horizon. The promenade is constructed of a rich array of materials from the water's edge to the building facades, creating an attractive area for multiple uses by local residents and outside visitors. A berm of stone boulders forms a rugged buffer separating the promenade from the water's edge, with periodic interruptions of stadium-like steps and isolated seating areas granting direct access to the water's edge. A wooden boardwalk runs along the top of the boulders for the entire length, backed by continuous stepped seating facing in both directions. The outside provides views of the sound, and the inside provides seating protected from the wind. The space between the continuous wooden seating and the buildings is made of small cobblestones with random strips of wood and glass insets. The area has become a favorite destination for the people of Malmö, reestablishing the city's link to the sea.

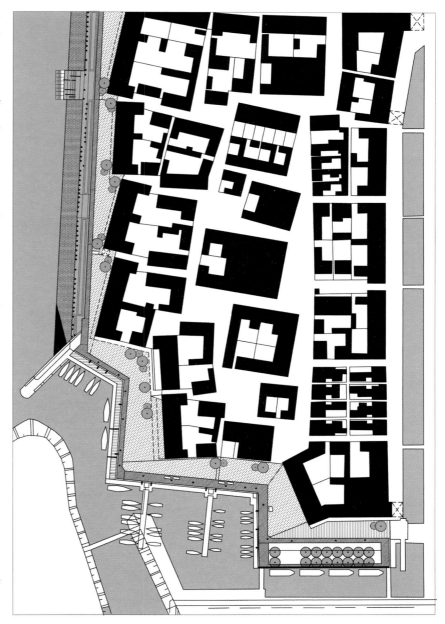

Figure 2.10. Blowup plan of the first block and promenade in B001. *(Source: Jeppe Aagaard Andersen. Redrawn by Ariel Utz.)*

Figure 2.11. View of promenade seating and edge buildings in Boo1. *(Photograph by Joakim Lloyd Raboff.)*

The buildings fronting the Sundspromenaden are five- to seven-story slabs, approximately fifty to sixty meters long, with small gaps between them. They have been positioned at slight angles to one another to deflect the wind. Buildings inside the block have been positioned to plug the gaps between the edge buildings. Together, the outside edge buildings and the inside buildings allow pedestrian access but create an effective windbreak, heightening the experience of contrast between outside and inside.

The inside of the large block plan has been subdivided into smaller development plots of different sizes, placed at shifted angles to one another. Each plot has been given to one of thirty-four different architect-developer teams for detailed design and development. The result is an experience of the block interior that has the feel of a medieval neighborhood, with random, angled paths and small squares, different architectural expressions with contrasts in scale, materials, and form. While the public is free to wander through this interior labyrinth, it is a quiet, sheltered zone that clearly belongs to the residents, in contrast to the outside promenade, which belongs to a larger public and affords distant views.

The east side of what can be described as the first of the larger blocks constructed in the overall plan fronts on a linear green space, with a saltwater canal running the entire length. It serves as a storm-water retention basin before the surplus water is returned to the sea at the north end and the small marina at the south end. Similarly to the west-side Sundspromenaden, the east side is divided into a diverse set of four- to five-story slab buildings, creating a continuous hard edge fronting the park, the Ankarparken. While the park and the continuous-edge buildings define the east side of a large block, the park itself can be understood as the interior space of an even larger block framed by a series of existing and new buildings. This double reading—what is outside for one part of the plan is inside for another—adds to the complexity of the urban experience. As an urban design strategy, it creates multiple and distinct orientation demands for each individual development site, encouraging diversity in architectural styles chosen in response.

This strategy of urban form can be described as a progression of a space within a space within a space, similar in concept to the nesting of Russian

Figure 2.12. View inside the first block of Bo01, looking south. *(Photograph by Jens Lindhe.)*

dolls. Each transition affords an opportunity for contrast, difference, and surprise. Under such circumstances, the treatment of the ground, the urban floor, and the proper treatment of storm water, both as an environmental issue and a design feature, play an important role in tracing the multiple transitions from inside to outside, from private to public.

The relatively low-rise, high-density mixed-use block plans are contrasted with one tall, predominantly residential tower, the Turning Torso. With fifty-four floors, it is the tallest residential building in Sweden. The net density on its block is 350 units per acre, in contrast to an average density of 34 units per acre for the low-rise blocks. Such a hypercontrast in both height and density (a factor of ten) makes a powerful contribution to the urban form. The height gives a point of reference to pedestrians inside the intricate block plans. At the same time, it serves as a landmark in the larger landscape of the city and the Öresund Strait, visible from Denmark and the Öresund Bridge. It has become a symbol of the rebirth of Malmö as an active player in a new regional economy.

The strategy of creating a hypercontrast in height and density has the advantage of celebrating the best qualities of both low-rise and high-rise development without compromising either. The intimacy and variety in low-rise high density is given a larger visual reference point in the tower, which provides orientation and a sense of scale. A singular high-rise tower has the advantage of not having its views interrupted by other towers, while its much higher density brings added human intensity to the neighborhood's ground-level streetscape. Such a strategy of urban form has a few highly successful

Figure 2.13. View of the Turning Torso in Boo1, the tallest residential building in Sweden. *(Photograph by Joakim Lloyd Raboff.)*

precedents on Wilshire Boulevard in Los Angeles and in São Paulo, Brazil. In both cases, a high-rise transit corridor sits in close proximity to low-rise residential neighborhoods. The qualities of both sit in stark contrast. Their proximity brings the advantages of both together while providing escape from each other's potential tyranny. This kind of hypercontrast in urban form is an underexplored strategy. The example of Boo1 is a reminder of its potential.

Green Space

In an effort to make Boo1 a "habitat-rich city district," the developers committed themselves to follow two different but related approaches. In the first, the developers committed to choose at least ten of thirty-five green points from a list prepared by Boo1 in partnership with the City of Malmö (see box 2.1).[13]

In the second approach, every building project was required to satisfy a green space factor,[14] calculated as an average of all the allowable factors. The factor gave a numerical rating for each surface of a project. Many of the weighted factors were for the elements on the green points listed in box 2.1. For Boo1, the average green space factor for all surfaces was required to be 0.5. For example, built and other sealed surfaces were given a rating of 1.0, while green materials on natural ground were given a factor of 0.0. If these were the only surfaces and their areas were equal, the green space factor would average to be 0.5. The area of all surfaces multiplied by their green space factor had to average 0.5 (see box 2.2).

Box 2.1. Green Points Criteria

1. A nesting box for every dwelling unit.
2. One biotope for specified insects (plant biotopes excluded) per 100 square meters (m²) of courtyard area.
3. Bat boxes inside the plot boundary.
4. No hardstanding in courtyards—all surfaces permeable to water.
5. All nonhard surfaces in the courtyard have soil deep and good enough for vegetable growing.
6. Courtyard includes a traditional cottage garden, complete with all its constituent parts.
7. Walls covered with climbing plants wherever possible or suitable.
8. A 1 m² pond for every 5 m² of hardstanding in the courtyard.
9. Courtyard vegetation specially selected to yield nectar for butterflies.
10. No more than five plants of the same species among the courtyard trees and bushes.
11. All courtyard biotopes designed to be fresh and moist.
12. All garden biotopes designed to be dry and lean.
13. Entire courtyard made up of biotopes modeled on biotopes occurring naturally.
14. All storm water captured to run aboveground for at least 10 m before being led off.
15. Green courtyard but no lawns.
16. All rainwater from buildings and courtyard paving collected and used for watering vegetation or for laundry, rinsing, and the like inside the buildings.
17. All plants suitable for domestic use in one way or another.
18. Batrachian biotopes in the courtyard, with hibernation possibilities.
19. In the courtyard or adjoining apartment buildings, at least 5 m² of orangery and greenhouse space per dwelling unit.
20. Bird food in the courtyard year-round.
21. At least two different traditional cultivated fruit and soft fruit varieties per 100 m² of courtyard space.
22. Swallow shelves on house fronts.
23. Entire courtyard used for growing vegetables, fruit, and soft fruit.
24. Developer or landscape architect to cooperate with ecological expertise and to shape the overall idea and the detailed solutions together with the ecological associate (choice of associate must be approved by B001 or the City of Malmö).
25. Gray water purified in the courtyard and reused.
26. All biodegradable domestic and garden waste composted and the entire compost output used within the property, in the courtyard, or in balcony boxes and the like.
27. All building material used in constructing the courtyard—surfacing, timber, masonry, furniture, equipment—has been used before.
28. At least 2 m² of permanent growing space on a balcony or in a flower box for every dwelling unit with no patio.
29. At least half the courtyard to be water.
30. Courtyard has a particular color as the theme for its plants, equipment, and material.
31. All trees in the courtyard to be fruit trees and all bushes fruit bushes.
32. Courtyard has topiary plants as its theme.
33. Part of the courtyard is allowed to run wild.
34. Courtyard has at least fifty wild Swedish flowering plants.
35. All roofs on the property are green, that is, clad in vegetation.

Box 2.2. Partial Factors for Greenery and for Paved Surfaces

Partial Factors for Greenery

1.0 Greenery on the ground

1.0 Bodies of water in ponds, streams, ditches

0.8 Green roofs

0.8 Plant bed on joists, >800 mm deep

0.6 Plant bed on joists, <800 mm deep

0.4 Tree with trunk circumference >35 cm (calculated for an area of not more than 25 m² of planting space per tree)

0.2 Solitary shrubs, multiple-trunk trees more than 3 m high (calculated for an area of not more than 5 m² of planting space per shrub or tree)

0.2 Climbing plants more than 2 m high (calculated for a wall area with width of 2 m per plant times the height of the plant)

Partial Factors for Paved Surfaces

0.4 Open paved surfaces (grass-reinforced areas, gravel, shingle, sand, etc.)

0.2 Paved areas (stone or slabs) with pointing

0.0 Impervious areas (roofing, asphalt, concrete, etc.)

Partial Factors for Hard Surfaces

0.2 Collection and retention of storm water (additional factor of sealed or hard surfaces with joints draining into a pond or magazine holding >20 L/m² of drained area)

0.1 Draining of sealed surfaces (to surrounding greenery on the ground)

In this manner, without solutions being specified, teams were encouraged to rethink all the surfaces of a project for their green potential and to come up with innovative designs. The overall goal was to make the properties and courtyards as green as possible and for storm water to be visible and used to enhance the courtyard environments.

The green space system for Västra Hamnen can be characterized as a network of parks and passages of different scales and uses that form an alternative network to the streets. Some are used for storm-water collection and retention and habitat creation; others are designed for active recreation. The system gives all residents access to a rich variety of green space within 300 meters of their dwellings. All the schools are located in proximity to the green space network so that students can choose to walk to school through the parks and not on the streets. Although not technically green space along its entire length, the system benefits from having continuous public access around the entire perimeter of the site along the shoreline.

In B001's urban landscape, rainwater is led from the roofs, in some cases to become a feature in a private garden court and in others into collectors and channels as open features inside the blocks. It is then channeled to streets, to

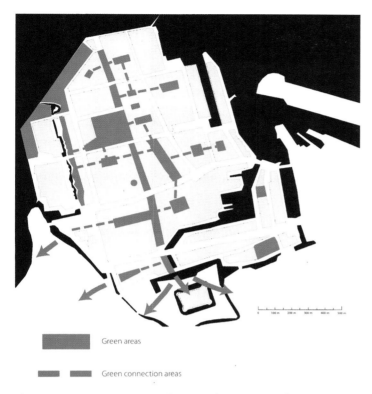

Figure 2.14. Green space plan for Boo1. *(Source: City of Malmö, "Design Principles.")*

Figure 2.15. Storm-water downspout in Boo1. *(Photograph by Bengt Persson.)*

landscape filtering areas, and then to the saltwater canal or the sea. When it rains, the place becomes alive with water sounds and flow. One's position in the neighborhood can be located in relation to storm water, enriching sensory awareness. Rather than being buried in pipes, storm water becomes an active spatial reference in the urban form.

Energy

One of the few quantitative requirements in the Quality Program is related to energy demand: "The target is for energy consumption on the properties not to exceed an average of 105 kWh/m² gross floor area per annum. This includes all property-related energy. Energy produced or recovered within the property is included. Responsibility: Developers."[15]

During negotiations between the City of Malmö and the developers on the Quality Program, the Boo1 organization wanted a stricter requirement than 105 kilowatt-hours per square meter per year, but the developers prevailed, arguing that 105 kWh/m²/y was more realistic and cost-effective.

Figure 2.16. Storm-water outlet to canal in Bo01. *(Photograph by Bengt Persson.)*

Figure 2.17. View of storm-water retention canal in Bo01. *(Photograph by Torben Petersen.)*

To achieve this goal, the architect-developer teams relied on their engineers, or "structural designers," to work out the appropriate technical solutions. The engineers used existing software to model the thermal performance of walls, roofs and ceilings, windows, solar and internal gains, air infiltration, and heating, ventilation, and air-conditioning systems until their calculations satisfied the requirement. As anyone involved in monitoring the energy performance of buildings knows, the steps between making energy calculations and achieving the same performance are complicated. To begin with, the calculations are in many cases an approximation of reality, in which resident behavior and operation can play an important role. Recognizing this fact, the Quality Program stipulated "educational measures" for residents of the new district.[16]

With the target of supplying all energy from local renewable sources, the SVEBO team knew that it would involve balancing two sides of an equation: energy demand and renewable energy supply. Obviously, this meant that the lower the demand, the easier it would be to supply energy from renewable sources. The target of 105 kWh/m²/y for total demand of the unit was a compromise between the developers and the SVEBO team in order to ensure cost feasibility. Nonetheless, it was significantly lower than the Swedish average at the time of 250 kWh/m²/y. The architect-developer team relied on its engineers to model the performance of alternative designs and technical systems until they could demonstrate that the units would achieve the target. It is clear from reports that designing to an energy demand target was a new experience for many architects. It involved paying close attention to (1) insulation values in wall and roof assemblies; (2) insulation value, size, and orientation of windows; (3) construction details for airtightness and thermal bridging; (4) heat exchange for ventilation; and (5) the quality of the heating system, its controls, and its commissioning. In the end, all ten of the buildings that had been measured for performance demonstrated calculated conformance equal to or better than 105 kWh/m²/y. Performance is another story, which involves many other variables discussed below.

As part of the assessment process, ten units were monitored between October 2002 and October 2003. The estimated total energy requirement, according to the Enorm energy calculations prepared by the developers, indicated that energy consumption would be better than the 105 kWh/m²/y for all properties except one, which showed 107 kWh/m²/y. The average calculated consump-

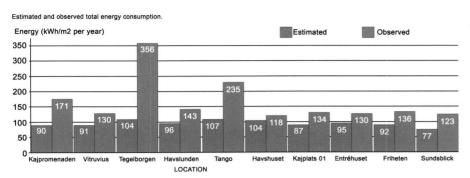

Figure 2.18. Estimated and observed total energy consumption in Boo1 units. *(Source: Formas. Redrawn by Ariel Utz.)*

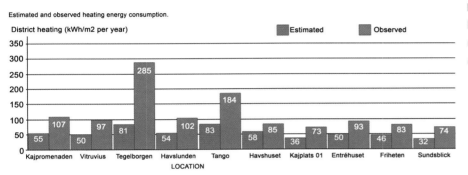

Figure 2.19. Estimated and observed heating energy consumption in Boo1 units. *(Source: Formas. Redrawn by Ariel Utz.)*

tion was 94.3 kWh/m²/y. By contrast, the average observed consumption is 167.6 kWh/m²/y. This represents a 77 percent increase over the calculated estimate and a 60 percent increase over the target. What is surprising is the range of deviation; two properties have total energy consumption of two to three times the target figure, 235 kWh/m²/y and 356 kWh/m²/y. By extrapolation from the data, the average calculated electricity consumption was estimated to be 38.6 kWh/m²/y, while the observed electricity consumption was 49.3 kWh/m²/y. This represents a 28 percent increase, which is significantly less than the increase of 77 percent for total energy. This indicates that while electricity consumption plays a role, heating is the primary cause of the consumption increase.

There is much speculation about what has caused the increase in energy consumption. Most likely it is a combination of factors, but the leading candidate from other research results is the units' air infiltration rate (number of air changes per hour, caused by cracks in the envelope), especially given the strong wind exposure of the site. Small flaws in construction can have a big effect on the air infiltration rate. Air infiltration resulting from poor construction can overwhelm the thermal transmittance of the walls, floors, roofs, and windows, even with higher than average transmittance values. It is not surprising, given this hypothesis, that the highest-consumption property is on the most exposed west corner of the site.

Another factor for the high heating consumption may be thermal bridges. These are structural details that conduct cold directly from outside to inside without a thermal break. Both of these conditions—high air infiltration rates and thermal bridging—certainly could have resulted from the rush to complete construction for the start of the expo.

An equally important factor may be the residents' behavior. Residents control domestic electricity consumption, hot-water use, and thermostat settings. Leaving lights and television on, taking long showers, and keeping the windows open with the radiator on can have a big effect on energy consumption. All of these behaviors suggest the need for better education and real-time feedback about energy consumption to encourage residents to change their behavior.

A final factor may be the lack of shading in some parts of the building, which increases the use of individual air-conditioning units. This is suggested by the fact that all the units with the highest electricity consumption have large areas of unshaded west-facing glass, which may trigger the unnecessary installation and use of air-conditioning. This hypothesis has not been tested, but it is suggested by the data.

In terms of energy supply, the first measurable requirement in the Quality Program was to provide 100 percent of the energy supply from renewable sources. Responsibility for achieving this goal was given to the local utility, Sydkraft, which came up with the unique combination of wind energy providing electricity for all the units while also powering a groundwater source heat pump for heating and cooling, supplemented by solar photovoltaics and evacuated tube solar water heating.

The B001 site has three important natural resources for renewable supply: a favorable average annual wind speed, good solar radiation, and seawater and a groundwater aquifer, which act as heat sinks. From these resources Sydkraft devised an innovative system that takes advantage of all three systems. A 2 megawatt (MW) wind turbine, located on the coast one mile north of the site, delivers electricity to the dwelling units and powers a large heat pump system that delivers hot and cold water to the neighborhood. A 120 m array of photovoltaic cells, located on buildings in the district, augments the electric supply. Heat is provided by the large heat pump. It uses the local groundwater aquifer and seawater as a heat sink, providing seasonal storage. Heat extracted from the units in the summer is stored in the aquifer until winter and then delivered by the heat pump. Cold extracted from the units in the winter is stored in the aquifer, and its cooling is delivered by the heat pump in the summer. In addition, 1,400 m² of solar collectors, both evacuated tube and flat plate, located on the roofs and facades of buildings supplements the district heating system.

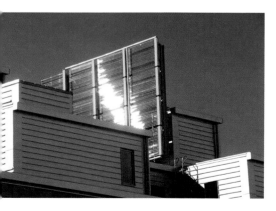

Figure 2.20. View of evacuated tube collectors in B001. *(Photograph by Jan-Erik Andersson.)*

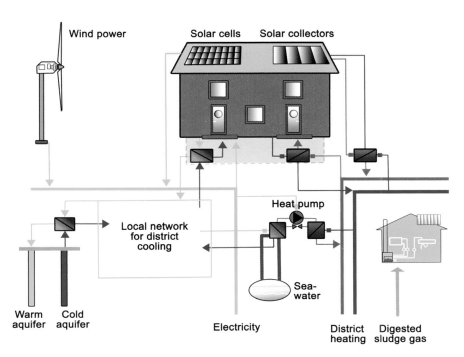

The electric, heating, and cooling supply systems are connected to the existing city grid and city heating and cooling district systems in order to have the city systems act as storage, offsetting any mismatch in production and consumption. When energy production of Boo1 exceeds consumption, the excess is sent to other parts of Malmö. When the local production of Boo1 is insufficient for the demand, the project receives energy from the city systems. The entire system is designed to have the local renewable supply equal the demand on an annual basis.

Figure 2.22 shows the balance of energy demand (use) and supply (production) based on calculations of the 1,000-plus units of housing in Boo1 constructed to meet the target of 105 kWh/m²/y. Figure 2.23 shows that, in spite of the measured increase in energy consumption from July 2002 to July 2003, the measured performance of both the wind machine and the aquifer-seawater heat pump system was sufficient to supply approximately all the energy for Boo1 from local renewable sources.

This energy balance does not include three potential sources of renewable energy generated by the neighborhood: combustible waste (delivered to the city's cogeneration plant), food waste, and sludge waste (delivered to the city's digestion plant). Even without these potential sources of renewable

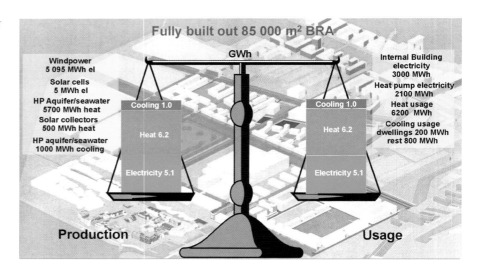

Figure 2.22. Estimated energy balance for B001. *(Source: Formas. Data from E.ON/ Sydkraft.)*

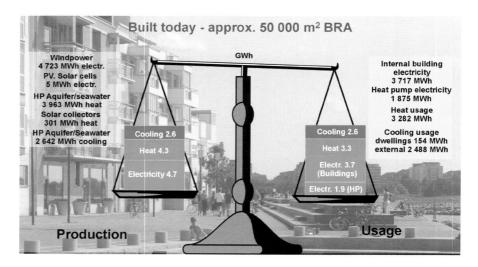

Figure 2.23. Measured energy balance for B001. *(Source: Formas. Data from E.ON/ Sydkraft.)*

supply included in the energy balance equation, B001 is one of the first neighborhoods in the world that can claim it supplies 100 percent of its energy from renewable sources and back it up with measured performance data. This means that except for carbon emissions from the use of private cars, the neighborhood is zero carbon in its operation. Assuming that the vehicle miles traveled per person are on average with those of other Swedish urban residents, the carbon dioxide (CO_2) emissions per person should be less than 2 metric tons per person-year.

Water

No specific goals for water usage were established in the Quality Program. The extent of water-conserving fixtures and appliances was left to the discretion of the developers. Water usage was expected to be approximately 200 liters per person-day, equivalent to Swedish standards at the time.

Potable water for the project is supplied by the city's water system; there is no rainwater capture or reuse for this purpose. Storm water is treated as an open landscape and urban design feature. It is cleaned and retained on-site before being channeled to the sea. Wastewater (sewage) is processed by the Malmö City Water and Wastewater Works. The city already has a system for removing the sludge and converting it to biogas by anaerobic digestion at the city's Sjölunda Wastewaster Treatment Plant. The biogas is supplied to the city's gas grid and contributes to cooking and electric generation. Its contribution to the energy balance equation has not been quantified.

Waste

The goals for waste in B001 were established through extensive system analysis of different waste and sewage systems as part of the LIP program. The approach, known as the B001 eco-cycle recycling system, had as its primary goal "achieving the greatest possible recovery and recycling of materials and resources." This overall goal spawned multiple innovative systems and experiments.

Since approximately half of all domestic refuse in Sweden is food waste, special attention was paid to the recovery and recycling of food waste as part of the B001 eco-cycle effort articulated in the Quality Program. A food waste collection system stands or falls on the success of separating the food waste from all other waste streams and containments. The B001 eco-cycle starts with a comprehensive system for household separation of glass, paper, metal, and plastic containers and newspapers as both a convenience and an incentive to isolate food waste. The Malmö City Water and Wastewater Works installed two large-scale food waste systems in order to compare the convenience and performance of (1) a vacuum collection system at collection points and (2) a food waste disposal system at each kitchen sink.

The vacuum collection system locates collection points near the housing units. Each point has two chutes with collection tanks—a green one for food waste and a gray one for the remaining combustible fraction. Residents sort their waste into special tear- and moisture-resistant bags and deposit them in the chutes. The tanks are emptied regularly by a vacuum collection vehicle. The combustible waste

Figure 2.24. Waste collection stations in B001. *(Photograph by Bengt Persson.)*

is delivered to the city's combustible cogeneration plant, and the food waste is delivered to a pretreatment plant before digestion in the city's existing sludge digestion plant.

The food waste disposal system is installed in fifty units. The waste disposers drain into a separate tank, and the food waste is separated by sedimentation. The water is drained off into the sewage system, and the remaining food waste is collected by a vacuum collection vehicle and conveyed directly to the central digestion plant. The comparative performance of the two systems is important for future applications and improvements.

The vacuum collection system was evaluated, and because small amounts of contaminants were discovered, as much as 60 percent by weight had to be discarded. As a result, the pretreatment technology was not deployed and digestion was not pursued. While the waste disposal system yielded food waste of high purity, the quantity from the small number of units (fifty) was too small to justify deploying the system, in part because residents may have disposed of food waste by other means. Nonetheless, since 15 percent of domestic refuse is organic food waste, it remains a significant potential source of biogas, enough to warrant further efforts to devise a system to capture its embedded energy and nutrients.

Materials

In regard to the selection of materials, the Quality Program used fairly unspecific language, "environmentally adapted" and "resource efficient," as the guiding environmental assessment standards for the architect-developer teams. These standards gave the teams considerable latitude in selecting materials. Since environmental assessment had not been used as a requirement for materials selection by designers before, in many cases the choice of materials was based on long-standing experience and practice. The Quality Program indicated the following regarding the environmental assessment of materials:

> **Materials Plan:** *Prior to the ordering of materials a materials plan shall be compiled . . . This plan shall show the materials which are planned [to be used]. The building materials used shall be assessed and reported in detail, if possible by the LCA methodology. Responsibility: Developers.*

> **Selection of Materials:** *Substances on the limitation and OBS lists of the National Chemicals Inspectorate shall be avoided . . . Responsibility: Developers.*[17]

Even though the developers relied on long-standing experience and practice in selecting materials, the fact that they had to submit a materials plan, assess the environmental impact of chosen materials, and avoid ecologically harmful banned substances made it a pioneering effort. Not only did it raise the awareness of the architect-developer teams to the large environmental impact of building materials in general; it also revealed the relatively undeveloped nature of the tools and methods of assessment and a glaring lack of reliable information about the content and processes of materials extraction, manufacturing, shipping, construction, recycling, and disposal, in other words, a "cradle-to-cradle" assessment.[18] In this sense, the Quality Program played an important role in highlighting the need for future research and development in the environmental assessment of building materials.

Social Agenda

The social agenda for B001 is imbedded in the goal of creating social sustainability by focusing on conditions essential for a high quality of life and by conceiving of B001 and the Western Harbor as leading Malmö's transition to an information society. Because time was so short for meeting the opening of the housing expo, an extended participatory process was not possible. Nonetheless, an informal test panel met regularly to react to the planners' proposals, and the developers were given an opportunity to influence the planning concepts. Many suggestions were made to create homes for seniors and for large families, collective housing, and half-finished flats that tenants could finish on their own, but none of these concepts have been realized. The customer profile given to the developers for B001 was "well-to-do, middle-aged empty nesters," but the plan also included 197 student homes and 376 student flats. B001 and the later phase of the Western Harbor have remained predominantly middle-class in their social agenda, in large part because of the higher infrastructure costs of development.

Lessons Learned

Creating "a national example of sustainable urban development" would not have been possible without strong leadership from the City of Malmö. The city's application and selection by SVEBO to host one of Sweden's housing expositions—the first European Millenium Housing Exposition—was the most important first step. Securing additional outside funding from SVEBO for the expo and additional funding from the Local Investment Program (LIP) and the European Union for the planning, design, and construction of the sustainable systems made project innovation possible.

The collaborative process between the SVEBO-appointed Expo Architect Committee, the City Planning Office and other agencies, the local utility, and interested property developers was essential in carrying out all the innovative concepts in the project. Selecting an outstanding urban designer, Klas Tham, to lead the project, supporting his vision, and selecting leading architects to carry out the vision were key elements in the project's success.

The City of Malmö's role as primary horizontal developer of all infrastructure and public spaces ensured conformance to the goals. As the landowner, the city was able to insist that developers sign on to the Quality Program as part of land acquisition agreements. In its role as primary developer, it was also able to coordinate development of the urban plan, soil decontamination, street and traffic designs, building standards, renewable energy systems, and the eco-cycle of waste and sewage systems. The added cost of development was recovered by the city through the sale of properties to the developers.

The transportation plan for Boo1 is an extension of a typical European city's traffic-planning model, with bus (and future tram) integration with the citywide system. What is unique is the provision of real-time information to residents about the schedule and arrival of vehicles, the priority given to pedestrians and cyclists by creating spaces where cars are allowed but are not given a designated right-of-way, the use of gas- or electric-powered public vehicles, and access to car sharing. The success of these systems is being applied to the whole city.

The goal of making the neighborhood "at least as convenient, attractive and beautiful as the (so-called) unsustainable city"[19] has been a surprising source of the success of Boo1's urban form. It has meant that sustainability strategies have not been at the expense of quality urban design. Although many sustainable strategies are deployed and visible—wind protection, solar collectors, open storm-water collection and retention—they are seamlessly integrated into the architecture and urban landscape with great design skill. Residents might not even think of them as sustainable strategies. They just enrich the urban experience. Here the goal of sustainability has been placed in the service of creating a high-quality urban environment.

The fact that the renewable energy systems plugged into the city's infrastructure before supplying the buildings freed the urban design from having to pay rigid attention to solar access and orientation. It freed the buildings and blocks to respond to other criteria of urban design. The concept of heightening the contrast between the inside and outside of the large urban blocks has been a major factor in the positive ratings of the neighborhood. The contrast is instrumental in the high ratings for factors such as "complexity" and "wholeness" and for creating "different types of places for encounters and solitude" and the possibility of "mystery, surprise, getting lost and wandering off."[20] The outside, seaside promenade is open and grand, with magnificent views and a variety of public activities engaging the water. The insides of the blocks are intimate, quiet, small in scale, and informal, with a labyrinth of paths and small squares.

The strategy of dividing the project into small-scale development plots, assigned to more than forty architect-developer teams, has created a richly diverse architectural experience, avoiding the monotony usually associated with a single developer. The selection of leading architects has led one reviewer to state, "What sets Boo1 apart is the high quality and consistent quality of its housing architecture."[21] There is no question that good contemporary architecture has enriched the urban experience.

Inclusion of the Turning Torso, a signature high-rise building by a signature designer, in the urban design strategy has created an identity, a modern and progressive image, for the project and the city. The building is effective as both a reference point and a landmark in the urban form, however controversial its design may be.

The green space plan with its open storm-water system has led an outside reviewer to state that "Boo1's concentration on the land areas, on the (urban) landscape and the gardens may be a real breakthrough" in urban design.[22] Boo1 shows that the urban landscape is one of the less explored, yet most promising, areas for advancing the dimensions of sustainable urban design.

The specific targets of 100 percent renewable energy supply and 105 kWh/m^2/y energy demand were extremely valuable in shaping the design process of the buildings and infrastructure. The architect-developer teams had to demonstrate how their building designs met the target for demand, and Sydkraft had to devise an integrated system that captured the potential of renewable sources, including primarily wind power and sea- and groundwater thermal energy, with modest contributions from solar power.

Getting actual energy performance to match a specified energy target remains one of the weak links in achieving a low-carbon future. There are so many steps in the process: the detailed design of the building envelope and systems, the accuracy of energy simulations, the quality of construction, the type and thoroughness of inspections, commissioning requirements and procedures, and user controls, operation, and education. Boo1 is a case in point, showing that slight flaws in any of these steps can increase energy use above a target goal. Once energy use exceeds a design target, the system of renewable energy may not have the design capacity to meet 100 percent of demand. Boo1 underscores the importance of improving every step in the process, from sustainable design to operation. A target for energy efficiency is important, but it is not enough.

Good sources of local renewable energy are a prerequisite for achieving 100 percent of the energy supply from renewables. While this is obvious, it is not always the case. Boo1 is fortunate in having both a strong local wind resource and a sea- and groundwater geothermal resource, yet it took an integrated systems approach by Sydkraft to combine and capture the potential of both. The wind machine provides the electric energy to drive the heat pump, which in turn uses the seawater and groundwater as a heat sink to increase the heat pump's coefficiency of performance. Whole-systems thinking was necessary to capture the synergy between these two local renewable resources.

The decision to have Sydkraft own and operate all the renewable systems, even those attached to private property, was essential. It freed homeowners from the risks of maintaining new, unfamiliar technologies, and it consolidated responsibility in an organization set up for the task.

The renewable systems had to be linked to the city's electric grid and its district hot- and cold-water infrastructure so these could act as storage, bridging the gap when the local renewable energy supply could not match neighborhood demand. Only by using the capacity in the city's infrastructure as storage is the neighborhood able to balance energy supply and demand on an annual basis.

On the basis of measured performance, Bo01 demonstrates that it is possible to provide 100 percent of energy supply from local, renewable sources for a small urban neighborhood-scale project. It is the first neighborhood in the world that can make such a claim.

The attention to and the use of storm water as a design feature in the public space is one of the hidden ways to create a more vibrant and animated public experience.

In the category of waste, the approach that emerged was dubbed the eco-cycle. The first step is reduction of waste, the second is recycling of waste, and the third is resource recovery from the waste flows. The third is the most important contribution to sustainability because it eliminates the concept of waste by making it a resource. Even though Bo01's experiments with collecting organic food waste for conversion to biogas failed, they point to the great potential this has for future development. Learning from the systems tested in Bo01 suggests the possibility of a new hybrid combination that captures the best intentions of both systems while being simpler and more cost-effective. Such a system would provide separate disposal bins in each kitchen for convenience. The contents could be dumped at nearby collection points and then delivered to a pretreatment plant before being processed in a digestion plant.

The effort to make Bo01 and the Western Harbor a "national example of sustainable urban development" was greatly assisted by the LIP funding in the eight initiative areas summarized above. It allowed the City of Malmö, the local utility, the SVEBO design team, and the architect-developer teams to think more carefully about what sustainable urban development means. Beyond the commitment to make a high-quality urban environment, the approach that emerged was simple: first reduce the demand for transport and energy and then meet the demand by the most environmentally responsive, renewable means. When Boo1's eco-cycle approach to recycling and resource recovery is included, this is one of the first articulations of what has come to be known as the three R's strategy—reduce, recycle, renew—now recognized as fundamental to sustainability.

The less specific targets were less effective as guiding instruments, especially for selecting and evaluating the environmental impact of building materials. The effort was challenged from the start by the lack of an accepted methodology but just as much by the lack of verified information about the "cradle-to-cradle" environmental impact of specific materials.

By all outward indications, Boo1 has been a financial success for the City of Malmö and the property developers. While no comprehensive financial analysis has been published, anecdotal reports indicate that the city and the developers have more than recovered their increased costs for sustainability. The rate of sales and prices of the properties indicate that it has become a very desirable neighborhood for middle- and upper-middle-income residents. The fact that low-carbon, 100 percent renewable operation is within the market range of middle- to upper-middle-income residents is an important finding. The financial success is why the city has been able to proceed with its subsequent phases. The potential for low-carbon neighborhoods to be affordable for lower-income groups will depend on whether the city can find the means to integrate them successfully into later phases of the project.

LEED-ND Rating

Use of the US Leadership in Energy and Environmental Design for Neighborhood Development (LEED-ND) rating system to evaluate European neighborhoods, such as Boo1, has its anomalies and reveals inherent biases in the LEED-ND system. For example, Boo1 receives no score for Certified Green Building (which requires a LEED-certified person), even though buildings were required to meet a strict energy performance standard in the design phase. It also lost points on Walkable Streets, Street Network, and Tree-Lined and Shaded Streets because the point system is based on a traditional US model of streets with trees and parking, whereas Boo1 has an innovative and sophisticated green rating system. Finally, LEED-ND gives a total of only 6 points for On-Site Renewable Energy Sources, District Heating and Cooling, and Infrastructure Energy Efficiency—just 6 points out of the total of 110, or only 5 percent. It also gives a total of only 7 points for Certified Green Buildings and Building Energy Efficiency, or 6 percent of the total. Given that these are important components in the whole-systems design concept that account for at least a 50 percent reduction in CO_2 emissions (everything but reduction in vehicular transit), they appear to be extremely undervalued at a total of just 11 percent. While Boo1 achieves a good rating of Gold, as the first neighborhood to be 100 percent renewable in energy operation, should it not have a Platinum rating? It would appear that the weighting of the LEED-ND point system should be revised.

Table 2.1. LEED-ND Rating for B001

Criteria	Maximum	Achieved
Smart Location and Linkage		
Prerequisite: Smart Location		X
Prerequisite: Imperiled Species and Ecological Communities		X
Prerequisite: Wetland and Water Body Conservation		X
Prerequisite: Agricultural Land Conservation		X
Prerequisite: Floodplain Avoidance		X
Credit: Preferred Locations	10	5
Credit: Brownfield Redevelopment	2	2
Credit: Locations with Reduced Automobile Dependence	7	7
Credit: Bicycle Network and Storage	1	1
Credit: Housing and Jobs Proximity	3	3
Credit: Steep Slope Protection	1	1
Credit: Site Design for Habitat or Wetland and Water Body Conservation	1	1
Credit: Restoration of Habitat or Wetlands and Water Bodies	1	0
Credit: Long-Term Conservation Management of Habitat or Wetlands and Water Bodies	1	1
Subtotal	27	21

Criteria	Maximum	Achieved
Neighborhood Pattern and Design		
Prerequisite: Walkable Streets		X
Prerequisite: Compact Development		X
Prerequisite: Connected and Open Community		X
Credit: Walkable Streets	12	10
Credit: Compact Development	6	5
Credit: Mixed-Use Neighborhood Centers	4	3
Credit: Mixed-Income Diverse Communities	7	3
Credit: Reduced Parking Footprint	1	1
Credit: Street Network	2	0
Credit: Transit Facilities	1	1
Credit: Transportation Demand Management	2	2
Credit: Access to Civic and Public Spaces	1	1
Credit: Access to Recreation Facilities	1	1
Credit: Visitability and Universal Design	1	1
Credit: Community Outreach and Involvement	2	1
Credit: Local Food Production	1	0
Credit: Tree-Lined and Shaded Streets	2	0
Credit: Neighborhood Schools	1	1
Subtotal	44	30

Table 2.1. LEED-ND Rating for Boo1 (continued)

Criteria	Maximum	Achieved
Green Infrastructure and Buildings		
Prerequisite: Certified Green Building		n/a
Prerequisite: Minimum Building Energy Efficiency		x
Prerequisite: Minimum Building Water Efficiency		x
Prerequisite: Construction Activity Pollution Prevention		x
Credit: Certified Green Buildings	5	n/a
Credit: Building Energy Efficiency	2	2
Credit: Building Water Efficiency	1	1
Credit: Water Efficient Landscaping	1	1
Credit: Existing Building Use	1	1
Credit: Historic Resource Preservation	1	0
Credit: Minimized Site Disturbance in Design and Construction	1	0
Credit: Stormwater Management	4	4
Credit: Heat Island Reduction	1	1
Credit: Solar Orientation	1	0
Credit: On-Site Renewable Energy Sources	3	3
Credit: District Heating and Cooling	2	2
Credit: Infrastructure Energy Efficiency	1	1
Credit: Wastewater Management	2	0
Credit: Recycled Content in Infrastructure	1	1
Credit: Solid Waste Management	1	1
Credit: Light Pollution Reduction	1	1
Subtotal	29	19

Innovation and Design Process		
Credit: Innovation and Exemplary Performance	5	3
Credit: LEED Accredited Professional	1	n/a
Subtotal	6	3

Regional Priority Credit		
Credit: Regional Priority Credit	4	n/a
Subtotal	4	0

Project Totals (Certification Estimates)		
Total Points	110	73
Certification Level	Platinum (80+) Gold (60–79) Silver (50–59) Certified (40–49)	Gold

Source: Harrison Fraker.

3. Hammarby Sjöstad, Stockholm, Sweden

Hammarby Sjöstad, "the town around the lake," is the largest mixed-use housing development undertaken by the city of Stockholm since the 1960s. It is also one of the most financially successful in the city as well as a recognized model of sustainable neighborhood development around the world. The site, which is reclaimed industrial land, is located in a valley with little wind power potential and has only a modest amount of winter solar radiation for Stockholm's cold climate. With such poor sources of renewable energy, how has the neighborhood become such a model of sustainable development? The secret lies in the waste flows and the city's integrated approach to the design of its infrastructure.

Figure 3.1. Aerial view of Hammarby Sjöstad, Stockholm, Sweden, looking south. *(Source: Stockholm City Planning Administration, "Hammarby Sjöstad" [Stockholm: City of Stockholm, 2007].)*

Figure 3.2. View of Sickla Canal in Hammarby Sjöstad. *(Photograph by Lennart Johansson.)*

While the project achieves only part of its goals for energy performance, its innovative approach to infrastructure design presents a promising and little-known potential for creating a low-carbon future.

Process and Plan

The impetus to build Hammarby Sjöstad coalesced because of Sweden's economic boom in 1992, which created a demand for new housing. The City of Stockholm responded by developing new planning strategies for the city. Even though they were not adopted until 1999, as the Stockholm City Plan 99, two of its fundamental strategies influenced the development of Hammarby Sjöstad: (1) to "build the city inward" (the City of Stockholm's central motto) and (2) to achieve "sustainable urban development in accordance with the international community as reflected in the 1996 Istanbul Habitat Agenda."[1]

The current plan was created in 1997 and will include 11,500 residential units for just over 26,000 people by 2017. The plan calls for approximately 250,000–350,000 square meters (m²) for commercial use, accommodating a total of 35,000 people who will live and work in the area.[2] Approximately 8,000 units had been completed as of 2012.

To showcase the strategy of "building inward," the City of Stockholm selected the old industrial harbor area around Lake Hammarby for construction of the new neighborhood. Recognizing that the project would require the expropriation of land; environmental remediation of contaminated soils; extensive reconstruction of infrastructure, including roads; and new public transit, the city assumed the role of master developer.

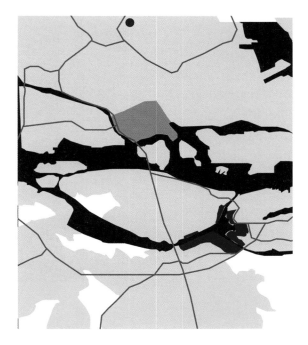

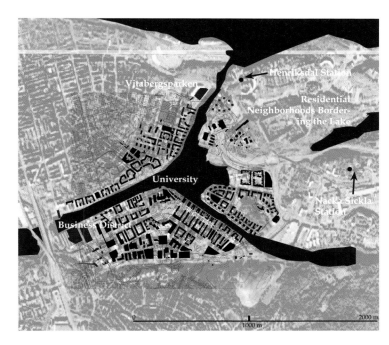

Figure 3.3. Location of Hammarby Sjöstad in Stockholm. *(Drawing by Jessica Yang.)*

Figure 3.4. Context plan of Stockholm. *(Drawing by Jessica Yang.)*

The city established the Hammarby Sjöstad Project Team, an organization within the Stockholm City Planning Administration, to bring together the many city and government agencies and private planning and design professionals hired to do the project. The team was given responsibility for planning, financing, land decontamination, and construction of bridges, streets, pipes, and parks within the district. The team (with consultants) prepared a master plan including physical designs and specifications for the streets, blocks, parks, open space (including quays), land use designations, density, coverage, setbacks, height restrictions, and the like, to guide construction (see "Urban Form" later in this chapter).

In 1998 the city expropriated the land, demolished a shantytown of corrugated steel structures, and began the process of decontamination under the guidance and monitoring of the City of Stockholm's Environment and Health Administration. During this period while the neighborhood plans were evolving, Stockholm decided to bid for the 2004 Summer Olympic Games and proposed the Hammarby Sjöstad area for the Olympic Village. Seeking to impress the Olympic Committee, the city proposed building the village according to an environmental strategy called "double-good,"[3] meaning energy use would be half that of a standard development. Even though Stockholm was not

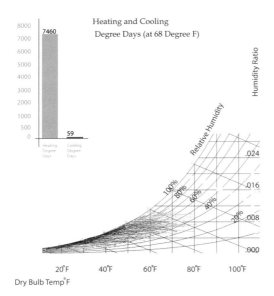

Figure 3.5. Psychrometric chart showing daily temperature ranges per year in Hammarby Sjöstad. The chart indicates that passive solar heating is an effective climate-responsive design strategy. There are 7,362 heating degree days (HDD) at 65°F and seven cooling degree days (CDD) at 72°F. *(Diagram by author. Data source: ESSB Weather Station, Stockholm Bromma, Stockholm, Sweden [17.95E, 59.35N].)*

selected, the environmental objectives survived and the city committed to making Hammarby Sjöstad twice as good, "a leading showcase of urban sustainability."

To ensure realization of the environmental objectives, the Project Team developed a special environmental program. Responsibility for meeting the program's objectives was delegated to the Stockholm Water Company, the energy company Fortum, and the city's Traffic and Waste Management Administration. Working in an integrated manner and under the oversight of the Project Team, they came up with what has become known as the Hammarby model. The key to the model has been described as "its holistic approach to infrastructure service provision and its integration of otherwise separate systems in order to accomplish the environmental objectives."[4] In simple terms, the utility companies found they could recover energy from each other's systems, energy that previously had been wasted. The Hammarby model was devised to supply 50 percent of demand from on-site sources. It is the most integrated whole-systems approach to the flows of energy, water, and waste among the four neighborhoods examined in this book. It was also the most comprehensive model of converting waste to energy known at the time.

The city has been building the master plan in increments, using the Hammarby model as a guide. Working in close partnership with multiple developers and architects chosen to develop individual plots within each block plan, the Project Team prepares a detailed Design Code document to represent the design quality for each designated subarea. The Design Code sets out principles in the following areas:[5]

- District character. Combining of inner-city built form with modern architecture influenced by the natural environment. Key to the character is the mix of uses and businesses, density, built form (blocks built around courtyards or play areas), public spaces, and relationship to water.

- Layout, form, and structure. Creation of specific design parameters for each block with the opportunity for innovation, including key landmark buildings, public spaces, and pedestrian routes.

- Architectural style

- Stockholm inner-city block form as a model

- Sjöstad local distinction—larger units, greater variation in height and form, and greater emphasis on outdoor spaces, balconies, terraces, and flat roofs

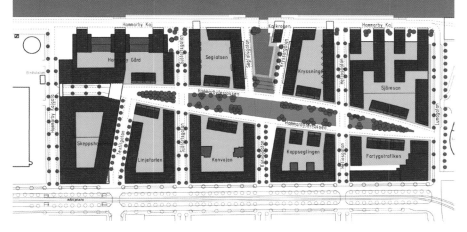

Figure 3.6. Hammarby Gård illustration plan, Hammarby Sjöstad. *(Source: Stockholm City Planning Administration, "Quality Programs for Design" [Stockholm: City of Stockholm].)*

- Building form to respond to its related open space
- Scale, order, and variation—density guidelines to be met but with emphasis on quality and variation
- Building types
- Building design principles
- Building elements
- Apartment standards
- Standards for additional services
- Building color and material
- Design of courtyards
- Design of public spaces, parks, and streets

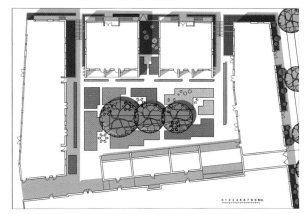

Figure 3.7. Kappseglingen courtyard plan, Hammarby Sjöstad. *(Source: Stockholm City Planning Administration, "Quality Programs for Design." Redrawn by Ariel Utz.)*

The Design Team continues to monitor the progress of construction and ensures that all of the Design Code criteria and environmental standards are met. By not allowing any block to be developed by a single developer or architect and by enforcing a specific design code, the process ensures that each development area achieves an authentic diversity of architectural expression while maintaining a coherent urban design integrity.

To ensure the principle of "twice as good," the Project Team articulated general environmental program goals to be followed by the architect-developer teams:[6]

- Maintain the local ecology.
- Minimize consumption of resources, including energy and water.
- Increase local energy generation.
- Utilize sewage for energy generation.
- Use renewable or recyclable building materials.
- Achieve total soil decontamination.

Figure 3.8. Kappseglingen courtyard section elevation, Hammarby Sjöstad. *(Source: Stockholm City Planning Administration, "Quality Programs for Design.")*

- Restore the lake.

- Reduce transport needs.

- Stimulate community cohesion and ecological responsibility of residents.

- Use implementation as a lever for development of new solutions.

- Use solutions that will not increase life-cycle costs.

- Generate knowledge, experience, and technology to contribute to sustainable development in other areas.

Since the environmental program goals are quite general, the Project Team developed a more specific set of criteria and targets for each of the topics discussed below.

Transportation

The more detailed goals for transportation included the following:[7]

- 80 percent of residents' and workers' journeys to be by foot, bicycle, or public transit (light-rail, bus, or ferry) by 2010.

- 15 percent of households to be signed up for carpooling by 2010.

- 5 percent of workplaces to be signed up to promote carpools by 2010.

In response, the City of Stockholm has made major investments in the road and transportation infrastructure to connect Hammarby Sjöstad with the rest of Stockholm. A new light-rail tram makes four stops along the main-street spine of the development and connects at each end directly to the Stockholm underground. The stops are positioned such that every residence is within 300 meters of a stop, and the frequency of trams is every twelve minutes. The small-scale blocks with generous sidewalks, paths through the park system, and pedestrian shortcuts make access highly convenient. Three bus lines stop in the neighborhood or in close proximity. A free, year-round ferry crosses the lake every fifteen minutes from early in the morning until late at night, connecting to the central city and existing transit lines.

Parking is supplied primarily in underground garages below the blocks, with limited on-street parking. The parking ratio is 0.7 space per unit,[8] which is higher than the Stockholm average (0.5 space per unit), and 62 percent of households own cars. In spite of the higher parking ratio and car ownership, daily trips by car are well below the Swedish average of approximately 50 percent, in large part because of the convenience and low cost of public transit, which make it an attractive alternative. This is supported by the studies reported below.

Preliminary transportation studies[9] report that by 2008, 52 percent of trips were by public transit (tram, bus, ferry), 27 percent were by foot or bicycle, and 21 percent were by private car. This indicates that the design goal of 80 percent of trips by foot, bike, and public transit has been largely achieved (79 percent). It is clear evidence that the integration of transit design and urban form is critical in an effort to reduce car usage and the related energy consumption and carbon emissions. The appropriate frequency, cost, and connectivity of transit design, integrated with small-scale blocks, pleasant sidewalks, and a pedestrian network through the parks with shortcuts through the blocks, were essential ingredients in creating this sustainable neighborhood. It is unclear whether the parking policy, the cost and ratio of 0.7 space per unit, has played a significant role in achieving the goal of 80 percent by foot, bike, and public transit.

Figure 3.9. Transit plan for Hammarby Sjöstad. *(Drawing by Nancy Nam.)*

Urban Form

The more detailed goals for urban form included the following:[10]

- Typical inner-city street dimensions (6–18-meter residential streets), block lengths (60–70 meters by 120–200 meters), and building heights (2–8 floors)
- Density and usage integrated with a contemporary airiness
- Water views from public space and residences
- Parks and sunlight
- A modified "modern architectural" agenda to include the following:
  - Restricted building depths, set-back penthouses, and multilevel apartments
  - Generous balconies and terraces, large windows, flat roofs, and pale plaster facades facing the water

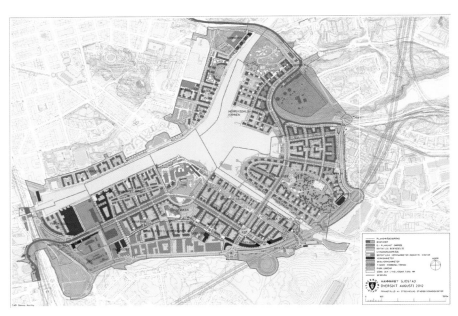

Figure 3.10. Master plan for Hammarby Sjöstad. *(Source: Stockholm City Planning Administration, "Hammarby Sjöstad.")*

Figure 3.11. Main street spine plan diagram, Hammarby Sjöstad. *(Drawing by Nancy Nam.)*

The urban form of Hammarby Sjöstad is modeled after the Stockholm city block and street typology. It is structured around a main street with vehicular traffic in both directions and a public tram down the center, creating a transit spine. The main street, together with cross streets, forms a grid pattern of urban blocks, which are zoned for narrow-perimeter buildings around courtyards. The street grid shifts in order to follow the multiple orientations of Lake Hammarby's shoreline. Because the shoreline's orientations are at oblique angles to the cardinal points of the compass, the street grid is at odd angles with the east–west, north–south orientation of classical city planning. The resulting orientations are not favorable to passive solar collection for many of the housing blocks. On the other hand, they do create a rich variety of sun and light conditions on the building facades and streets.

The main street parallels the shoreline on the edge of the Hammarby Gård district, shifts at a hinge-like plaza, and then follows the shoreline of the canal on the edge of the Sickla Kaj district until it turns to cross Sickla Canal to the Sickla Udde district. The total length of the commercial frontage is 1,800 meters, with four tram stops, including a covered main station. The cross section of the street locates commercial space on the first two floors and housing above, totaling five or six floors.

The pattern of streets and blocks is modulated by a syncopated rhythm of urban landscape open spaces. In the cross section leading to the lake, there is an alternating structure of main street, block, open space, block, water's edge. In this manner, each block has a singular identity, and all blocks are separated by public open space. In the cross section parallel to the lake, the blocks are separated by the cross streets, but these are distinguished

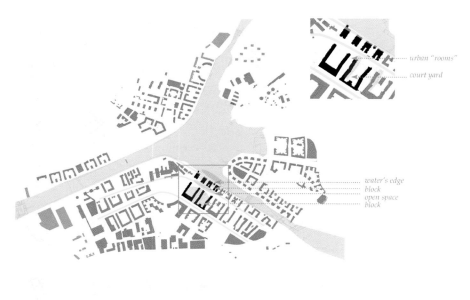

urban "rooms"
court yard

water's edge
block
open space
block

Figure 3.12. Street plan for Hammarby Sjöstad. *(Drawing by Nancy Nam.)*

through angled setbacks of building facades creating distinct urban "rooms," further articulated by different treatments of the landscape and street parking.

The Stockholm perimeter block concept has been altered by opening the side facing the lake, creating U-shaped courtyards with views to the lake. The buildings located on the blocks at the water's edge are positioned to maintain view corridors, maximizing the number of units with oblique lake views, deep into the plan. The building designs take advantage of the views with multiple types of balconies and terraces. The scale of the lakeshore makes the courtyards semipublic. The blocks are relatively small in dimension, in the range of 60–80 meters by 100–120 meters (at the property lines), adding to the pedestrian-friendly nature of the neighborhood.

Specific design guidelines for each development district define the urban form of each block in the district. The design guidelines are extremely detailed and prescriptive in content. Not only do they dictate the shape, height, width, and setback of buildings, but they also prescribe detailed articulations in plan and section. In addition, they specify materials, colors, and window and door details while also giving a full set of landscape plans and details for the courtyards.

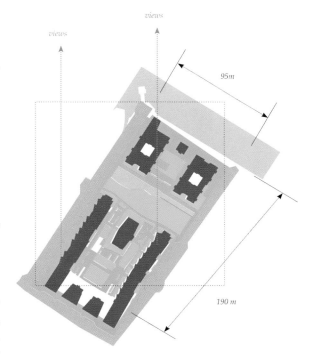

views
views
95m
190 m

Figure 3.13. Block plan for Hammarby Sjöstad. *(Drawing by Harrison Fraker.)*

Figure 3.14. View of balconies facing the lake in Hammarby Sjöstad. *(Photograph by Lennart Johansson.)*

Green Space

The specific goals for the green space system included the following:[11]

- Reuse, clean up, and transform the brownfield into an attractive mixed-use residential district with parks and public spaces.
- Adhere to an open space standard of at least 15 square meters of courtyard space and a total of 25–30 square meters of courtyard and park space within 300 meters of every apartment.
- Protect natural areas of particular value.
- If undeveloped green space is developed, replace it with biotopes that increase the area's biodiversity.

The green open spaces that divide the blocks vary in landscape type, creating distinct districts. In the Sickla Kaj district, the open space is a linear park with different uses and landscape treatments at each block. A storm-water bioswale runs the whole length of the seven blocks, unifying the ensemble with an architectonic feature that serves the important environmental function of detaining storm water before it descends into the lake via a water ladder. In the Sickla Udde district, the open space is more like a picturesque English park with meandering paths that wind through stands of trees and over hilly contours, creating interesting views of the site. The open space in Hammarby Gård is a long, narrow, mews-like oval with smaller-scale housing units fronting it.

Figure 3.15. Green space plan for Hammarby Sjöstad. *(Drawing by Nancy Nam.)*

The green space concept takes advantage of extensive water frontage along the lake (approximately 5.8 kilometers) with public access on its entire length. The treatment varies from natural wetlands to highly structured quays to small harbors for docking and boating, creating a rich experience of the water's edge. The whole system provides an exceptional amenity for running, walking, cycling, and simple passive recreation.

Energy

The energy efficiency goals set by the Project Team included the following:[12]

Figure 3.16. View of the edge of Sickla Canal in Hammarby Sjöstad. *(Photograph by Lennart Johansson.)*

- Total energy consumption was to be 105 kilowatt-hours per square meter per year (kWh/m²/y), achieved through conservation and tight construction. (A more ambitious goal of 60 kWh/m²/y was modified to meet the requirement that "solutions should not increase cost.")

- The goal for total energy use was set at 105 kWh/m²/y, in contrast to the Swedish average at the time, 270 kWh/m²/y. As mentioned, a much more ambitious 60 kWh/m²/y was considered but was deemed not to be cost-effective. Nonetheless, to achieve 105 kWh/m²/y requires higher standards of insulation, better-quality windows (especially in U-value and air infiltration rating), and tighter construction to reduce air infiltration overall. It also requires more energy-efficient appliances and lighting. These higher standards are integrated into the development process by inclusion in the Design Code for each development district. The Project Team continues to monitor the progress of construction to ensure that the Design Code standards are met.

Figure 3.17. View of the lake-edge pedestrian walkway in Hammarby Sjöstad. *(Photograph by Lennart Johansson.)*

Performance data for energy consumption were collected for 2005.[13] The data represent the actual consumption of both electric and thermal energy as measured by the residential meters. The goal of 105 kWh/m²/y is assumed to be divided into 35 kWh/m²/y for electricity and 70 kWh/m²/y for thermal energy. The original aggressive goal of 60 kWh/m²/y is divided in the same proportions for further comparison. Table 3.1 displays the two goals against the average measured performance and the ranges of variation.

As can be seen in table 3.1, energy consumption was approximately 50 percent higher (157 kWh/m²/y) than the goal (105 kWh/m²/y). This has been attributed to several factors:[14] (1) larger glass areas to take advantage of lake views resulted in greater heat loss in the winter (without passive solar gains because of predominantly north, east, and west orientations); (2) greater solar gain in the summer (east- and west-facing glass) increased cooling loads; and (3) not all residents purchased high-performance appliances and lighting fixtures. This is a clear example in which urban design decisions about orientation to capture views have compromised energy performance.

The energy supply goals set by the Project Team included the following:[15]

- Supply 50 percent of the energy demand on-site.
- Supply district heating by a heat recovery plant that uses purified wastewater from the site as a heat source.
- Provide district heating and electricity by a cogeneration plant that burns combustible waste from the site, with additional biofuel obtained off-site.
- Incorporate limited arrays of solar photovoltaic cells and solar hot-water panels to demonstrate and test new technology.
- Generate biogas from wastewater sludge for city vehicles.

In the Hammarby model, energy is captured from three different waste flows. First, combustible garbage is burned in the Högdalen cogeneration

Table 3.1. Energy Goals versus Measured Performance

	Goal	(Goal)	Measured (2005)	Range (2005)
Electric	35 kWh/m²/y	(20 kWh/m²/y)	46 kWh/m²/y	40–51 kWh/m²/y
Thermal	70 kWh/m²/y	(40 kWh/m²/y)	111 kWh/m²/y	47–177 kWh/m²/y
Total	105 kWh/m²/y	(60 kWh/m²/y)	157 kWh/m²/y	87–228 kWh/m²/y

plant, delivering district heating and electricity. Second, wastewater (sewage) is treated in the Sjöstaden's and Henriksdal's wastewater treatment plants. Before the sewage is returned to the sea, the heat is recovered by a heat pump in the Hammarby thermal power station, which contributes to the district heating and cooling systems. Third, the sludge in the Sjöstaden's and Henriksdal's treatment plants is digested and converted to biogas for cooking, to generate electricity, and to power city buses.

The goal of supplying 50 percent of the energy demand from on-site sources is ambitious and is also highly dependent on reaching the energy-demand reduction goals. As we have seen, these have not been met.

The other half of the equation, determining the amount of energy supplied from on-site sources, is complicated by the multiple steps in the waste-to-energy processes employed and the fact that most of the steps are not

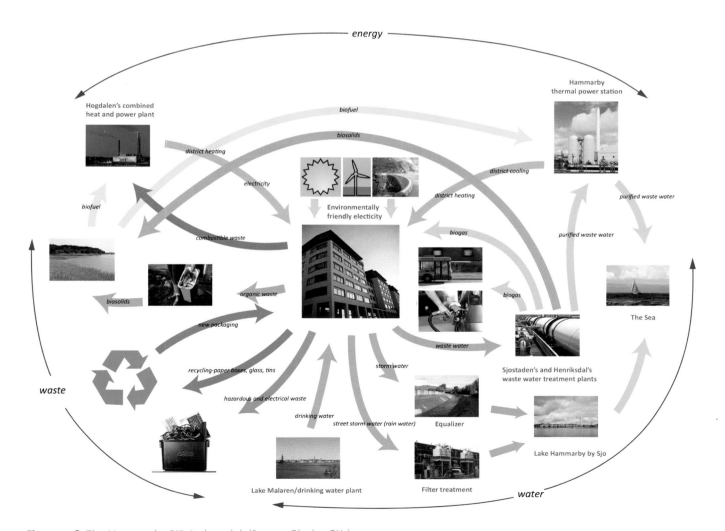

Figure 3.18. The Hammarby Sjöstad model. *(Source: GlashusEtt.)*

metered. However, by knowing the average amount of wastewater generated per person per year, the average amount of municipal solid waste produced per person per year, and the reported, measured efficiencies of the various processes, it is possible to calculate the amount of energy produced by each person's waste stream. Table 3.2 summarizes this energy production.[16]

The energy supplied by each person can now be converted to the average-sized dwelling unit of 80 square meters with an average of 2.27 occupants, as shown in table 3.3.

The total amount of energy supplied by the waste streams can now be compared with the two different goals for energy demand and the measured data on energy demand, as shown in table 3.4.

When the amount of electric energy supplied by solar photovoltaics is added to the equation, with it estimated (not measured) at 5 percent of demand, the percentage of energy supplied by on-site sources (both waste and solar) increases by only 1–2 percent.

It is clear from the measured performance that the goal of 50 percent energy supply from on-site sources has not been met; indeed, only 20 percent of the measured demand has been attained. However, if the initial goal of 60 kWh/m²/y had been maintained and achieved, the goal of 50 percent supply from on-site sources would have been exceeded (54 percent, including photovoltaics). What this shows is that achieving aggressive energy conservation goals is a critical factor in being able to supply a high percentage of energy from on-site sources.

Even though the goal of 50 percent energy supply from on-site sources has not been achieved, the amount of energy supplied by on-site waste flows is not trivial by any measure. Twenty percent of the actual measured demand is significant. As an added benefit, it comes from a source of continuous flow, and thus, unlike wind and solar energy, it can be used to meet base loads. The

Table 3.2. Energy Production from Waste Streams per Person

Source	Heat (kWh/y)	Electricity (kWh/y)
54,750 L wastewater/person-year	0.396	n/a
4.1 m³ biogas from wastewater/person-year	8.5	5.7
450 kg combustible municipal solid waste/person-year	886.0	202.0
Total	894.9	207.7
	895 kWh/y	208 kWh/y

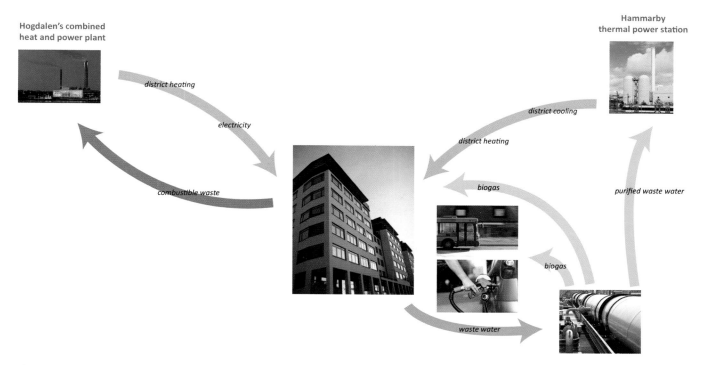

Figure 3.19. Waste-to-energy cycle, Hammarby Sjöstad. *(Source: GlashusEtt, Hammarby Sjöstad: A Unique Environmental Project in Stockholm [Stockholm: City of Stockholm, 2007].)*

Table 3.3. Total Energy from Waste

Heating	$\dfrac{895\ \text{kWh/y} \times 2.27}{80\ \text{m}^2} = 25.4\ \text{kWh/m}^2/\text{y}$
Electricity	$\dfrac{208\ \text{kWh/y} \times 2.27}{80\ \text{m}^2} = 5.9\ \text{kWh/m}^2/\text{y}$
Total	31.3 kWh/m²/y

Table 3.4. Percentage of Energy Supplied by Waste Compared with Different Demand Goals and Measured Performance

Supply (waste)	31.3 kWh/m²/y = 52%
Demand goal (initial)	60.0 kWh/m²/y
Supply (waste)	31.3 kWh/m²/y = 30%
Demand goal (revised)	105.0 kWh/m²/y
Supply (waste)	31.3 kWh/m²/y = 20%
Demand (measured)	157.0 kWh/m²/y

Note: Data show that 50% of the energy supply could have been delivered from waste if the original goal of 60 kWh/m²/y had been achieved.

Figure 3.20. View of photovoltaic facade screen in Hammarby Sjöstad. *(Photograph by Lennart Johansson.)*

potential impact for sustainable city building is transformative. Rather than paying to truck municipal solid waste to landfills, cities can use the waste to provide a large fraction of the base load for heating and electricity.

Water

The overarching goal for water is to reduce demand by 50 percent (through water-conserving fixtures)[17] to 100 liters per person-day.

Reducing water use is the simplest way to address the wasteful flow-through model of water consumption and treatment. By setting the goal of reducing water usage by 50 percent, Hammarby Sjöstad initiated the first step in a more sustainable approach to water supply. The reduction is achieved by requiring in the design guidelines that each architect-developer team install low-flow toilets and fixtures in all housing units. Water consumption[18] has been measured to be 150 liters per person-day, halfway to the goal of 100 liters per person-day.

The Hammarby model does not include any rainwater capture or any system to recycle storm water or treated sewage for irrigation or potable water. Water is supplied by the city's central system.

The goal for wastewater is for treatment to be provided by the city plant. Hammarby Sjöstad's wastewater (sewage) is treated at Stockholm's Henriksdal's plant. It is treated to the highest standards of the World Health Organization. Energy and fertilizer are extracted from it before it is released into the bay. A new experimental treatment plant is testing innovative alternative systems.

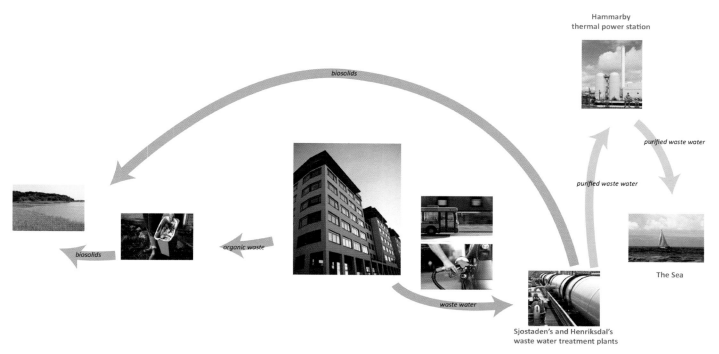

Figure 3.21. Wastewater cycle, Hammarby Sjöstad. *(Source: GlashusEtt, Hammarby Sjöstad.)*

The goal for storm water is that it be treated in bioswales as a landscape feature. This is managed in a variety of ways. Storm water from buildings and courtyards is detained in a storm-water bioswale canal and in paved gutters before being released into Lake Hammarby via a water ladder. The goal for street-water runoff is that it be collected on-site in settling tanks and filtered. In this way, all rainwater and snowmelt from streets is drained into holding basins and then into settling tanks. It remains there for several hours, allowing contaminants to sink to the bottom, before being drained into the canals.

Waste

The goals for waste included the following:[19]

- Reduce solid waste by 15 percent by weight and recycle it using an automated system with vacuum chutes, block-based recycling rooms, and area-based collection points for residents to sort newspaper, glass, plastic, and metals.
- Collect combustible waste and convert it into district heating and electricity.

Figure 3.22. View of storm-water bioswale in Hammarby Sjöstad. *(Photograph by Lennart Johansson.)*

Figure 3.23. View of storm-water retention in Hammarby Sjöstad. *(Photograph by Lennart Johansson.)*

Figure 3.24. View of storm-water ladder in Hammarby Sjöstad. *(Photograph by Lennart Johansson.)*

- Compost organic waste (garbage) and use it as fertilizer.
- Collect hazardous waste for off-site disposal.

Eliminating the concept of waste is the most comprehensive approach to waste removal; however, reducing the initial flow of waste is an important first step. Hammarby Sjöstad set the goal of reducing solid waste by 15 percent by weight and, further, has taken the most comprehensive approach by recycling or reusing all the remaining flows. These goals are as follows:

- Sort and collect all solid waste (glass, plastics, metals, and newspaper), using a vacuum system at locations around the site, and then recycle it. The system is employed to eliminate the transportation energy use and pollution caused by garbage trucks.

- Collect combustible waste and convert it into district heating and electricity (see "Energy," above).
- Collect and compost garbage (organic waste).

Following are the goals for materials that relate to waste avoidance or disposal:

- Use recycled materials where environmentally and economically feasible.
- Deposit no more than 20 percent of construction waste in landfills.

Social Agenda

The social intentions for the project included the following:[20]

- Designate the new residential district as mixed-use.
- Provide "comfortable living" with good lake views.
- Promote healthy living in a natural setting.
- Balance comfortable living and environmental sustainability.
- Mix jobs and housing.

At the beginning of the project, the city assumed that the new neighborhood would be primarily for elderly residents moving back to the city from the suburbs, but that assumption was wrong. In Sweden, financial assistance for housing is provided directly to low- and moderate-income families[21] on the basis of income, so they are free to find suitable housing in the marketplace. As a result of this policy and because of the pedestrian- and environmentally friendly qualities of the neighborhood, from the very beginning the neighborhood was attractive to young families with children. Fortunately, the city was able to respond by revising the plan to include schools and community facilities suited to their needs. A detailed demographic analysis has not been found except for a report that the average income in the neighborhood is approximately 20 percent above the average citywide.[22]

Lessons Learned

The critical role that city government played in achieving an innovative approach to sustainable neighborhood development is the most important lesson learned. By acting as the primary, horizontal, developer, the city was able to insist that the utilities, the agencies involved in providing energy, water, waste removal, sewage treatment, and transportation, work together

Figure 3.25. View of vacuum waste system stations in Hammarby Sjöstad. *(Photograph by Lennart Johansson.)*

Figure 3.26. View of vacuum waste system collection in Hammarby Sjöstad. *(Photograph by Lennart Johansson.)*

to come up with an integrated approach to the neighborhood's infrastructure. This resulted in the Hammarby model, described earlier. It remains one of the most integrated whole-systems approaches to sustainable neighborhood infrastructure yet built.

By acting as the lead developer, the city was also able to establish aggressive energy efficiency goals that go beyond the current standards in Stockholm. This is the first means of lowering energy demand and one of the most cost-effective, essential in achieving sustainability and lowering carbon footprint. To this end, the city established detailed design guidelines for each development parcel in order to achieve more aggressive energy efficiency goals, urban design qualities, and architectural character. The city used the normal permitting process to review whether guidelines were being met. This level of control did not discourage participation in the process by architect-developer teams.

Any approach to sustainable neighborhoods must begin with the relationship between transportation, urban form (the streets and blocks), and mixed use. Creating a high-quality pedestrian environment with convenient and close proximity to transit stops is essential for achieving a high percentage of trips by public transit. Providing a sufficient mix of convenient local shopping and local jobs limits the need for trips outside the neighborhood. Simply stated, creating a pedestrian-friendly environment matters in reducing dependence on the car as the primary mode of transit. From the perspective of achieving sustainability or reducing carbon emissions, "there is no car like no car." While the site is relatively isolated by its topography and the lake, the public transit system of tram, buses, and ferries, along with a focus on pedestrians and bikes, has fully integrated Hammarby Sjöstad into the city, reducing the use of the car to satisfy daily needs.

Building orientation, along with glazing size and orientation, also matters. These factors can have a critical effect on energy consumption. When a desire to take advantage of attractive views conflicts with the most favorable window orientation for energy conservation, it is important to provide dynamic solar control and nighttime insulation to mitigate increased energy losses and gains. In Hammarby Sjöstad, the lack of such environmentally responsive building systems has been cited as the reason for measured energy consumption exceeding the desired goal for energy demand.

In part because each block has been built by more than one architect-developer team, the highly prescriptive guidelines have not produced a sterile or repetitive environment. On the contrary, because the guidelines have left just enough room for the multiple architect-developer teams to innovate in their own right, the urban design ensemble is rich and fresh, with authentic differences in expression.

The strategy of combining a traditional urban design concept of streets and blocks with the development of a modern architectural expression has produced an uncommon synthesis of urban design. This is not a neo-traditional neighborhood, nor is it a stereotypical, sterile modern planned neighborhood of the 1950s. It is a rich, contemporary expression of urban development with up-to-date construction techniques and materials. One of the side benefits of the modern architectural expression and detailing is that the limited application of the solar photovoltaics and hot-water collectors is seamless and perceived as a natural outgrowth of the environmental goals of the project.

The idea of trying to create a low-carbon community primarily from the waste streams generated by the high-density housing has meant that the urban design, the form of the blocks and buildings, can respond more to capturing the special qualities of the site, rather than being shaped by the need to optimize sustainable technologies such as solar collectors or wind machines.

The urban form of Hammarby Sjöstad has been successful on multiple levels. The lake has become an engaging asset, creating a unique sense of place. The provision of mixed use—a library, schools, health-care facilities, recreational facilities, restaurants, and local commercial establishments—creates a complete sense of community. The neighborhood is successfully served by transit anchored by the main-street tram. On the other hand, with the increased width of the street to accommodate the tram and the psychological separation it creates, the commercial area may function more as two one-sided commercial strips. Even though the street is activated by the tram, it is not clear whether its division into two sides and separate sections will allow the synergy among shops necessary for it to be a successful commercial street. The question is raised in part at this stage of development because not all of the shops have been built and only approximately 8,000 of the 12,000 units of housing have been built, but the problem has been exacerbated by the fact that functions such as the library and some restaurants have been located along the lakeshore, further drawing energy away from the commercial street.

The green space system for Hammarby Sjöstad has had a positive effect on the experience of residents. Almost every housing unit is less than one block from a park, each with its own landscape identity, and less than three blocks from the lakefront. The result is a green space system that is just as dominant as the streets and buildings. When this is combined with the streets and pedestrian paths that open to the lake, the public space of Hammarby Sjöstad is as much about a lake and park as it is about the city—it is urbanism with a markedly higher proportion of green, and this is why it has been so attractive to residents.

The Hammarby model is one of the best examples of using neighborhood waste streams for generating energy and recovering heat. It is the closest any system has come to eliminating the concept of waste. Combustible solid waste is collected and burned to provide district heating and electricity. Any toxic waste from combustion is captured in the flues, contained, and disposed of off-site. The sludge from sewage is converted to gas in an anaerobic digester and used for multiple purposes: it powers city buses, provides cooking gas for 1,000 homes, and generates some electricity. The organic garbage is composted. Heat is recovered from the treated sewage effluent before it is returned to the bay. All glass, metal, plastics, and newspapers are recycled. Only a small amount of toxic material (from television sets and other electronics) is collected and carefully disposed of.

The performance data from Hammarby Sjöstad show that a significant portion (20 percent) of neighborhood heating and electric demand can be provided from local neighborhood waste. This is a particularly important lesson learned, especially for cities or neighborhoods that pay a premium to have their waste trucked to landfills and their sewage treated and dumped without recovering any energy.

Even though the goal of generating 50 percent of the neighborhood's energy needs from local sources was not achieved, this was not caused by the performance of the waste recovery systems. It is attributed to the fact that the energy-demand reduction goal was not achieved; that is, the denominator in the equation came in too high to achieve the 50 percent goal. This underscores the important lesson that reducing energy demand to the lowest level economically possible is a secret to generating the highest percentage of energy from local sources. This is the first principle in the idea of "closing the circle," of making a neighborhood self-sufficient in operation, running only on its local sources of energy.

Hammarby Sjöstad is one of the first models to demonstrate the potential role of natural storm-water treatment as a design feature of the urban landscape. The storm-water canal and bioswale running the length of Sickla Kaj gives a special identity and animation to almost one-third of the district. It brings nature alive in the city.

The waste-to-energy program demonstrates the potential of whole-systems thinking as a path to a low-carbon future. The next step in whole-systems thinking will be to capture the energy in organic garbage by converting it to biogas rather than fertilizer.

The combination of transit-oriented, mixed-use, green space, and urban design strategies with lake views has created a vibrant middle-class community where sustainability strategies are a background feature. Affordability has been subsidized directly to families by the government. The result has paid off for the city as each development phase has sold out almost immediately, confirming its social desirability for a cross section of Swedish society.

LEED-ND Rating

Using the US Leadership in Energy and Environmental Design for Neighborhood Development (LEED-ND) rating system to evaluate European neighborhoods, such as Hammarby Sjöstad, has its anomalies and reveals inherent biases in the LEED-ND system. For example, Hammarby receives no score for Certified Green Building (which requires a LEED-certified person), even though buildings were required to meet a strict energy performance standard in the design phase. It also lost points on Walkable Streets, Street Network, and Tree-Lined and Shaded Streets because the point system is based on a traditional US model of streets with trees and parking, whereas Hammarby Sjöstad has an elaborate green space system integrated into the block system. Finally, LEED-ND gives a total of only 6 points for On-Site Renewable Energy Sources, District Heating and Cooling, and Infrastructure Energy Efficiency—just 6 points out of the total of 110, or only 5 percent. It also gives a total of only 7 points for Certified Green Buildings and Building Energy Efficiency, or 6 percent of the total. Since these are important components in the whole-systems design concept that account for at least a 50 percent reduction in carbon dioxide (CO_2) emissions (everything but reduction in vehicular transit), it appears to be extremely undervalued at a total of just 11 percent. While Hammarby Sjöstad achieves a rating of Gold, this rating seems high, given that only 20 percent of the energy comes from on-site renewables. It would appear that the weighting of the LEED-ND point system should be revised.

Table 3.5. LEED-ND Rating for Hammarby Sjöstad

Criteria	Maximum	Achieved
Smart Location and Linkage		
Prerequisite: Smart Location		X
Prerequisite: Imperiled Species and Ecological Communities		X
Prerequisite: Wetland and Water Body Conservation		X
Prerequisite: Agricultural Land Conservation		X
Prerequisite: Floodplain Avoidance		X
Credit: Preferred Locations	10	5
Credit: Brownfield Redevelopment	2	2
Credit: Locations with Reduced Automobile Dependence	7	7
Credit: Bicycle Network and Storage	1	1
Credit: Housing and Jobs Proximity	3	3
Credit: Steep Slope Protection	1	1
Credit: Site Design for Habitat or Wetland and Water Body Conservation	1	1
Credit: Restoration of Habitat or Wetlands and Water Bodies	1	1
Credit: Long-Term Conservation Management of Habitat or Wetlands and Water Bodies	1	1
Subtotal	27	22

Neighborhood Pattern and Design		
Prerequisite: Walkable Streets		X
Prerequisite: Compact Development		X
Prerequisite: Connected and Open Community		X
Credit: Walkable Streets	12	10
Credit: Compact Development	6	5
Credit: Mixed-Use Neighborhood Centers	4	4
Credit: Mixed-Income Diverse Communities	7	3
Credit: Reduced Parking Footprint	1	1
Credit: Street Network	2	0
Credit: Transit Facilities	1	1
Credit: Transportation Demand Management	2	2
Credit: Access to Civic and Public Spaces	1	1
Credit: Access to Recreation Facilities	1	1
Credit: Visitability and Universal Design	1	1
Credit: Community Outreach and Involvement	2	1
Credit: Local Food Production	1	0
Credit: Tree-Lined and Shaded Streets	2	1
Credit: Neighborhood Schools	1	1
Subtotal	44	32

Table 3.5. LEED-ND Rating for Hammarby Sjöstad (continued)

Criteria	Maximum	Achieved
Green Infrastructure and Buildings		
Prerequisite: Certified Green Building		n/a
Prerequisite: Minimum Building Energy Efficiency		x
Prerequisite: Minimum Building Water Efficiency		x
Prerequisite: Construction Activity Pollution Prevention		x
Credit: Certified Green Buildings	5	n/a
Credit: Building Energy Efficiency	2	2
Credit: Building Water Efficiency	1	1
Credit: Water Efficient Landscaping	1	1
Credit: Existing Building Use	1	1
Credit: Historic Resource Preservation	1	0
Credit: Minimized Site Disturbance in Design and Construction	1	0
Credit: Stormwater Management	4	4
Credit: Heat Island Reduction	1	1
Credit: Solar Orientation	1	0
Credit: On-Site Renewable Energy Sources	3	3
Credit: District Heating and Cooling	2	2
Credit: Infrastructure Energy Efficiency	1	1
Credit: Wastewater Management	2	2
Credit: Recycled Content in Infrastructure	1	1
Credit: Solid Waste Management	1	1
Credit: Light Pollution Reduction	1	1
Subtotal	29	21
Innovation and Design Process		
Credit: Innovation and Exemplary Performance	5	3
Credit: LEED Accredited Professional	1	n/a
Subtotal	6	3
Regional Priority Credit		
Credit: Regional Priority Credit	4	n/a
Subtotal	4	0

Project Totals (Certification Estimates)

	Maximum	Achieved
Total Points	**110**	**78**
Certification Level	Platinum (80+) Gold (60–79) Silver (50–59) Certified (40–49)	Gold

Source: Harrison Fraker.

4. Kronsberg, Hannover, Germany

In developing the new Kronsberg district, the City of Hannover sought to address a serious housing shortage in the 1990s and, at the same time, to present a comprehensive example of visionary urban planning and construction as its part of the EXPO 2000 World Exposition. Consistent with the exposition's motto, "Humankind-Nature-Technology," the city wanted to apply "all available knowledge of ecological optimization in construction and habitation, consistently and holistically throughout the area according to the principles of Agenda 21."[1] The city planned the district itself to become an exhibit.

The plan was to provide 3,000 dwellings in the first phase (by EXPO 2000) and eventually 6,000 units for a total of 12,000–15,000 people from a wide range of economic and social backgrounds. Construction of the community was projected to create 2,000 jobs. With ambitious goals, demands for quality, and a tight schedule, the City of Hannover had to come up with special planning procedures. It set binding quality standards for all planning measures in pursuing its goals. The specific planning instruments developed as part of the process have been successful not only in creating a high quality of life in the district, as reported by residents, but also in achieving most of the goals for sustainability. More than ten years after the opening of EXPO 2000, these procedures and instruments hold important secrets for how to achieve real, measured, sustainable low-carbon operation. They represent a different model that is transferable to other development projects.

Figure 4.1. Aerial view of Kronsberg, Hannover, Germany, from the southwest. *(Photograph by Karl Johaentges.)*

Figure 4.2. View of eastern-edge pedestrian and bike allée in Kronsberg. *(Photograph by Karl Johaentges.)*

Process and Plan

The planning jurisdiction for all of the Kronsberg area was transferred to the City of Hannover as part of a local government redistricting in 1974. It provided a large development opportunity (140 hectares) on a greenfield at the edge of the city. Hannover's selection for the EXPO 2000 World Exposition in 1990 became the occasion to develop the site chosen for the exposition in 1991. As the primary landowner with planning jurisdiction, the city took the lead in the planning process.

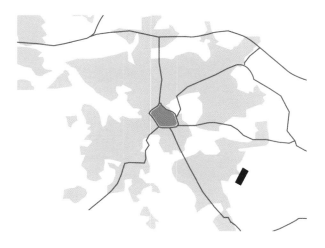

Figure 4.3. Location of Kronsberg within Hannover. *(Drawing by Jessica Yang.)*

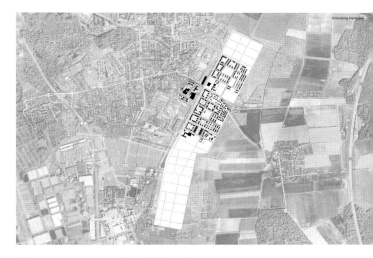

Figure 4.4. Context plan of Kronsberg. *(Drawing by Jessica Yang.)*

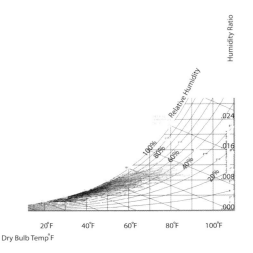

Figure 4.5. Psychrometric chart showing daily temperature ranges per year in Kronsberg. The chart indicates passive solar heating as an effective climate-responsive design strategy. Heating degree days (HDD) at 65°F = 5,717; cooling degree days (CDD) at 72°F = 91. *(Diagram by Harrison Fraker. Data source: EDDV Weather Station, Hannover, Germany [9.68E, 52.47N].)*

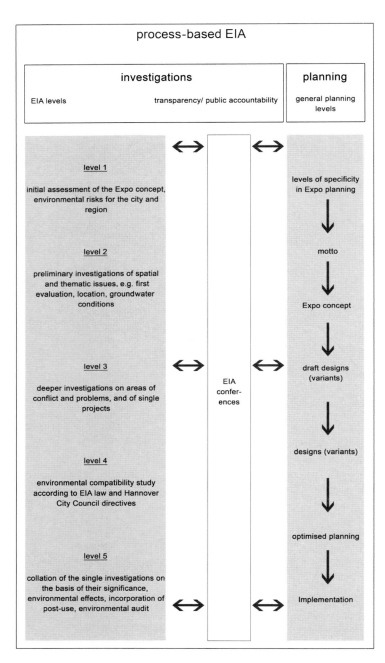

Figure 4.6. Process-based environmental impact analysis. *(Source: Karin Rumming, ed., Hannover Kronsberg Handbook: Planning and Realisation [Leipzig: Jütte Druck, 2004]. Redrawn by Ariel Utz.)*

The plan for Kronsberg follows the regional planning principle that residential development should expand along local public rail transit routes and be concentrated at urban densities in the catchment areas around stops. The plan calls for a ribbon of commercial development with a parallel ribbon of residential development.

Faced with a very tight schedule for opening the exposition in 2000, the city needed to streamline typical development procedures. It responded by creating an innovative, cooperative planning process that can best be described as running multiple processes in parallel, which required a tremendous cooperative effort on the part of the city.

The core process of developing the plan for Kronsberg followed a linear sequence. As long ago as the 1950s, various planning concepts were drawn up for the Kronsberg area, continuing through the 1980s and culminating in 1992 with an Urban Landscape and Planning Competition held by the city. The winning design concept was revised by a more detailed Urban Design and Construction Competition, the results of which were further modified by a Landscape Study, leading to a Zoning Plan and a final Development Plan in 1994.

The planning and design of Kronsberg were shaped by two broad principles: the City of Hannover's 1992 plan to reduce carbon dioxide (CO_2) emissions by 25 percent from 1990 levels and the principles and spirit of Agenda 21, "a vision for development that simultaneously promotes economic growth, improved quality of life and environmental protection." The city received financial assistance from EXPO 2000 Hannover GmbH to pursue these aims in three areas:[2]

1. Ecological optimization
2. City as garden
3. City as social habitat

The goal was to create a district that maximized the residents' quality of life while minimizing their use of resources. The focus was to provide a practical district designed to meet the needs of residents—to develop and apply new ecological, social, and economic standards that would act as an exemplary model for other developments.

At every step of the way, this core process was informed by the following independent, parallel efforts: (1) an environmental impact analysis (EIA), conducted by the city with consultants, provided continuous assessment by experts of potential environmental consequences, with public input at EIA hearings; (2) the Kronsberg Advisory Council, a group of appointed planning and design experts, focused on ensuring the quality of the planning and design concepts for the district; (3) a planning ombudsman, appointed as a planning advocate, coordinated citizen participation; and (4) the Kronsberg Environmental Liaison Agency (KUKA) was charged with supporting the whole process and informing the public through training programs, workshops, instruction manuals, and publications for both professionals (in planning, design, and construction) and the public.[3]

Responsibility for optimizing Kronsberg's ecological development was led by a specialist planning group within the city's Directorate of Environmental Services. A special Kronsberg Standard[4] was devised for the greening of all residential and commercial buildings and open space.

This standard was incorporated into land sale contracts, development plans, and regulations. It involved environmentally compatible energy systems combined with environmentally sound construction and conservation of natural systems in the following areas: energy efficiency optimization, water management, waste management, soil management, and environmental communication and education. Within this framework, development of an energy concept was coordinated by a steering group composed of staff from the city utility (Stadtwerke Hannover AG), the City Planning Directorate, and the City Environment Director-

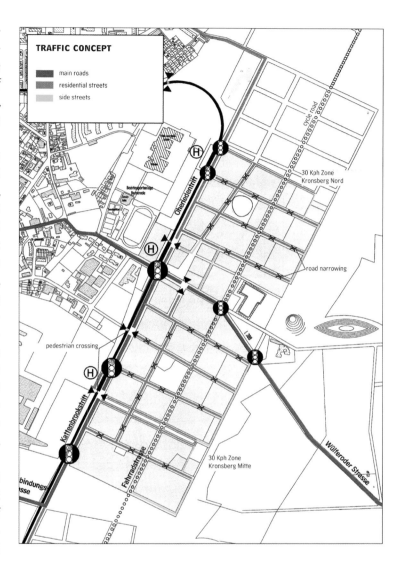

Figure 4.7. Kronsberg traffic concept plan. *(Source: Rumming, Hannover Kronsberg Handbook.)*

ate. The city commissioned a local consultancy to conduct a systematic analysis of options for energy supply and energy demand side reductions. The criteria for selecting a system included climate impact (reduction of CO_2 emissions) and economic viability. The resulting Kronsberg Energy Concept[5] was consistent with the city's energy policy aims of 1992, the objectives of which were to (1) give priority to energy efficiency; (2) make efficient use of primary energy through combined heat and power (CHP) systems, that is, cogeneration; and (3) increase renewable energy supply. It resulted in the Low Energy House (LEH) standard,[6] district heating from a decentralized CHP plant, an electricity savings program, and innovative applications of renewable energy systems.

In the process of planning, designing, and constructing Kronsberg, the city devised specific planning instruments for accomplishing its goals. In order to ensure social diversity, the City of Hannover and the State of Lower Saxony extended subsidy programs for home building in Kronsberg. Twenty-seven hundred houses and apartments out of the 3,000 built in the first phase received some form of public support, making rents affordable for residents from a wide range of economic backgrounds. Next, the city defined the ecological standards for developers through clauses in the land sale contracts. These mandated low-energy construction, use of the Kronsberg calculation method[7] to show conformance with the LEH standard, connection to the city's sewage network, approval of building materials, participation in soil management, and regulations for tree planting. Low-energy construction was defined in more detail by the LEH standard.[8] The standard was extremely prescriptive in specifying insulation U-values for walls, roofs, and windows; air infiltration rates; ventilation rates; heating technology performance; and construction details to avoid thermal bridging and air infiltration. All contractors had to use the Kronsberg calculation method to verify conformance before receiving a building permit. The LEH standard was supported by instructional handbooks and training workshops presented by KUKA for all developers and planners. In addition, KUKA presented workshops and prepared educational material for all residents on sustainable and resource-efficient living.

As a final step, the city implemented a Quality Assurance Program (QAP).[9] It procured funds from EXPO 2000 Hannover GmbH and the European Union to provide subsidies for the extra costs of quality assurance monitoring and partial subsidies for the extra cost of energy-efficient technologies. The obligations of property developers through the QAP included the following:

- Provision of proof of the heating index
- Meeting of airtightness requirements (approximately one-half air change per hour)
- Submission of defined planning documentation
- Inspection and checking of work

While implementation of the program was the responsibility of the Environmental Planning Group of EXPO 2000, a quality assurance work group was appointed from seven independent engineering firms to create common guidelines on the following:

- Inspection methods
- Details of the calculation method
- Evaluation of construction details

It also incorporated the following objectives:

- Guarantee of the LEH standard
- Minimization of thermal bridging and use of airtight construction to avoid heat loss
- Comfortable accommodation
- Correlation of planning with construction quality guarantee for the owner and user

The QAP was applied in five stages during construction:

1. Checking adherence to the required energy index
2. Checking detailed planning
3. Checking work on-site with documentation
4. Measuring adherence to limit values for airtightness (blower door test)
5. Certification

Certification was a prerequisite for all property sales. Initially there was resistance from the construction companies to the QAP, but this was overcome by intensive discussions with inspectors during the early stages. Participation by KUKA, which organized site meetings at short notice among all participants, made it possible to discuss and devise solutions to any problems promptly with an outside mediator. Kronsberg's attention to the planning process and the development of specific planning instruments to achieve its goals paid significant dividends.

Transportation

The goal for Kronsberg was to provide an environmentally responsible transportation system that minimized the use of the private car, to provide a roughly equal spread between pedestrians, bikes, trams, buses, and private cars. While

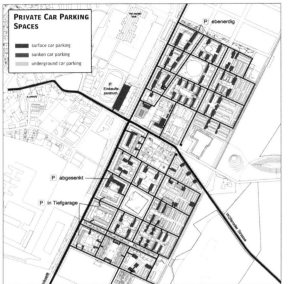

Figure 4.8. Kronsberg private car parking plan. *(Source: Rumming, Hannover Kronsberg Handbook.)*

not specified, this goal translates into roughly 20 percent of daily trips by car. It is consistent with the European tradition of creating pedestrian- and bicycle-friendly districts that are transit oriented. In many ways, it was treated as a given.

In its effort to create an environmentally responsible transport system with a balance among transit modes, the city deployed a full array of strategies. The new tramline is the backbone, providing a 20-minute link between Kronsberg and the Hannover city center. Service is provided at 8- to 12-minute intervals, with five stops at 300-meter intervals, making no resident more than 400 meters from a stop. In the first phase, three tram stops were built, located at the middle and two ends along the district's west edge. The tramline is supplemented by an east–west regional bus route, which stops at the main district square. The relatively small blocks, at 75 square meters, and the tree-lined streets make walking a convenient and pleasant experience.

The street system has traffic-narrowing provisions at the center of each block and street parking to assist in traffic calming. Parking is provided in both surface and underground spaces at a ratio of 0.8 car per housing unit. In addition, no street in the grid goes straight through the district in the north–south direction. The only direct north–south route is a bicycle path,

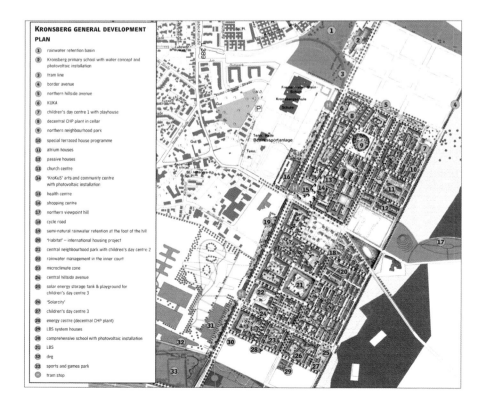

Figure 4.9. Kronsberg general development plan. *(Source: Rumming, Hannover Kronsberg Handbook.)*

which runs down the middle of the development. All of these provisions give priority to walking and biking as preferred modes of circulation within the district.

No comprehensive transport survey of residents has been reported; thus, realization of the goal of achieving a balanced split between walking, biking, public transit, and use of private cars cannot be confirmed. Nonetheless, anecdotal observations and walking tours of the district suggest that the comprehensive strategy to limit the use of private cars has been successful. There is only occasional internal automobile circulation observed within the district. The tram and bus services are used regularly, with residents observed coming and going throughout the day. This suggests that traffic-calming provisions, the lack of north–south through streets, and the convenience of walking and biking have made the strategy successful. From these observations, it is hard to imagine that reduction in car use to approximately 20–25 percent of all trips has not been achieved.

Urban Form

The goals for Kronsberg's urban form grew out of an urban construction competition to define planning for the new district in 1993. The winning scheme proposed a simple grid of streets and blocks, punctuated by parks and open space running through the district. The concept allowed flexibility in specifying the zoning requirements for the mixed-use development and evolved into the following design concepts.

The district stretches from north to south along the west slope of Kronsberg Hill and is divided into two neighborhoods, north and south. Its geometric form is derived in part from its alignment along the new tramline, which runs between Hannover and the EXPO 2000 site. An additional important forming concept from the beginning was to create clear external borders. The resulting rectilinear form measures approximately 1.5 kilometers long by 0.5 kilometer wide in the first phase.

The program for the district called for the creation of a compact, multiuse, high-density development containing 6,000 dwellings for 12,000–15,000 people when completed. The first phase contains 3,000 units for approximately 6,000 people and a full mix of commercial and social services, with 2,000 jobs located adjacent to the project.

A one-sided, mixed-use residential-over-commercial strip is located along the entire length of the tram line.

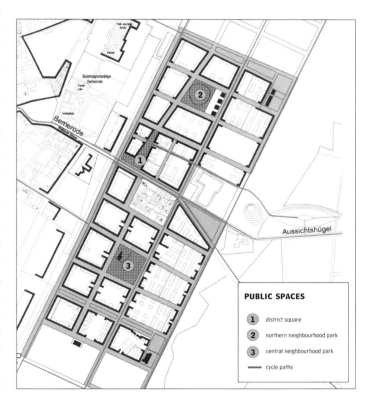

Figure 4.10. Kronsberg public spaces plan. *(Source: Rumming, Hannover Kronsberg Handbook. Redrawn by Ariel Utz.)*

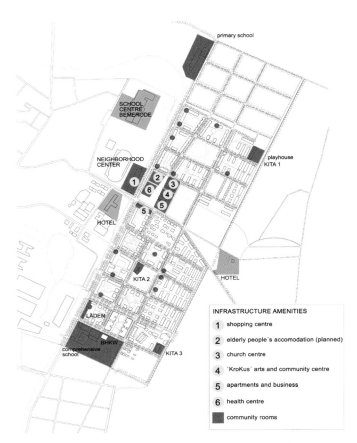

Figure 4.11. Kronsberg infrastructure and amenities plan. *(Source: Rumming, Hannover Kronsberg Handbook. Redrawn by Ariel Utz.)*

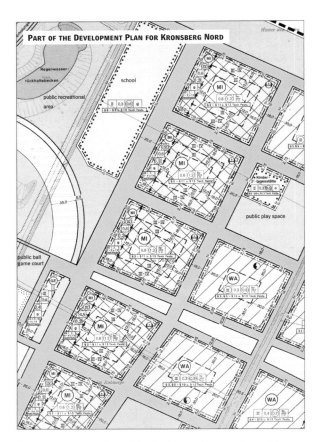

Figure 4.12. Kronsberg block plan instrument used to give design guidelines for development. *(Source: Rumming, Hannover Kronsberg Handbook.)*

It is served by the major access road, a boulevard with local street parking on its east side, separating the pedestrian sidewalk from the tram line. A district square is located in the middle, opposite the tram stop, with a shopping center and most of the social amenities located around it, including an arts and community center, a health center, an ecumenical church, a youth club, and community social services.

The district is structured further around a grid of streets creating blocks measuring approximately 75 by 75 meters and 1.2–1.8 hectares in area. This limits the public access space (rights-of-way) to approximately 19 percent of the area. The grid layout of the blocks, the hierarchy of streets, and the open space planning create a unifying framework with many different architectural vocabularies and construction materials. More than forty architecture and landscape architecture offices applied different approaches and design solutions, many chosen by design competition. The purpose was to create a truly diverse spatial experience in the district while maintaining an overall unity.

The zoning structure follows the principle of decreasing density and building heights as one approaches the countryside on the east edge. Development along the main access road consists of relatively compact four- to five-story blocks with a net density of 200 units per hectare. As one progresses up the slope, the development becomes more open, with three-story blocks and pavilion structures giving way to two-story terraced housing with a net density of 48 units per hectare. The zoning plan designated compulsory building lines on the street frontage and mandated that the ends, the corners, of each block must be developed in order to define the corner with built form.

Green Space

Consistent with the idea of the "city as garden," the overall goals for green space planning were to "incorporate ecological concerns in an exemplary manner" in all dimensions of the project. The essential planning aims related to green space were "(1) a shift to ecologically responsible agriculture, (2) enhancement of species diversity, (3) biotope protection by creating habitats for flora and fauna, and (4) improvements to the local recreation amenity value by enhancing the natural qualities of the landscape."[10] The objective was to improve environmental quality in spite of the change in use, aiming for an ecological balance that would represent a net environmental gain for the Kronsberg countryside. It involved regulations for tree planting and compensation measures according to the Lower Saxony nature conservation law.

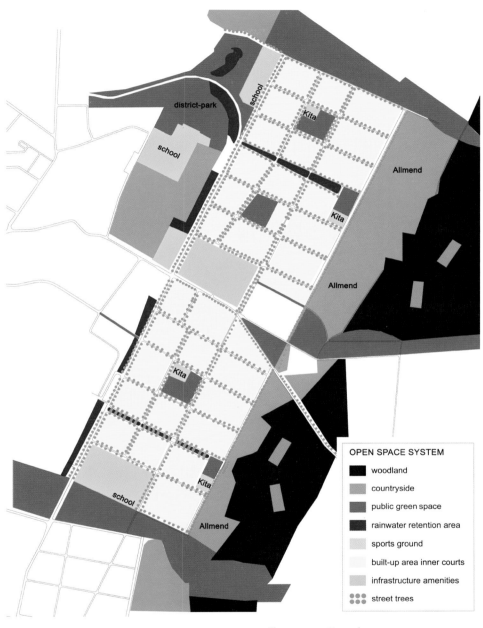

OPEN SPACE SYSTEM

- woodland
- countryside
- public green space
- rainwater retention area
- sports ground
- built-up area inner courts
- infrastructure amenities
- street trees

Figure 4.13. Kronsberg open space system plan. *(Source: Rumming, Hannover Kronsberg Handbook. Redrawn by Ariel Utz.)*

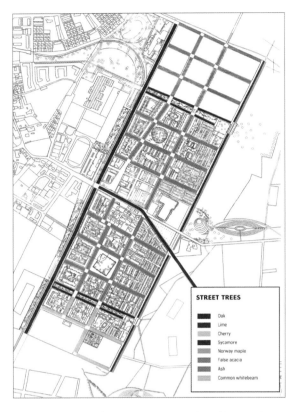

Figure 4.14. Kronsberg street trees plan. *(Source: Rumming, Hannover Kronsberg Handbook.)*

Both the north and the south neighborhoods are organized around neighborhood parks, each creating its own unique identity. The interior of each block is a communal courtyard designed to create an even finer-grain identity and difference. A continuous tree-lined alley defines the east boundary of the development, creating a sharp edge with the rural landscape. The grid of streets and blocks is differentiated further by five transverse green space corridors that connect the residential areas with the hilltop ridge and the woodland park along the entire length, each continuing into the countryside. These corridors have both dividing and unifying functions. They are distinctly landscaped, functioning as part of the open rainwater treatment system and creating urban habitat in contrast to the surrounding countryside. There are breaks in the alley and hilltop woodland park where they intersect with the transverse corridors. Viewing mounds, formed by excavated soils, are placed at the top of each park corridor, providing overlooks of the city and countryside. While the neighborhoods are defined by these corridors, they are further distinguished by having different street tree species planted in each—sycamore in the north, ash in the south, lime and Norway maple framing the east alley. Lime trees define the transverse corridors, and oaks are planted along the commercial street on the west. With these multiple design strategies (parks, alley, corridors, hilltop woodland, viewing mounds, and street trees), the urban landscape plays a major role in shaping and enriching the urban form.

Figure 4.15. Kronsberg, view to the countryside. *(Photograph by Karl Johaentges.)*

Figure 4.16. Kronsberg, view of viewing mounds. *(Photograph by Karl Johaentges.)*

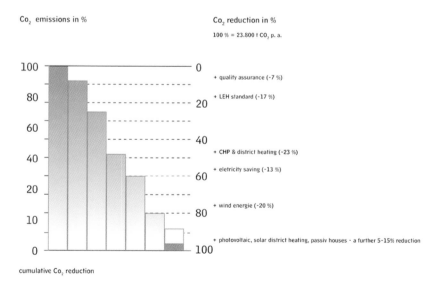

Figure 4.17. Kronsberg, reduction in CO_2 emissions. *(Source: Rumming, Hannover Kronsberg Handbook.)*

Energy

The Kronsberg energy concept was drawn up and coordinated by a city steering group. The energy target was to reduce CO_2 emissions by 60 percent[11] compared with those dictated by national construction standards without increasing the up-front costs much or at all. This was to be accomplished by giving priority to energy savings and the efficiencies of a combined heat and power (CHP) system. The city council sought to further reduce CO_2 emissions to 80 percent; the additional 20 percent savings was to be achieved by the innovative use of renewable energy, primarily from wind.

With the priority given to energy efficiency, the city developed the Kronsberg Low Energy House (LEH)[12] standard, to be applied to all buildings. The goal of the standard was to reduce CO_2 emissions by 17 percent, and the local authorities provided subsidies to help accomplish this. All developers and clients were obliged through the land sale contracts to conform to the following measures:

- Heating energy index of 50 kilowatt-hours per square meter per year ($kWh/m^2/y$) as the target value
- This figure not to be exceeded by a maximum of 10 percent (limit value)
- Calculation method for heating energy index defined (Kronsberg calculation method)
- Monitoring by qualified engineers

If the limit was exceeded, the developers and clients faced a penalty payment of 5 euros per square meter. These requirements led to more prescriptive standards for insulation, airtightness, ventilation, and heating system technology. Conformance with these standards was ensured by the Quality Assurance Program described earlier. The goal for improving electric energy efficiency was to reduce CO_2 emissions by 13 percent through incentives for installing high-efficiency lighting and appliances.

Reductions were achieved by low-energy building construction as mandated in the LEH standard. The standard prescribed very detailed requirements for managing conductive heat loss, air infiltration, and heating technologies, all reinforced by the careful Quality Assurance Program. Heating efficiency was supplemented by a program of subsidies to reduce electricity consumption. The subsidies provided free high-efficiency lightbulbs and partial subsidies for energy-efficient appliances. The program was aggressively promoted by KUKA with brochures and educational sessions for residents on the benefits, ways, and means of efficiency.

The Quality Assurance Program was essential in achieving the goal of 50–55 $kWh/m^2/y$ for heating. Reported measurements from the QAP show that both the airtightness standard and the insulation values for specific building components were met or exceeded on average. This resulted in measured energy consumption for heating in 2001 of 56 kWh/m²/y[13] in the audited area, essentially at the goal. The strategy of focusing on optimizing energy efficiency has paid large dividends.

On the other hand, the target goal of reducing electric energy consumption by 30 percent (from 32 kWh/m²/y to 22 kWh/m²/y) has not been achieved. The measured consumption of 30 kWh/m²/y is only a 5–6 percent reduction.[14] The difference is attributed to the fact that only a small portion of the households measured opted to purchase the most energy-efficient appliances under the electricity savings program promoted by KUKA. Replacing older appliances with new, energy-efficient ones represents a long-term savings potential.

The target of energy consumption for domestic hot water was achieved at 15 kWh/m²/y,[15] but the target for supply line losses from the district heating system was not achieved. The target for total energy consumption (105 kWh/m²/y) was exceeded by 12–18 percent, at 125 kWh/m²/y, primarily from combined heating and power (CHP) line losses and higher than predicted electricity consumption.

One major strategy for reducing CO_2 emissions was to generate both electricity and hot water from one fuel source in a CHP plant. In such a power plant, a fuel source (such as gas) is burned to generate steam, which drives an electric generator. The waste heat in the form of hot water is then circulated to the buildings to become the source for heating and hot water. The goal for the CHP system was to reduce CO_2 emissions by 23 percent. Further reductions of 20 percent were targeted through the use of wind energy, and additional renewable energy systems were targeted to deliver 5–15 percent reductions. The total goal for CO_2 reductions is summarized in the graph.

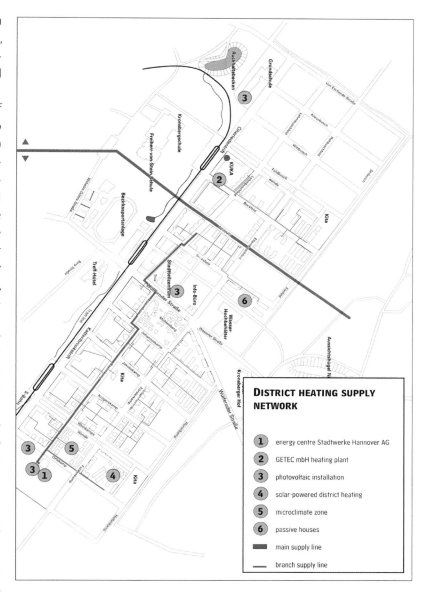

DISTRICT HEATING SUPPLY NETWORK

1. energy centre Stadtwerke Hannover AG
2. GETEC mbH heating plant
3. photovoltaic installation
4. solar-powered district heating
5. microclimate zone
6. passive houses

▬▬▬ main supply line

──── branch supply line

Figure 4.18. Kronsberg district heating plan. *(Source: Rumming, Hannover Kronsberg Handbook.)*

Figure 4.19. View of wind turbines in Kronsberg. *(Photograph by Karl Johaentges.)*

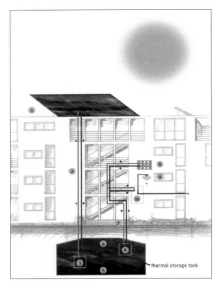

How it works ...

1. solar collectors
2. heat circulation
3. heat exchanger
4. water temperature 90° C
5. water temperature 40° C
6. heat exchanger
7. hot water circuit for apartments
8. radiator
9. hot water supply
10. heat exchanger

Figure 4.20. Solar thermal seasonal storage diagram for Kronsberg. *(Source: Rumming, Hannover Kronsberg Handbook.)*

The energy supply system for Kronsberg is anchored by two decentralized CHP stations. The stations are extremely efficient converters of primary energy (gas) to end use, generating both electric energy and hot water. Capturing the latent heat of exhaust gases adds to overall efficiency such that the two CHP plants are over 94 percent efficient. Four-fifths of the district is served by a CHP plant at the south end of the site and one-fifth by a plant at the north end.

The south CHP plant provides domestic hot water and base-load heating by gas-powered generators with a thermal capacity of 1,650 kilowatts (kW) and an electric capacity of 1,250 kW. Peak heating load is handled by two 5,000 kW gas-powered boilers. The total heating capacity of the two boilers and the generators is 11.7 megawatts (MW).

In the south plant, the base load is provided by two gas generators with a thermal performance of 440 kW and an electric capacity of 220 kW. Peak heating is covered by two gas-fired boilers at 1,650 kW each. Total heating capacity from the boilers and generators is 3,740 kW.

The heat from both plants is carried in a loop of water pipes to the buildings. The temperature of the supply cycle is 75°C–90°C, and the return cycle is 40°C. At transfer stations in each building the district hot water supply passes through a heat exchanger, delivering heating and domestic hot water to consumers.

The majority of Kronsberg's electricity is supplied by wind power. A small existing wind turbine delivering 280 kW has been augmented by two more turbines producing 1.5 and 1.8 MW, respectively. In addition, solar power is converted to electricity totaling 45 kW by four photovoltaic installations located on the primary school, the district arts and community center, the shopping center, and the south Stadtwerke energy center. Together, both wind and solar energy deliver a total of 3.6 MW of renewable electric supply. This amounts to 3.6 MW out of 5.0 MW, or 72 percent of the neighborhood's total electric capacity.

Three other innovative systems have been piloted at Kronsberg: seasonal solar storage, a microclimate environmental filter, and the passive house.

For seasonal solar storage, a 1,350 m² flat-plate hot water collector array serves 104 apartments in the Solar City complex. Solar energy is collected in the summer and piped to a well-insulated 2,750 m³ cistern, providing seasonal storage. The system provides around 40 percent of the complex's heating demand.

The microclimate environmental filter involves a "microclimate zone," an atrium created between two rows of housing blocks to act as an environmen-

Figure 4.21. View of seasonal solar thermal storage neighborhood in Kronsberg. *(Photograph by Karl Johaentges.)*

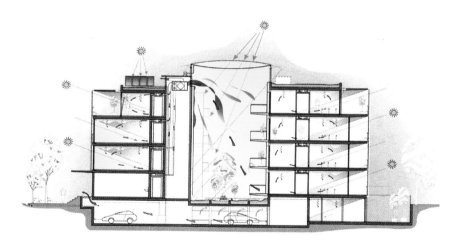

Figure 4.22. "Microclimate zone" section in Kronsberg. *(Source: Inge Schottkowski-Bahre, ed., Modell Kronsberg: Sustainable Building for the Future [Leipzig: Jütte Druck, 2000].)*

tal buffer and filter. In the summer, the movable reflective layer on the atrium's roof reflects solar heat. In the winter, solar energy is allowed to penetrate and heat the microclimate zone. The adjoining heavy walls act as thermal storage, absorbing about 75 percent of the solar energy and releasing it uniformly. The microclimate zone serves as a buffer, reducing heat loss from the units by 20 percent. It also serves as a preheater for mechanical ventilation in the winter. Beyond its energy function, the microclimate zone creates a spacious, light-filled communal green space for residents.

Figure 4.23. View of microclimate zone interior in Kronsberg. *(Photograph by Karl Johaentges.)*

Figure 4.24. View of microclimate zone east-side entrance in Kronsberg. *(Photograph by Karl Johaentges.)*

Figure 4.25. Kronsberg passive house diagram. *(Source: Rumming, Hannover Kronsberg Handbook.)*

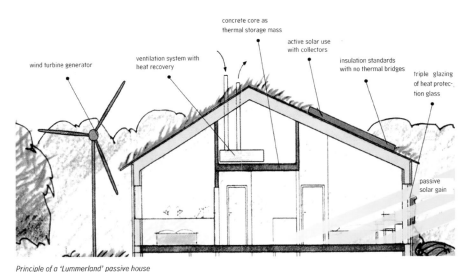

Principle of a 'Lummerland' passive house

Kronsberg features eight terraced houses constructed to the "passive house" standards (15 kWh/m²/y). Heat loss is reduced to the extent that direct solar energy through the south-facing windows and internal heat sources provide for most of the heating needs. The reduction in heat loss is achieved through super insulators with K-values of 0.15 watts per square meter per Kelvin (W/m²/K) or less and insulation thicknesses of 30–40 centimeters. The windows are triple glazed and have insulated frames, air infiltration is reduced to one-half air change per hour, and ventilation involves a heat recovery system. In the depths of winter, the passive house uses a small amount of heat from the district system, amounting to about 15 kWh/m²/y. Thus, a passive house uses one-seventh the energy of a conventional house and one-fourth the energy of the LEH standard.

The goal of reducing CO_2 emissions by 60 percent has been 14 percent below target. The measured performance in 2001 indicated approximately a 46 percent reduction.[16] As discussed earlier, the higher than predicted electricity consumption and CHP line losses are the cause. When the virtually zero-emission energy production from the wind machines (37 kWh/m²/y) and solar photovoltaics (0.04 kWh/m²/y) are factored into the equation, the carbon emissions are 71 percent, approaching the goal of 80 percent reduction. In spite of not reaching the targets, these are excellent performance results.

The results can be translated into a measure of CO_2 emissions per person per year. Judging by the buildings' performance, this averages approximately 1.05 metric tons of CO_2 per year. If CO_2 emission estimates for transportation are added, it gives a good indication of CO_2 emissions that can be attributed to the urban design strategy of the district. Judging by transportation statistics from the city of Hannover, and given the pedestrian-friendly, transit-oriented design of Kronsberg, it is safe to assume that the average mode split is 48 percent car, 29 percent transit, 8 percent walking, and 14 percent other (bike, etc.). Also, using average daily travel distances of 13.3 kilometers per person and European Union average emissions of 1,869 metric tons of CO_2 per kilometer, the CO_2 emission per person for car transport is approximately 0.99 metric ton of CO_2 per person per year. Together, CO_2 emissions from building plus transport equal 2.04 metric tons per person. If the mode split for Kronsberg is less than the Hannover average, closer to the observed approximation of 25 percent car usage, then the CO_2 emission would be closer to 1.5 metric tons of CO_2 per person.

Water

The goals and objectives for the Kronsberg water system fall into three categories: (1) a seminatural decentralized rainwater management system designed "to preserve as far as possible the original natural drainage situation," (2) drinking water economies as much as possible through water-saving devices, and (3) raising of residents' awareness of water issues through education and information provided by KUKA.[17]

Figure 4.26. View of passive house in Kronsberg. *(Photograph by Karl Johaentges.)*

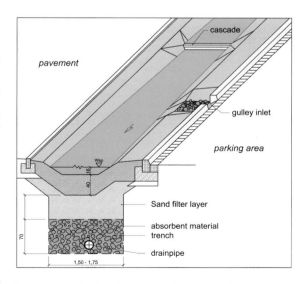

Figure 4.27. Mulden-Rigolen system, Kronsberg, section 1. *(Source: Rumming, Hannover Kronsberg Handbook. Redrawn by Ariel Utz.)*

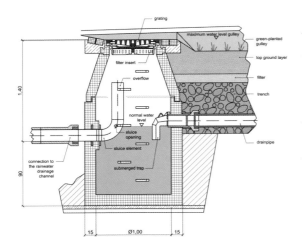

Figure 4.28. Mulden-Rigolen system, Kronsberg, section 2. *(Source: Rumming, Hannover Kronsberg Handbook. Redrawn by Ariel Utz.)*

Figure 4.29. View of Mulden-Rigolen bioswale street in Kronsberg. *(Photograph by Karl Johaentges.)*

Reductions in drinking water consumption were pursued by fairly standard measures: installation of water-saving devices such as water-air mixers, flow limiters, and constant flow devices, as well as installation of water meters in all apartments. The system was intended to give residents the information and the devices they needed to reduce consumption, supported by extensive educational programs. The reduction in potable water usage has not been reported, so it is impossible to assess the effectiveness of provisions for low-flow fixtures and devices.

The seminatural decentralized rainwater management system is much more elaborate. First, it restricts the use of impervious paving in the streets to driving lanes. All parking and sidewalk paving is permeable. Rainwater drainage from the streets is collected not in storm-water pipes but in an open drainage system—the Mulden-Rigolen system. The runoff is channeled into grassed hollows and retained by a series of cascade dams. The water is allowed to soak through a layer of topsoil and a filter, collecting in a stone-filled trench, from which it can infiltrate the soil. In cases of extreme rainfall, an overflow system pipes the water to large retention areas. In other landscape areas, hollow and trench drains retain water and channel it to retention ponds, which are landscape features. To collect data and optimize construction details, a 1:1 scale demonstration stretch of the Mulden-Rigolen system was built before the infrastructure of streets was installed. This enabled fine-tuning of the system to fit the slope of the land and optimize the size and number of regulated openings. The full-scale test also indicated that the goal of limiting drainage runoff to three liters per second per hectare would be attained, especially with the provision of large retention areas for extreme occurrences. As a result, the Mulden-Rigolen system was installed in all public streets.

No rainwater capture and reuse systems were employed, nor were any local gray water treatment systems.

Waste

The overall aim of the Kronsberg waste concept was "preventive waste management," wherein the objective was to achieve consistent waste avoidance and recycling. The waste concept focused on two areas: construction waste and domestic and commercial waste. The aim for domestic and commercial waste was to reduce quantities by 50 percent.[18] A complete system for waste separation, drop-off, and pickup was deployed at convenient locations throughout

Figure 4.30. View of storm-water retention pond in Kronsberg. *(Photograph by Karl Johaentges.)*

Figure 4.31. View of Southern Avenue bioswale in Kronsberg. *(Photograph by Karl Johaentges.)*

Figure 4.32. View of waste system collection area in Kronsberg. *(Photograph by Karl Johaentges.)*

Figure 4.33. Aerial view of blocks, streets, courts, and parks in Kronsberg. *(Photograph by Karl Johaentges.)*

the district. The goal was to reduce construction waste by as much as 80 percent through avoidance and provisions for recycling. Consistent with the concept of waste reuse, the city developed an ecological soil management plan. The concept was to use 100 percent of the excavated soil for landscape and environmental enhancements in the local vicinity, avoiding the cost, CO_2 emissions, and pollution of trucking it to landfills out of the area.[19]

The provisions for sorting and collecting material waste during construction generated an 80 percent reduction in construction material waste leaving the site. The provisions for reducing and recycling domestic and commercial waste resulted in recycling rates of approximately 80 percent.

The soil management program recycled 100 percent of all excavated soils from construction for landscaping and environmental enhancement in the district. This eliminated approximately 100,000 truckloads leaving the district, thus reducing dust, noise, and CO_2 emissions.

Social Agenda

The goal was to create "a broad social mix for the district"[20] and further "to avoid social segregation by mixing various forms of housing finance and ownership."[21] These broad goals translated into more specific requirements to provide flexible accommodations to cope with changing housing needs by providing a mixture of large and small apartments and apartments suitable for families and new lifestyles. The effort of achieving a broad social mix was supported by creating a mixed-use and multiuse program for the district including a full range of social and commercial services, easy access to local jobs, and connectivity to the larger city of Hannover. The program included three kindergartens, a primary school with an after-school center and a sports hall, a shopping center and commercial space, a health center, a church, a senior center, an arts center, and community rooms distributed in the neighborhood districts.

The goal of creating a district with a broad social mix that avoids social segregation and provides affordable rents has largely been achieved. In the end, nearly 50 percent of the housing is subsidized, making rents affordable and the population diverse; one-third of the residents are immigrants; one-fourth are under the age of eighteen; sixteen apartments accommodate residents with disabilities; a large number of residents receive senior services; and 10 percent of the units are social housing.

Lessons Learned

The parallel and evolutionary planning and design process, led by the city, was notably effective in creating collaboration, cooperation, and continuous learning but also in enabling efficient approvals within a tight schedule. The contractually binding Quality Assurance Program with real physical tests to obtain construction certification was instrumental in achieving the target of 50–55 kWh/m²/y for heating energy demand. Ongoing training of developers and construction contractors with exemplary details and standards was key to achieving the QAP standards. Special attention to educating residents about energy and water conservation, including the provision of formal incentives, was also critical in achieving measured performance targets.

The spirit of Agenda 21—balancing human needs with ecological responsibility by taking a holistic approach—was an important guiding principle that produced Kronsberg's very practical approach. The specific target of 50–55 kWh/m²/y for heating demand was an essential component in the effort to achieve a 60 percent reduction in CO_2 emissions. The goal of 60 percent reduction in CO_2 emissions produced the strategy of combining a CHP district system with wind power to supply both electricity and hot water.

The urban form of Kronsberg is based on a simple street grid and block structure. The sharp definition of its compact rectilinear perimeter gives the district a clear identity and wholeness. The diversity of architectural expression from some forty different firms adds rich variety to the strict framework. The progression from a layer of higher-density closed-perimeter blocks along the main street on the west edge to open-perimeter blocks in the middle zone to terraced housing along the uphill, higher east edge provides a stepped progression from city to countryside, in concept similar to the transect. Because two-thirds of the blocks also have openings in their edges, the feeling is more that of a rural town than an urban area.

The most distinguishing qualities of the district are created by the different urban landscape design strategies. Organizing the north and south neighborhoods around neighborhood parks not only breaks the monotony of the grid but also gives a focus to each with distinct landscape design features. The fact that the blocks have different communal courtyards adds even greater richness and distinct identities. The design of the sloping east–west streets with their rainwater swales and the insertion of three east–west landscape corridors, also treating rainwater and creating urban habitat, give further identity and difference to the street grid. The success of the urban design is its straightforward simplicity. At first glance it appears to be an uninteresting typical grid and block plan, but in experience and use it becomes a richly interesting and diverse place to live.

Kronsberg demonstrates that energy efficiency strategies, even at the aggressive standard of the passive house, are still the most cost-effective means of reducing CO_2 emissions. It also demonstrates that local district CHP systems are an excellent means for reducing CO_2 emissions because they deliver both heat and electricity from the primary fuel source—a two-for-one. In the CHP process, twice as much heat as electric energy is generated. The Kronsberg system makes up the difference by combining the CHP system with wind power. This is an excellent example of how renewable systems can be combined with a traditional energy supply system, balancing the supply profiles of each to meet demand.

Kronsberg demonstrates that it is possible to reduce CO_2 emissions by close to 80 percent, to less than two metric tons per person, which is below the average global standard to stabilize climate change.

While the use of bioswales to slow and retain storm water is a more common practice today, the effectiveness of the Mulden-Rigolen system has made it a model for bioswale design on sloping sites. The water-conserving toilets and fixtures are an effective means of reducing water consumption and are standard practice today.

The waste reduction and recycling systems implemented in Kronsberg are effective and are standard practice in Europe. The use of all the soil from construction excavation to create landscape features (such as viewing mounds) is both an effective way to reduce CO_2 emissions and a potential innovative landscape design concept with wide application.

Social integration and sustainability are enhanced in large part by the full mix of services provided. With a shopping center, local shopping and commercial space, a health-care center, an ecumenical church, an arts and community center, a senior center, and community rooms located throughout the district, residents can satisfy most of their daily needs locally. In no small way, the three kindergartens and the primary school complete the needs of young families, for which school becomes the focus of community participation.

The ecological dimensions of Kronsberg are one of the multiple factors cited by residents as contributing to the high quality of the living space and the neighborhood. An academic study of Kronsberg confirms the social sustainability of the community. Eighty percent of residents surveyed (40 percent of the population) stated that they would choose to move to Kronsberg again, primarily because of the low rents, original architecture, practical apartment layouts, green surroundings, family-friendliness, and access to work.

LEED-ND Rating

Use of the US Leadership in Energy and Environmental Design for Neighborhood Development (LEED-ND) rating system to evaluate European neighborhoods, such as Kronsberg, has its anomalies and reveals inherent biases in the LEED-ND system. For example, Kronsberg receives no score for Certified Green Building (which requires a LEED-certified person), even though buildings were required to meet a strict energy performance standard in all phases of development, including a blower door test, before getting a certificate of occupancy. It also lost points on Walkable Streets and Street Network because the point system is based on a traditional US model of streets with trees and parking, whereas Kronsberg streets are based on a different model. Finally, LEED-ND gives a total of only 6 points for On-Site Renewable Energy Sources, District Heating and Cooling, and Infrastructure Energy Efficiency—just 6 points out of the total of 110, or only 5 percent. It also gives a total of only 7 points for Certified Green Buildings and Building Energy Efficiency, or 6 percent of the total. Since these are important components in the whole-systems design concept that account for at least a 50 percent reduction in CO_2 emissions (everything but reduction in vehicular transit), it appears to be extremely undervalued at a total of just 11 percent. While Kronsberg achieves a rating of Gold, it would be Platinum if it had been given more weight for its building energy efficiency, renewables, and district heating system. It would appear that the weighting of the LEED-ND point system should be revised.

Table 4.1. LEED-ND Rating for Kronsberg

Criteria	Maximum	Achieved
Smart Location and Linkage		
Prerequisite: Smart Location		X
Prerequisite: Imperiled Species and Ecological Communities		X
Prerequisite: Wetland and Water Body Conservation		X
Prerequisite: Agricultural Land Conservation		X
Prerequisite: Floodplain Avoidance		X
Credit: Preferred Locations	10	0
Credit: Brownfield Redevelopment	2	0
Credit: Locations with Reduced Automobile Dependence	7	7
Credit: Bicycle Network and Storage	1	1
Credit: Housing and Jobs Proximity	3	3
Credit: Steep Slope Protection	1	1
Credit: Site Design for Habitat or Wetland and Water Body Conservation	1	1
Credit: Restoration of Habitat or Wetlands and Water Bodies	1	0
Credit: Long-Term Conservation Management of Habitat or Wetlands and Water Bodies	1	1
Subtotal	27	14

Criteria	Maximum	Achieved
Neighborhood Pattern and Design		
Prerequisite: Walkable Streets		X
Prerequisite: Compact Development		X
Prerequisite: Connected and Open Community		X
Credit: Walkable Streets	12	10
Credit: Compact Development	6	4
Credit: Mixed-Use Neighborhood Centers	4	4
Credit: Mixed-Income Diverse Communities	7	7
Credit: Reduced Parking Footprint	1	1
Credit: Street Network	2	0
Credit: Transit Facilities	1	1
Credit: Transportation Demand Management	2	2
Credit: Access to Civic and Public Spaces	1	1
Credit: Access to Recreation Facilities	1	1
Credit: Visitability and Universal Design	1	1
Credit: Community Outreach and Involvement	2	2
Credit: Local Food Production	1	1
Credit: Tree-Lined and Shaded Streets	2	2
Credit: Neighborhood Schools	1	1
Subtotal	44	38

Table 4.1. LEED-ND Rating for Kronsberg (continued)

Criteria	Maximum	Achieved
Green Infrastructure and Buildings		
Prerequisite: Certified Green Building		n/a
Prerequisite: Minimum Building Energy Efficiency		x
Prerequisite: Minimum Building Water Efficiency		x
Prerequisite: Construction Activity Pollution Prevention		x
Credit: Certified Green Buildings	5	n/a
Credit: Building Energy Efficiency	2	2
Credit: Building Water Efficiency	1	1
Credit: Water Efficient Landscaping	1	1
Credit: Existing Building Use	1	0
Credit: Historic Resource Preservation	1	0
Credit: Minimized Site Disturbance in Design and Construction	1	0
Credit: Stormwater Management	4	4
Credit: Heat Island Reduction	1	1
Credit: Solar Orientation	1	0
Credit: On-Site Renewable Energy Sources	3	3
Credit: District Heating and Cooling	2	2
Credit: Infrastructure Energy Efficiency	1	1
Credit: Wastewater Management	2	0
Credit: Recycled Content in Infrastructure	1	1
Credit: Solid Waste Management	1	1
Credit: Light Pollution Reduction	1	1
Subtotal	29	18

Innovation and Design Process		
Credit: Innovation and Exemplary Performance	5	3
Credit: LEED Accredited Professional	1	n/a
Subtotal	6	3

Regional Priority Credit		
Credit: Regional Priority Credit	4	n/a
Subtotal	4	0

Project Totals (Certification Estimates)		
Total Points	110	73
Certification Level	Platinum (80+) Gold (60–79) Silver (50–59) Certified (40–49)	Gold

Source: Harrison Fraker.

5. Vauban, Freiburg, Germany

Vauban is a mixed-use neighborhood located in the southwest corner of Freiburg, Germany, a three-kilometer tram ride from the city center. Vauban is no ordinary neighborhood, and in no ordinary city. Although it is located at the west edge of the Black Forest, Freiburg is blessed with one of Germany's highest incidences of annual solar radiation. Not surprisingly, it is home to Europe's top independent solar research laboratory (the Fraunhofer Institute for Solar Energy Systems ISE) and enjoys enough photovoltaic instal-lations (including a solar-powered bicycle shed at the main train stations) to be

Figure 5.1. Aerial view of Vauban, Freiburg, Germany. *(Photograph by Transurban: Thomas Schroepfer and Christian Werthman, with Limin Hee.)*

Figure 5.2. View of main park-boulevard in Vauban. *(Photograph by Transurban: Thomas Schroepfer and Christian Werthman, with Limin Hee.)*

branded "solar region Freiburg." Freiburg has been at the forefront of the environmental movement since the 1970s, and its city council boasts the largest number of Green Party members in all of Germany. It is also home to architect Rolf Disch's Heliotrope house, among the first anywhere to produce more energy than it uses.

When Freiburg began the process of creating a new city district on the site of a former French military barracks in 1993, its main goal was to build a mixed-income neighborhood for approximately 5,000 residents. What emerged is one of the most unusual and enlightened examples of sustainable urban design. The story of Vauban is as much about the people and process as it is about the successful application of technology. As Disch has said, "It is not a question of the Technik—we have the Technik, but it is a question of the mind. We have the problem [of how] to do it."[1] The story of Vauban reveals some of those vital how-to secrets.

Process and Plan

The City of Freiburg bought the property of a former French barracks from the federal authorities and began planning a new district of forty-two hectares in 1993 to accommodate a growing population. As landowner, the city was responsible for planning and development of the site, but the goal was much more than creating a mixed-income, mixed-use housing project for 5,000 people and creating 600 jobs. Because the site is located at the city's edge, surrounded by natural beauty, there was much local interest in how the land would be developed.

Because of this great community interest, the city adopted a principle called "learning while planning"[2] and embarked on an experimental and enlightened urban design process, intended to engage direct community participation throughout. In 1994, the city held an urban design competition to bring out a range of ideas from the community. The results became the foundation for the development plan.

The process was formalized when the citizens' association Forum Vauban[3] applied to coordinate the participation process and was legally recognized as its participatory planning body by the City of Freiburg in 1995. Forum Vauban was founded not only to organize far-reaching citizen participation but also to support the implementation of community-based building projects called Baugruppen,[4] wherein groups of future building owners were recruited and directed their own cooperative building projects. Forum Vauban also played a key role in creating and implementing ecological standards, especially in the areas of traffic and energy, for what it described as a "sustainable model city district." As the formal liaison to the city planning board and the city council, Forum Vauban initiated the "car-free living"[5] concept and saw it through to realization in forming a car-sharing association, the Freiburger Auto-Gemeinschaft.[6]

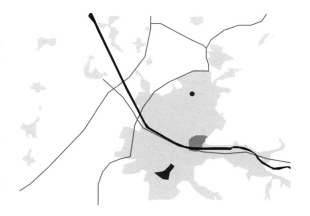

Figure 5.3. Location of Vauban within Freiburg. *(Drawing by Jessica Yang.)*

As the construction phase progressed, Forum Vauban transferred much of the support of the Baugruppen efforts to various nonprofit organizations, such as the building cooperative Vauban, Genova eG and Buergerbau AG (Citizens' Building Stock Corporation). Their services included identifying appropriate sites within the project for development; advertising until future building owners' groups (Baugruppen) were filled; guiding the groups during all phases of the planning and building process; managing the construction phases; controlling costs, schedule, and quality; and being responsible for financing and for the accounts of the project.

Forum Vauban was (and continues to be) financed by member fees, donations, and public grants (German Environment Foundation). With this funding, Forum Vauban publishes the magazine *Vauban actuel* to advertise local events, publicize the ecological design strategies of the various Baugruppen, and support group initiatives, including a neighborhood center and farmer's market. As the project progressed, Forum Vauban gradually shifted from addressing ecological concerns in the planning and building process to enhancing the social and cultural dynamic of residents.

As landowner and government agency responsible for planning and development, the City of Freiburg set up a special committee, the City Council Vauban Committee, to be the forum of discussion with Forum Vauban and to prepare recommendations for city council approval. One of the most important early decisions was to divide the project into small plots, facilitating the sale of land directly to final owners rather than to intermediary developers. This decision cut out the cost of middlemen and paved the way for multiple Baugruppen projects (fifteen in the first phase and over forty in total). Central to the success of this model was that the chief urban planner, Sven von Ungern-

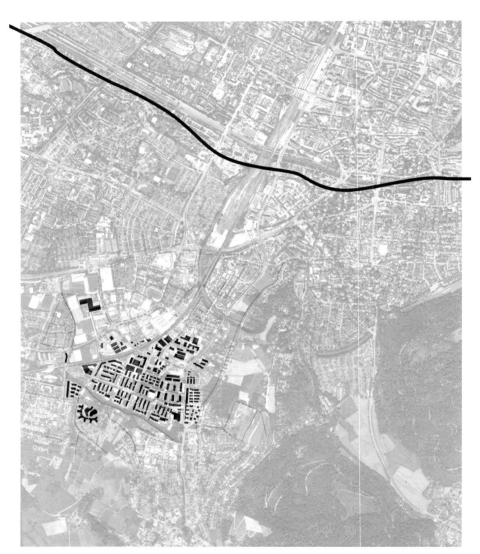

Figure 5.4. Context plan for Vauban.
(Drawing by Jessica Yang.)

Sternberg, was open to allowing the development plan to change as a result of continuous learning and evolving standards of the Baugruppen and Forum Vauban. As goals and standards evolved, the city was able to incorporate them by putting new restrictions on builders in the sale contracts, thus controlling development. Further, as landowner and manager of the process, the city controlled the risk associated with its acceptance or failure. The city set up a separate budget for the project to more easily monitor the level of funds being recouped through the sale of lots and outside grants for special projects associated with the development.

Through citizen participation in Forum Vauban and enlightened leadership by the chief urban planner and city council, together those actors worked to create an eco-community in a participatory fashion, meeting a unique set of social, economic, environmental (transportation, energy, water, waste), and design goals.

The overall principle of "learning while planning" enabled the project's goals and objectives to emerge naturally out of the far-reaching participatory process. Most important, because the homeowners played a critical role in developing the goals and objectives, they had knowledge, understanding, and a stake in their successful implementation.

Transportation

While the project goals and objectives for transportation are typical of transit-oriented development, the Vauban district pioneered the concept of car-free living, with the intention of reducing car use throughout the district to the benefit of all—not to create a small car-free enclave. The goals and objectives are summarized as follows:[7]

- Priority is given to pedestrians, cyclists, and public transportation.
- All schools, businesses, shopping centers, food cooperatives, and recreation centers and 600 jobs are within short walking and cycling distances (less than ten minutes' travel) of residential Baugruppen areas.
- No parking—only drop-off (including deliveries) and pickup—is allowed at residential doorsteps. Parking for residents' cars is available in community facilities located nearby at the periphery.
- The speed limit on the district's main street is 30 kilometers per hour (less than 20 miles per hour), and in residential areas it is limited to "walking speeds" of 3–5 miles per hour.
- Car sharing is available.
- Access is provided to public transit—both trams and buses.

Vauban's development plan prohibits the building of parking spaces on private property. Parking is provided in four multistory garages at the periphery of the residential areas. The cost of a parking space is substantial (approximately US$40,000),[8] and car owners have to accept walking short distances to their cars. Residents without cars do not have to contribute to the cost of providing parking. They can gain access to cars through a car-sharing company offering five cars and a van at the community parking area. Residents who join the car-sharing program receive one-year free passes for all public transportation. The only continuous network is for bicyclists and pedestrians, giving them priority over cars, which are restricted to the discontinuous street network.

The backbone of the public transportation system is the tram that runs on the center of the park-boulevard, with stops at the west end, in the middle, and at the east intersection with Merzhauser Strasse such that each residence is within a 300-meter walk of a stop. The tram connects in ten minutes to downtown Freiburg. The headways average approximately eight minutes, with real-time information on arrival times at each stop. The regional bus system stops in front of the Sonnenschiff development along Merzhauser Strasse to link to the tram.

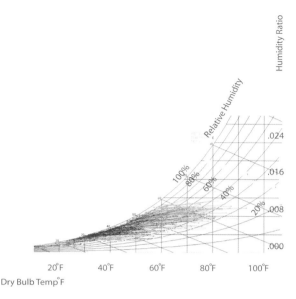

Figure 5.5. Psychrometric chart showing daily temperature ranges per year in Vauban. The chart indicates passive solar power as the primary climate-responsive design strategy. Heating degree days (HDD) at 65°F = 9,327; cooling degree days (CDD) at 72°F = 5. *(Diagram by Harrison Fraker. Data source: Freiburg-Schwarzwald, Baden-Württemberger, Germany [8.00E, 47.88N].)*

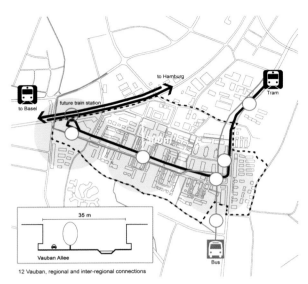

Figure 5.6. Public transit in Vauban. *(Source: Transurban: Thomas Schroepfer and Christian Werthman, with Limin Hee. Redrawn by Ariel Utz.)*

Figure 5.7. Parking in Vauban. *(Source: Szibbo and Reinhalter.)*

No comprehensive transportation survey of residents has been reported that indicates the mode split between walking, biking, public transit, car sharing, and private cars. However, the fact that a primary school, kindergartens, markets, and shops, as well as 600 jobs, are all on-site makes the vision of a walkable "district of short distances" a reality. Seventy percent of Vauban's families do not own cars. This results in 250 cars per 1,000 inhabitants[9] (one-third the national average). These statistics suggest that only 10–15 percent of daily trips in Vauban are by car, compared with the average mode split in Germany of approximately 50 percent of daily trips by car (90 percent in the United States).

Urban Form

The goals for Vauban's urban form have not been explicitly reported. The shape of Vauban was guided by concepts developed out of the open design competition and by the zoning guidelines of the city. These provided a general framework for individual developments on small plots.

The urban form of Vauban that emerged can best be understood as a T shape made by its primary public spaces: a one-sided commercial street at the head of the east entry to the site connected to a long green spine running east–west through the heart of the development as the tail. The commercial street at the entry is the main connection to the city and the region. It has commercial space on the first three floors, with a unique design of solar townhouses above. It is served by a solar parking garage on the opposite side of the street.

The green spine has an unusual hybrid urban form. It could be thought of as a boulevard with two-way traffic on one side of a linear green space that incorporates the tracks of a tram and a storm-water swale or as a linear green park in which the tram and cars are a necessary but minor intrusion. The experience and interpretation of the spine as a park is reinforced by several additional urban design elements. Almost all buildings along the spine are placed at right angles to it, with only their ends fronting on the space. This provides access and opens views into residential enclaves beyond. In addition, there are three defined open spaces across the spine at specific locations along the length linking both sides. Unlike the situation on typical boulevards with continuous buildings lining both sides, the edges of this space are

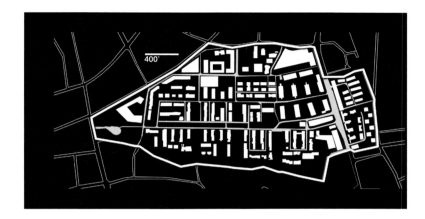

Figure 5.8. Vauban block pattern.
(Source: Szibbo and Reinhalter.)

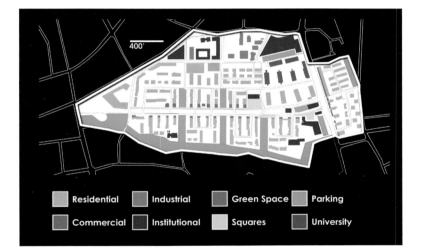

Figure 5.9. Land use in Vauban. *(Source: Szibbo and Reinhalter.)*

Figure 5.10. View of commercial building ends in Vauban. *(Photograph by Transurban: Thomas Schroepfer and Christian Werthman, with Limin Hee.)*

Figure 5.11. View of public plaza in Vauban. *(Photograph by Transurban: Thomas Schroepfer and Christian Werthman, with Limin Hee.)*

porous and predominately open. And yet the space has a commercial function on both sides because the ends of the buildings facing the linear park provide commercial uses on the ground floor. The result is a curious double reading—when one walks along the side, because of the foreshortened perspective, it feels like a continuous commercial street with urban density (approximately thirty units per acre) to support it. Yet when one looks across the spine, it feels like a residential park with occasional commercial conveniences dotted along its edge.

In many ways, the green spine acts as a trolley-car boulevard providing both access to the city by transit users and neighborhood convenience (shopping at the three stops), and yet its design is a new urban type: partly open linear park, partly urban neighborhood, partly boulevard.

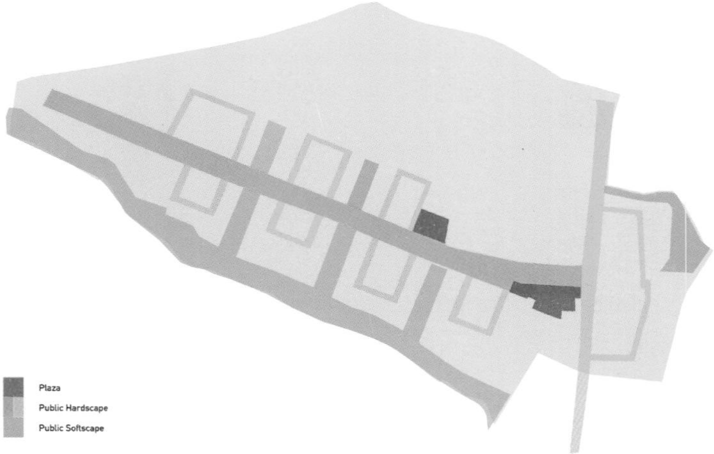

In addition to the green spaces that cross the linear park-boulevard, there is a community plaza set back on the north side approximately one-third of the way along its length. This is the community meeting place, served by a south-facing building with a restaurant and pub, community meeting rooms, the offices of Forum Vauban and its magazine, and a small hostel.

The block structure of the neighborhood is atypical. On the south side of the park-boulevard, U-shaped roads provide access to the Baugruppen build-

Plaza
Public Hardscape
Public Softscape

Figure 5.12. Public open space in Vauban. *(Source: Transurban: Thomas Schroepfer and Christian Werthmann, with Limin Hee.)*

ings (figure 5.8). On the north side there are three layers of buildings. In the first layer, similarly to the south side, access is provided by U-shaped streets. In the other two layers, there is a more typical pattern of streets and blocks, yet the streets do not go through. They shift at each block or terminate in a dead end. With the automobile street pattern on both sides discontinuous, pedestrians and bicyclists are given the only continuous routes, which provide the easiest, most convenient access to the neighborhood.

Green Space

As a result of the goal to make Vauban "densely built, yet green"[10] and with the public green spaces to be designed together with the local residents, the public open space of Vauban has one of the greener feelings of almost any neighborhood built to urban densities (more than thirty units per acre). This is achieved by a remarkable range of design strategies, from the most subtle to the most obvious. In the park-boulevard spine, the tramway tracks are not in a paved roadway but in grass, and the existing mature trees have been maintained. In addition, the tram's right-of-way is unfenced. Crossing of the tracks is limited to cross streets because the storm-water swale running parallel to the tracks is too deep to cross. The result is a virtually uninterrupted green space where the tram is an incidental occurrence.

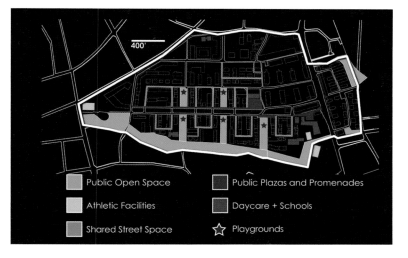

The three green spaces that cross the park-boulevard at right angles not only open the boulevard to the north and south neighborhoods but also provide linkage and access to the "regenerated biotope," the Sankt-Georgen stream, a key greenbelt and nature preserve along the entire length of the south edge.

The greening of the public spaces is further enhanced by the way the semipublic space, attached to the ground level of the Baugruppen, has been used for private gardens and custom-designed bicycle sheds, with all paving being permeable. The greening of the public space is not limited to the ground. Many of the Baugruppen employ vertical greening—vines and plants maintained by residents create a "living facade" that provides cooling in the summer and beauty year-round. To top it off, over 50 percent of the buildings have some sort of green roof to provide insulation and rainwater retention or solar collectors for hot water or electric generation. The overwhelming sense is that this urban neighborhood, as defined by its density, mixed use, and transit orientation, has become a multiple-level park.

Figure 5.13. Vauban green space and amenities. *(Source: Szibbo and Reinhalter.)*

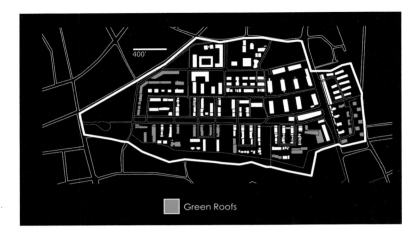

Figure 5.14. Green roofs in Vauban. *(Source: Szibbo and Reinhalter.)*

Figure 5.15. View of a vertical green in Vauban. *(Photograph by Carsten Sperling.)*

Figure 5.16. Vegetation in Vauban. *(Source: Szibbo and Reinhalter.)*

Energy

The goals for energy use in Vauban were guided by national and local policies that encourage energy efficiency (use redistribution) at the neighborhood scale, passively designed buildings to take advantage of the climate, and energy supply through district cogeneration systems and renewable sources. This framework was implemented in Vauban as follows:[11]

- All buildings were to be built to the improved low-energy standards of no greater than 65 kilowatt-hours per square meter per year (kWh/m²/y) for heating. This standard compares with 100 kWh/m²/y for buildings built between 1995 and 2000 and 200 kWh/m²/y for homes built prior to 1995. The standard was calculated using the Swiss SIA 380/1 standard (equivalent to 48–55 kWh/m²/y in a German standard).

- Energy supply was to be provided by a local high-efficiency cogeneration plant operating on wood chips and natural gas, with a short-distance heating network with the electricity produced supplied to the local grid.

- Solar energy supply was encouraged by creative financing in two modes: solar hot-water systems were incorporated in many of the Baugruppen projects to assist in heating and provision of domestic hot water, and photovoltaics (450 square meters in the first phase) were also installed on the Baugruppen buildings, with the two largest arrays on the parking garages. A total of 662 kilowatts-peak (kWp) was installed.

- Each Baugruppe was free to better the energy standards in its projects as a kind of friendly competition. This produced over a hundred units that met the passive house standard of 15 kWh/m²/y for heating, including the first two four-story passive multiunit apartment buildings built in Germany. The friendly competition also generated seventy-five units of the Plus Energy house (designed and developed by Rolf Disch as a demonstration of the principles in his Heliotrope house), which return the equivalent of 15 percent of the house's energy use per year to the city.

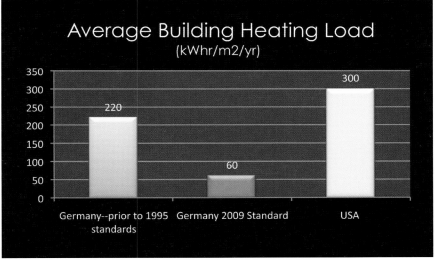

Figure 5.17. Vauban heating standards. *(Source: Szibbo and Reinhalter.)*

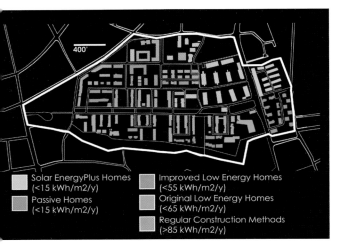

Solar EnergyPlus Homes
(<15 kWh/m2/y)

Passive Homes
(<15 kWh/m2/y)

Improved Low Energy Homes
(<55 kWh/m2/y)

Original Low Energy Homes
(<65 kWh/m2/y)

Regular Construction Methods
(>85 kWh/m2/y)

Figure 5.18. Vauban housing typologies. *(Source: Szibbo and Reinhalter.)*

Figure 5.19. Aerial view of original phase one Baugruppen housing units in Vauban, including original low-energy houses. *(Photograph by Thomas Fabian, City of Freiburg.)*

Figure 5.20. View of Passive House in Vauban, the first multistory, multiunit passive apartment block in Germany. *(Photograph by Carsten Sperling.)*

Figure 5.21. View of plus-energy houses in Vauban. *(Photograph by Daniel Schoenen.)*

Since all forty Baugruppen set their own goals and strategies for achieving or exceeding the mandatory low-energy standard, the only way to measure total performance is to monitor consumption in each building, and no such monitoring has been reported. Nonetheless, since 200 units (12 percent) were designed to the passive-house standard of 15 kWh/m²/y (some were designed for zero energy consumption), 100 units (6 percent) were designed to a standard of 55 kWh/m²/y for heating, and many solar hot-water systems were installed to reduce hot-water demand, it is reasonable to argue that the neighborhood performed well below the overall goal. By extrapolation, average total performance can be estimated as shown in table 5.1. The estimate shown is 24 percent below the approximated goal of 105 kWh/m²/y.

Both hot water and electricity are supplied by a district cogeneration plant (combined heat and power, or CHP) using wood chips and natural gas as fuel. Hot water is supplied to all the buildings by a district hot-water system, and electricity is fed through the city grid.

Table 5.1. Projected Energy Consumption for Vauban

Heating	46 kWh/m²/y	(65)
Electricity	22 kWh/m²/y	(30)
Hot water	12 kWh/m²/y	(15)
Total	80 kWh/m²/y	

Figure 5.22. Cogeneration Plant 1 in Vauban. *(Photograph by Carsten Sperling.)*

So far, eighty-nine solar photovoltaic systems equaling 1,200 m² have been installed on buildings throughout the project.[12] The largest arrays are on the solar parking garage and in the Solarsiedlung district, which was designed, developed, and financed by Rolf Disch with subsidies from the energy company Badenova.

The hot-water supply has been supplemented by solar collectors on the roofs of many Baugruppen projects. Baugruppe Kleehauser, one of the first multistory passive apartment buildings in Germany, has gone a step further toward a "zero home" by having its own small-scale CHP system, which provides backup heating to the passive solar systems and all electricity for the units.

Figure 5.23. Solar power plan for Vauban. *(Source: Szibbo and Reinhalter.)*

Figure 5.24. View of solar collectors in Vauban. *(Photograph by Carsten Sperling.)*

It is reported that 100 percent of the heating demand and 60 percent of the electricity demand has been supplied by the CHP system (using wood chips).[13] In addition, it has been reported that the solar photovoltaic systems generate 621,636 kWh/m²/y. This produces the total annual energy supply breakdown shown in table 5.2.

In other words, the neighborhood's energy demand is supplied by approximately 93 percent renewables!

Table 5.2. Percentage of Annual Renewable Energy Supply in Vauban

	Energy Supplied	Percentage of Total
Heating (wood chips)	10,399,400 kWh/y	73%
Electricity (wood chips)	2,366,760 kWh/y	16%
Electricity (photovoltaics)	621,636 kWh/y	4%
Electricity (gas)	956,204 kWh/y	7%
Total	14,344,000 kWh/y	

Water

The goals for water conservation, water reuse, and rainwater capture were not specified but were left up to the design objectives developed by each Baugruppe. Not surprisingly, given the climate of innovation and creativity promoted by Forum Vauban, many of the Baugruppen projects have employed innovative systems in all three areas: conservation, reuse, and rainwater capture. It also generated one pilot project in wastewater treatment to produce biogas for cooking.

The goals for storm-water treatment have not been specifically stated, but the system is designed to promote infiltration of rainwater into the ground over 90 percent of the site; in other words, it has a primary goal of groundwater recharge.

With the encouragement of Forum Vauban, many Baugruppen installed innovative water systems. Rainwater capture systems were installed and used for landscape irrigation, including the vertical green shading system. Rainwater capture is also used to flush toilets in the primary school. Vacuum toilets (using 0.5–1.0 liter, versus 5–9 liters for conventional toilets) were used in several Baugruppen, dramatically reducing water consumption. In Baugruppe Wohnen und Arbeiten, a vacuum system delivers the solids to an anaerobic digester, which ferments the solids along with food waste, generating biogas for cooking. The remaining wastewater is cleaned in biofilm plants and returned to the water cycle.

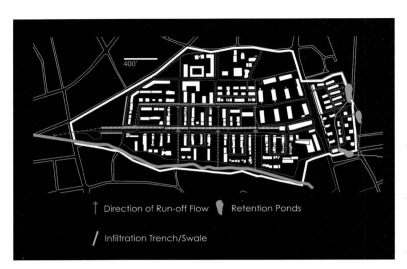

Figure 5.25. Storm-water management plan for Vauban. *(Source: Szibbo and Reinhalter.)*

There are no specific goals for the reduction in water usage, and no data have been reported on actual water use. Nonetheless, water usage can be assumed to be below the average for new German construction because of the application of vacuum toilets and rainwater capture and reuse. The innovative pilot program of reusing treated toilet water is too small to be counted, but its feasibility should be noted.

A simple rainwater retention system reduces the need for storm-water piping. The grading plan for the site directs all storm water into two linear "dry" trench-swales: one in the center of the park-boulevard, Vauban allée, and the other parallel to the pedestrian and bike path one block to the north. Both detain the storm water, allowing natural infiltration, and in the event of a severe (hundred-year) storm, the two swales will drain into the village creek at the west end of the site. Storm water on the east side of Merzhauser Strasse is detained in a dry swale and directed to a landscape protection area in the northeast.

No data have been reported on the rainwater recharge system. Anecdotal information indicates that the system has been working with only minimal discharge into the village creek. The reduction in storm-water runoff achieved by the use of green roofs (50 percent of dwellings have some form of green roof), permeable paving, and rainwater capture contributes to the success of the two linear infiltration trench-swales.

Waste

As with water, no specific goals regarding waste were stated for the project. The strategies for waste reduction, recycling, and reuse were developed by each Baugruppe. But again, the education provided by Forum Vauban about ecological principles of building and living provided a full menu of strategies, which were implemented throughout the development.

Provisions for waste reduction are not well publicized for Vauban. Nonetheless, a number of waste mitigation initiatives were implemented, especially in the area of cobuilding, or Baugruppen development. With the help of Forum Vauban, the community developed brochures on how to avoid construction waste and handed them out to developers. They also provided recycling stations for the disposal of scrap metal and construction waste. The neighborhood is served by the city of Freiburg's waste and recycling collection system.

Figure 5.26. View of central storm-water swale in Vauban. *(Photograph by Transurban: Thomas Schroepfer and Christian Werthmann, with Limin Hee.)*

The impact of providing recycling stations during construction and circulating brochures on how to reduce construction waste has not been reported in quantitative terms. Furthermore, data on the waste collection and recycling provided by the city of Freiburg have not been reported.

Social Agenda

The goal from the beginning was to integrate the legal, political, social, and economic actors from the grassroots level up to the city government, with an emphasis on including future homeowners in a participatory development process. Two of Vauban's most important social aims were (1) to achieve diversity in the living styles of residents and (2) to enable people from many strata of society to purchase their own homes. The following goals were developed to further the social and cultural dimensions of the neighborhood:[14]

- A balance of living and working areas
- A balance of social groups
- A mixed-use district center with shops for daily needs
- A primary school and kindergarten
- Family- and child-friendliness in the design of public space
- A neighborhood center for meetings, events, and guests
- A farmer's market

The most important process in helping to achieve these goals was the Baugruppen formation of a collective of future homeowners to purchase a designated site and then design and direct the building of their own housing, with the assistance of Forum Vauban.

Lessons Learned

The continuous participatory planning and design process, "planning that learns," was instrumental not only in achieving the goals of energy efficiency and renewable energy supply but also in promoting the goals of a socially integrated living and working neighborhood that is friendly to families, children, and elderly residents. Providing seed funding from the city and the federal government to support Forum Vauban and establishing it as the legally constituted representative of the citizens' groups was essential in the project's success. Creating small lots, which were sold directly to the homeowners' groups (Baugruppen), which functioned as their own developers and builders, was effective in making the housing more affordable by cutting out "middle-man" developers.

The Baugruppen collective building process promoted individual innovation, sharing of best practices through Forum Vauban, and real ownership and understanding of the operation and maintenance of building systems. The participatory design process was central in developing the innovative car-free living concept and creating public and semipublic spaces that are pedestrian and bicycle friendly, with special attention to the needs of children and elders.

Permitting only drop-offs, not long-term parking, at each residence, while providing parking in nearby garages, dramatically reduces the presence of the car in the public realm. Placing a high price on parking spaces in the garages, giving public transit subsidies to residents who do not own cars, and providing easy access to car sharing has produced one of the largest percentages of households without car ownership (70 percent) ever reported. When these strategies are combined with the design of public spaces to promote walking and biking, Vauban points the way to a less car-dependent future.

The participatory design and building process evolved naturally into the creation of social organizations that have promoted a stable, integrated, and participatory neighborhood culture.

The "learning while planning" framework prompted innovation, empowering residents to take responsibility for design qualities of their neighborhoods. In such a climate of innovation, the only compulsory standard—65 kWh/m²/y for heating, written into all the land sales agreements—became a mere baseline. Many of the Baugruppen and private developers set their own, more aggressive standards; exceeding the compulsory standard demonstrated the feasibility of much lower targets.

The urban form of Vauban is a new kind of hybrid. With block densities that range from 50 to 106 units per acre, Vauban meets the criterion of being urban in density. Yet the urban form is structured to create the experience of an urban park, with green space flowing through the blocks. Clearly this has created an open, flowing green identity and design quality that is valued by the residents. On the other hand, the openness and typical block pattern (i.e., not closed-perimeter blocks) is vexing to urban designers. The question arises, Is Vauban really urban when its streets are not so clearly defined by buildings and its public space is so open and free-flowing?

Placing most of the Baugruppen buildings at right angles to the park-boulevard has produced many residential units with east–west orientations. Their green facades have mitigated the potential cooling problem in the summer, but the orientation, while enhancing the green open space connections, does not take advantage of passive solar gain in the winter. It is important to note that the zero-energy passive homes and the plus-energy passive homes all have the classic north–south orientation, with full glazing on the south walls and well-insulated north walls with few windows. Thus, the urban design strategy of the east- and west-facing buildings is a clear trade-off on energy performance.

Having over forty different Baugruppen, each with its own program, objectives, and individual architects, has produced a rich variety of architectural expression, unified by the dominant green expression of the three-dimensional landscape.

The way in which the urban form has been opened to emphasize the flow of landscape open space, the prevalence of green facades, the saving of mature trees, and the glimpse of green roofs have all been successful in giving Vauban its overwhelming green design quality. The public realm is shaped in large part by a living green floor, green walls, and green roofs. Vauban's public space has a different feel from that in most cities. Even though it would not be considered high design, the urban landscape with all its sensory richness dominates the buildings, creating a very different kind of urbanism. Making the storm-water system visible and an active part of the public space gives greater definition and sensory enrichment to public life.

Vauban demonstrates that successful whole-systems performance has to begin with energy efficiency, passive solar design, and natural ventilation at the building scale. This is underscored by the zero-energy passive house and the plus-energy houses in the solar district. Once energy demand has been reduced, Vauban demonstrates the feasibility of a small-district CHP system to supply most of the hot water for heating and a portion of the electricity, using wood chips as its primary fuel. When the CHP is combined with a significant amount of solar photovoltaic generation, the whole system is powered by a high ratio of renewables with low carbon emissions.

The biodigester demonstration project, which uses sludge and food waste to generate biogas for cooking, has great promise for other potential applications, especially when thought of in relation to the building-scale cogeneration system in Baugruppe Kleehauser. It points to an entirely new and promising whole-systems approach for generating energy from waste. If the gas for the building-scale cogeneration system could be generated by a neighborhood anaerobic digester using neighborhood food waste, sludge, and digestible green waste, the biogas could replace the city gas and power the cogeneration system from local waste flows. The anaerobic digester pilot project has promising implications for application at the larger system and neighborhood scales.

The social goals for Vauban have been achieved in large part from the outset by the innovative participatory design and collective building process promoted by Forum Vauban. Through extensive public relations, meetings, and the district's magazine, *Vauban actuel*, Forum Vauban assisted in the formation of building collectives and fostered citizen participation in residential street design (stressing access and children's safety). It also helped in conceptualization of the neighborhood center Haus 037 and its weekly market. In addition, the neighborhood formed a Vauban district association to promote social and cultural activities including neighborhood lunches, annual celebrations, fund-raising runs, children's cinema, flea markets, football and boule tournaments, art shows, music and art classes, and the like. The result of these organizational efforts is one of the more socially diverse, mixed-use, and supportive communities, which is family and children friendly and welcoming to seniors, as indicated by the following statistics:[15]

- Thirty percent of the 5,100 district residents (1,530) are under the age of eighteen, supported by two facilities for toddlers and five day care centers.

- The district's 400 teenagers are designing and building a teen center to accommodate their growth to 800 in the near future.

- The neighborhood will accommodate more than 300 individuals over the age of sixty with transgenerational apartments and barrier-free access.

- Ten barrack buildings were converted to low-income dormitories for 600 students in the initial phase of the project.

- Over 500 jobs are located in the development area, not counting the home-based jobs held by many residents.

- The neighborhood is home to the following businesses and services: a large supermarket, a cooperative organic food store, an organic supermarket, two bakeries, a small organic wine and cheese shop, a weekly farmer's market (another supermarket is planned at the tram turning loop), one restaurant, two canteens, a pub, a kebab shop, two ice cream parlors, a drug store and pharmacy, a stationery shop, a bicycle shop, a computer repair shop, two hair salons, a shoe repair shop, the practices of several family physicians, pediatricians, and dentists, and multiple physical therapy and alternative healing practices.

LEED-ND Rating

Use of the US Leadership in Energy and Environmental Design for Neighborhood Development (LEED-ND) rating to evaluate European neighborhoods, such as Vauban, has its anomalies and reveals inherent biases in the LEED-ND system. For example, Vauban received no score for Certified Green Building (which requires a LEED-certified person), even though the Baugruppen buildings' performance has exceeded the energy efficiency standards. It also lost points on Walkable Streets and Street Network because the point system is based on a traditional US model streets grid with trees and parking, whereas Kronsberg's streets are based on car-free living. Finally, LEED-ND gives a total of only 6 points for On-Site Renewable Energy Sources, District Heating and Cooling, and Infrastructure Energy Efficiency—just 6 points out of the total of 110, or only 5 percent. It also gives a total of only 7 points for Certified Green Buildings and Building Energy Efficiency, or 6 percent of the total. Since these are important components in the whole-systems design concept that account for at least a 50 percent reduction in CO_2 emissions (everything but reduction in vehicular transit), it appears to be extremely undervalued at a total of just 11 percent. Even though Vauban achieves a Platinum rating, it is based on an accumulation of points for things that do not have a major effect on reduction of CO_2 emissions. This shows that a high rating can be achieved without addressing one of the most important environmental measures. It would appear that the weighting of the LEED-ND point system should be revised.

Table 5.3. LEED-ND Rating for Vauban

Criteria	Maximum	Achieved
Smart Location and Linkage		
Prerequisite: Smart Location		X
Prerequisite: Imperiled Species and Ecological Communities		X
Prerequisite: Wetland and Water Body Conservation		X
Prerequisite: Agricultural Land Conservation		X
Prerequisite: Floodplain Avoidance		X
Credit: Preferred Locations	10	5
Credit: Brownfield Redevelopment	2	0
Credit: Locations with Reduced Automobile Dependence	7	7
Credit: Bicycle Network and Storage	1	1
Credit: Housing and Jobs Proximity	3	3
Credit: Steep Slope Protection	1	1
Credit: Site Design for Habitat or Wetland and Water Body Conservation	1	1
Credit: Restoration of Habitat or Wetlands and Water Bodies	1	1
Credit: Long-Term Conservation Management of Habitat or Wetlands and Water Bodies	1	1
Subtotal	27	20

Criteria	Maximum	Achieved
Neighborhood Pattern and Design		
Prerequisite: Walkable Streets		X
Prerequisite: Compact Development		X
Prerequisite: Connected and Open Community		X
Credit: Walkable Streets	12	10
Credit: Compact Development	6	5
Credit: Mixed-Use Neighborhood Centers	4	4
Credit: Mixed-Income Diverse Communities	7	7
Credit: Reduced Parking Footprint	1	1
Credit: Street Network	2	0
Credit: Transit Facilities	1	1
Credit: Transportation Demand Management	2	2
Credit: Access to Civic and Public Spaces	1	1
Credit: Access to Recreation Facilities	1	1
Credit: Visitability and Universal Design	1	1
Credit: Community Outreach and Involvement	2	2
Credit: Local Food Production	1	1
Credit: Tree-Lined and Shaded Streets	2	2
Credit: Neighborhood Schools	1	1
Subtotal	44	39

Table 5.3. LEED-ND Rating for Vauban (continued)

Criteria	Maximum	Achieved
Green Infrastructure and Buildings		
Prerequisite: Certified Green Building		n/a
Prerequisite: Minimum Building Energy Efficiency		x
Prerequisite: Minimum Building Water Efficiency		x
Prerequisite: Construction Activity Pollution Prevention		x
Credit: Certified Green Buildings	5	n/a
Credit: Building Energy Efficiency	2	2
Credit: Building Water Efficiency	1	1
Credit: Water Efficient Landscaping	1	1
Credit: Existing Building Use	1	1
Credit: Historic Resource Preservation	1	1
Credit: Minimized Site Disturbance in Design and Construction	1	1
Credit: Stormwater Management	4	4
Credit: Heat Island Reduction	1	1
Credit: Solar Orientation	1	0
Credit: On-Site Renewable Energy Sources	3	3
Credit: District Heating and Cooling	2	2
Credit: Infrastructure Energy Efficiency	1	1
Credit: Wastewater Management	2	1
Credit: Recycled Content in Infrastructure	1	1
Credit: Solid Waste Management	1	1
Credit: Light Pollution Reduction	1	1
Subtotal	29	22
Innovation and Design Process		
Credit: Innovation and Exemplary Performance	5	3
Credit: LEED Accredited Professional	1	n/a
Subtotal	6	3
Regional Priority Credit		
Credit: Regional Priority Credit	4	n/a
Subtotal	4	0

Project Totals (Certification Estimates)

Total Points	110	84
Certification Level	Platinum (80+) Gold (60–79) Silver (50–59) Certified (40–49)	Platinum

Source: Harrison Fraker.

6. Observations across Neighborhoods

The planning for all four neighborhoods began in the mid- to late 1990s, approximately fifteen years ago. This time gap begs the question as to why it has taken so long for the lessons learned to find their way into new developments. The answer is complicated. Three of the four were developed in the context of major international events—the European Millenium Housing Exposition (Boo1), an Olympic bid (Hammarby Sjöstad), the EXPO 2000 World Exposition (Kronsberg)—and the fourth was part of a city with visionary environmental goals (Vauban).

These special circumstances inspired efforts to explore new, exemplary development practices, to depart from business as usual, to create demonstrations of a more sustainable and livable urban future. All four neighborhoods received considerable seed funding from their host cities, their federal governments, and the European Union to defray the added cost of initiating a more integrated, interagency, and interdisciplinary professional development process. It is this additional funding that made it possible to explore new alternatives, to overcome what Lord Nicholas Stern has described as the inertia, risk aversion, and incentives in current development practices. Most development projects do not have access to special seed funding, nor are they conceived with international expectations of innovation and change.

The length of time needed for each project and the timing in terms of events that influenced the projects were also factors. The process of planning, designing, and building urban neighborhoods is complicated and lengthy. It can take up to ten years from the start of planning to have enough of a neighborhood built and operating long enough to have collected performance data. Reports on the projects did not start to appear until 2004 for some and 2005 or 2006 for others. Just as the results were being disseminated and absorbed by the professions, the global financial crisis brought most development around the world to a halt. At the time there were many next-generation, innovative, and integrated sustainable development projects on the boards, as indicated by the number of projects chosen for inclusion in the efforts of the Clinton Climate Initiative (CCI) to promote integrated whole-systems thinking at the neighborhood or district scale. Originally, the CCI selected neighborhood- or district-scale projects in ten countries on six continents to "demonstrate models for sustainable urban growth,"[1] with the intention of monitoring and sharing best practices. The program has now been integrated within the C40 Cities Climate Leadership Group.[2] Only now are some of these proceeding, and in many cases in a more scaled-back form. The global financial crisis had the added effect of overwhelming any urgency about environmental concerns and climate change as a driving force for innovation in real estate development. Coping with a deep recession, massive foreclosures in housing markets, banks unwilling to make loans and hoarding capital, countries on the verge of bankruptcy from debt crises: such concerns overwhelm any sense of urgency about responding to environmental issues.

Just as the US economy has begun emerging slowly from the "Great Recession," the devastation of recent severe climate events has renewed a sense of urgency about how we should respond to climate change. The question now is, How will issues of sustainability or low-carbon operation be transformed by the added need for adaptability and greater resilience? Even with the renewed urgency of climate change as a driving force, it may not last long. Fortunately, many dimensions of these first-generation neighborhoods hold secrets to a more holistic urbanism, one that enriches the health and well-being of people's everyday lives, where climate change is not a necessary driving force. Given that these four case studies are the first neighborhoods with real performance data, the lessons learned and the conclusions that can be drawn across the neighborhoods are even more relevant. They point the way not only to achieving whole-systems "wizardry under the hood" for low-carbon operation but also to achieving the design qualities that engage people's imaginations. With these dimensions, the design of sustainable neighborhoods may not be driven solely by a threat (climate change and environmental degradation) but may become an object of desire for design qualities and quality of life, which are an integral part of the whole-systems design approach.

Process and Plan

In each of the four neighborhoods, the city, its planning agency, and its political leaders played a critical role in integrating the process. As landowners, the cities had the legal responsibility and authority for development of the projects. Using their political power and leadership, they were able to raise outside seed funding from federal agencies, use city funds, and, if needed, borrow funds at low interest rates to support the projects. In all cases, the cities created special development committees, usually with their planning agencies, which were given planning authority and leadership over the projects. All of the committees were interdisciplinary, with representation from internal agencies, outside consultants, citizens' groups, and the responsible utilities. Each committee developed specific goals and objectives for projects that were critical in driving innovative planning and design. The goals and objectives also represent the first targets and benchmarks for performance of sustainable neighborhoods.

Using their legal authority, the cities charged the responsible utilities—energy, water, sewage, and waste—with developing an integrated plan that met the specific goals of the projects. In most cases, the utilities used their internal expertise and outside consultants to devise new integrated approaches, all supported by additional seed funding funneled through the cities.

The cities developed overall master plans using outside consultants or by competition. They developed detailed development and engineering plans for the public spaces: the streets, the parks, the transit systems, and all the infrastructure—energy, water, storm water, and waste. The cities bid and contracted for construction of the public infrastructure and paid for it with a combination of city funds and construction loans. In this manner, the cities acted as the master "horizontal" developer, assuming the financial risk for each project.

Figure 6.1. Master plan of B001. *(Drawing courtesy of Stockholm City Planning Administration.)*

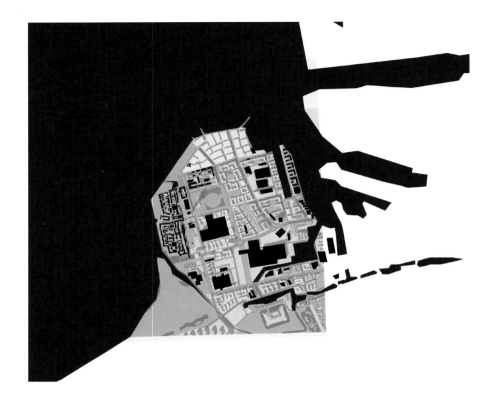

Figure 6.2. Master plan of Hammarby Sjöstad. *(Drawing courtesy of Stockholm City Planning Administration.)*

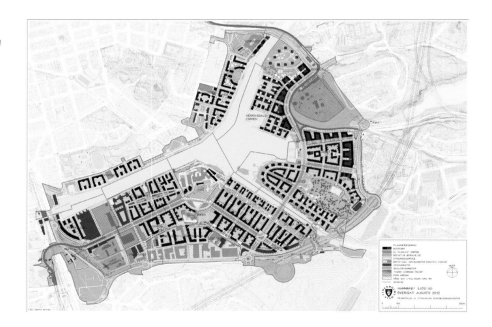

Figure 6.3. Master plan of Kronsberg. *(Source: Karin Rumming, ed., Hannover Kronsberg Handbook: Planning and Realisation [Leipzig: Jütte Druck, 2004].)*

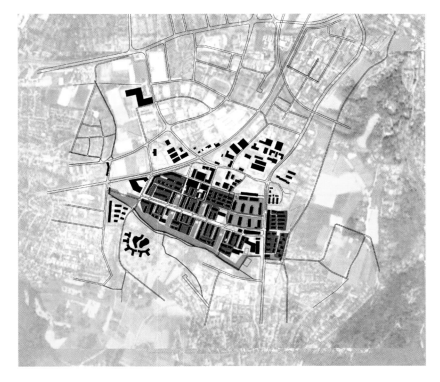

Figure 6.4. Master plan of Vauban. *(Drawing by Jessica Yang.)*

All four cities divided the developments into small plots, which were sold to multiple architect-developer teams. By maintaining continuous control over the projects, the cities were able to write specific goals and objectives and planning and inspection procedures into the land sale agreements. Even though many developers warned the cities against imposing these additional requirements and threatened not to bid on the projects, in the end almost all participated enthusiastically. The fact that new requirements were legally mandated, not optional or negotiable, did not jeopardize development.

The biggest difference in process among the four case studies was the degree of resident involvement in Vauban's "learning while planning" participation process managed by Forum Vauban. In Bo01, Hammarby Sjöstad, and Kronsberg, the cities engaged architect-developer teams with input from future residents as part of a city-run process to develop goals and objectives. Construction was carried out by traditional builder-developer contracts, either selling or renting properties to future residents. On the other hand, in Vauban, although the city enabled the process, much greater participation was given to residents in Baugruppen to set higher standards, select the architect, direct the design, and manage the construction. The higher performance results in Vauban demonstrate the value and innovation possible with more resident participation in the process.

The role of the cities in acting as master horizontal developer cannot be underestimated in the success of the projects. The cities held the power and legal authority and took all the risk in demanding a new integrated approach to sustainability. In all four cases, this role paid off financially. While no comprehensive financial analysis of the projects has been published, anecdotal reports from the city planning officials indicate that the cities profited sufficiently from the land sales to fund subsequent phases of development.[3] In other words, the neighborhoods created their own ongoing financial sustainability.

Transportation

All four neighborhoods demonstrate the well-known principles and values of mixed-use and transit-oriented development. Each has a public transit system (bus or tram) as an essential component of development, with the following characteristics:

- Transit stops are at convenient locations within 300–400 meters of residences.
- Headways are at intervals of six to eight minutes.
- Transit stops offer climate shelter and real-time information on schedules.

- Connections are provided to desired destinations.
- Neighborhoods have limited parking ratios of 0.2–0.8 space per unit.
- Each has street designs with traffic-calming measures and street networks that give priority to pedestrians and bikes.
- Each has a relatively fine-grain street and block pattern with frequent pedestrian shortcuts.
- Each has taken care in the design of the pedestrian environment and provided dedicated bike paths and bike parking.
- Each has provided a healthy balance of jobs and housing, with a significant mix of uses and services, to minimize the need for trips outside the neighborhood.

The net effect of these measures is that car trips in all the neighborhoods are below the European average of 50 percent, with Hammarby Sjöstad and Vauban achieving 20 percent and 10–15 percent, respectively. As a result, vehicle miles traveled (VMT) per year recorded are significantly (40–60 percent) less (orders of magnitude below the US average of 14,000 VMT per year). The impact on carbon dioxide (CO_2) emissions is also significant, ranging from 1.5 to 2.0 metric tons of CO_2 per person.[4] While the transition to alternative biofuels and electric vehicles will surely be a part of our low-carbon future, pedestrian-, bike-, and transit-oriented neighborhoods are the most cost-effective strategy for lowering CO_2 emissions from transportation because, as the bumper sticker says, "There is no car like no car!"

One of the underappreciated, hidden dimensions is the health benefit from a significant increase in walking and biking. It has not been quantified or studied for each neighborhood. However, if 80 percent of daily trips are by walking, biking, or public transit, or a combination thereof (as in both Vauban and Hammarby Sjöstad), the amount of moderate daily exercise is significant. The US Centers for Disease Control and Prevention (CDC) prescribes 150 minutes per week (2.5 hours) of moderate exercise (e.g., walking at a pace of three miles per hour) as a way to lower the risk of heart disease, stroke, high blood pressure, high cholesterol, type 2 diabetes, metabolic syndrome, colon cancer, breast cancer, and obesity.[5] If four trips per day involve 10 minutes of walking as part of commuting and doing errands, they result in more than 4 hours of moderate exercise per week. Even though this is a very conservative estimate of the amount of exercise involved in the daily trips of these neighborhoods, it exceeds the CDC recommendations by a large margin. This simple illustration highlights what Richard Jackson, former director of the CDC's National Center for Environmental Health, has been claiming: that the design of our neighborhoods and communities can play a significant role in promoting a healthier lifestyle.[6]

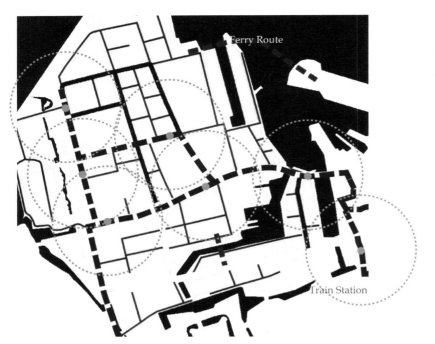

Ferry Route

Train Station

Boo1

+ 1 Miles Away from City Center

+ Main Transportation Lines in Boo1

1/4 Mile Radius from Bus Stops

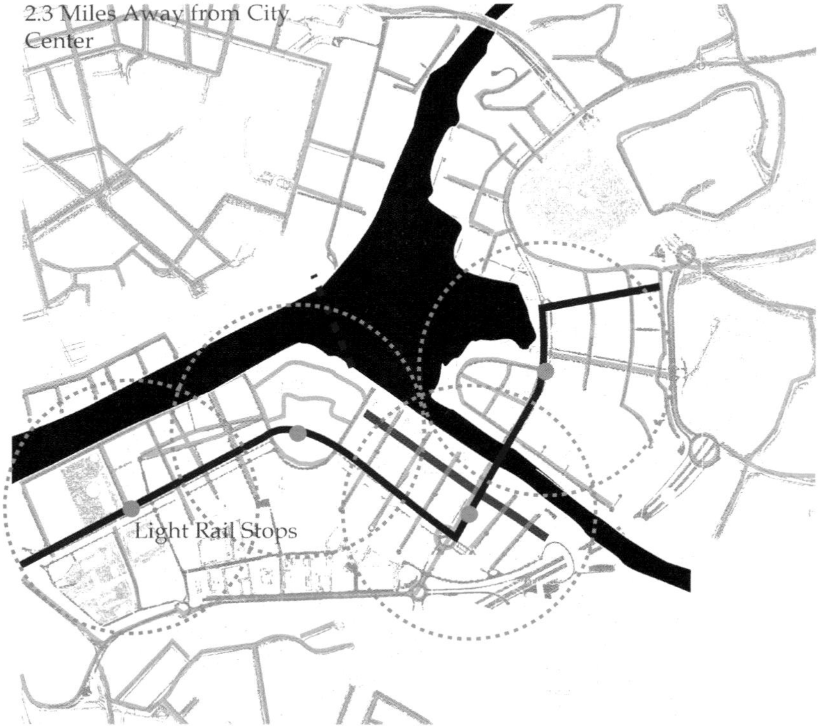

Figure 6.5. Transportation plan for Boo1. *(Drawing by Mahammad Momin.)*

2.3 Miles Away from City Center

Light Rail Stops

Hammarby

+ 2.3 Miles Away from City Center

+ Main Transportation Lines in Hammarby

1/4 Mile Radius from Light-Rail Stops

Figure 6.6. Transportation plan for Hammarby Sjöstad. *(Drawing by Mahammad Momin.)*

Kronsberg

+ 5 Miles Away from City Center
+ Main Transportation Lines in Kronsberg
1/4 Mile Radius from Bus Stops

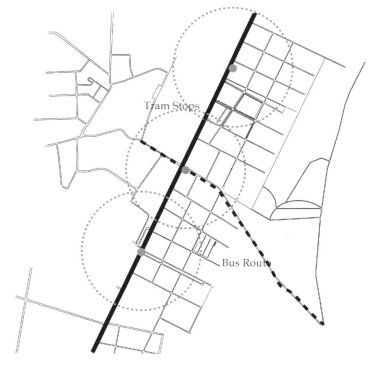

Figure 6.7. Transportation plan for Kronsberg. *(Drawing by Mahammad Momin.)*

Vauban

+ 2 Miles Away from City Center
+ Main Transportation Lines in Vauban
1/4 Mile Radius from Bus Stops

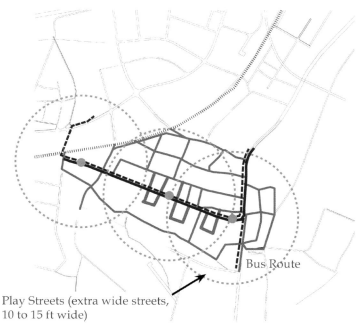

Figure 6.8. Transportation plan for Vauban. *(Drawing by Mahammad Momin.)*

Urban Form

On many levels, the urban form of the four neighborhoods is a testimony to the principles of smart growth being promoted in the United States, but of course each derives more from the traditional compact, walkable, transit-oriented, mixed-use European urban neighborhood, the antecedent of smart growth. Each has moderate urban densities, ranging from a low of 34 units per acre (net, Boo1) to a high of 350 units per acre (net, Turning Torso, Boo1), but averaging 80–100 units per acre (net). The densities support a high-quality public transit system that in three of the four neighborhoods (Hammarby Sjöstad, Kronsberg, and Vauban) has been the generator of a compact linear configuration related to a transit spine. The bus network at Boo1 has been developed to serve its site, which has a more two-directional urban grid, a two-dimensional field rather than a line.

Each has given priority to pedestrian and bike circulation, with a relatively fine-grain pattern of streets and blocks with frequent pedestrian shortcuts through blocks or green parks. Each has a healthy ratio of mixed uses, including shops, schools, and services with a generous balance of jobs and housing. All of these strategies reduce the need for trips beyond the neighborhood.

The building blocks of each neighborhood are based on a traditional urban perimeter block type, but each has been transformed to capture specific qualities of its site: Boo1 employs a larger block type with a strong contrast between inside and outside—between quiet, intimate spaces and public spaces with expansive water views. Hammarby Sjöstad opens one side of the block for views to the lake. Kronsberg develops a progression of block types from closed to open, from a one-sided commercial strip to a more open landscape edge. Vauban employs open "finger" blocks with commercial ends defining an intermittent commercial street. The range of block types in the case studies confirms the capacity of the urban block typology to generate a rich and diverse range of urban experience tailored to the specifics of each site. The block types are further enriched in all four neighborhoods by their having been divided into smaller development plots, each assigned to a different architect-developer team. The result is a diverse yet controlled expression of contemporary architectural ideas, capturing aesthetic differences similarly to the way historic cities accrue difference over time. The difference in block types displayed is relatively small and subtle compared with many more radical block types currently published in the architectural press. The four case studies are confirmation of the street–urban perimeter block typology as a robust strategy of city building that could easily accommodate some of the more radical block types.

Green Space

What distinguishes the four neighborhoods is the more emergent and potentially radical and expanded role of the urban landscape. Unlike urban neighborhoods with occasional pocket parks, almost every urban block in the four neighborhoods has direct access to part of an expanded urban landscape, leaving aside the green courtyards inside the blocks. The ratio of hardscape to landscape is radically different from that in the traditional city, greatly changing the perception and feel of each neighborhood. In the neighborhoods, as much as 40–50 percent (as high as 70 percent in Vauban) of the surface area is pervious and green. The increased landscape surface area not only is decorative but also provides multiple ecological services: (1) it retains storm water in a variety of bioswales and retention ponds; (2) it greatly expands the urban habitat of flora and fauna; (3) the trees' shade and green surface change the microclimate, reducing the heat island effect in summer and providing shelter in winter; and (4) the increased flora greatly improves air quality, absorbs CO_2, and, most important, creates a dramatically different olfactory environment. This increased flora also provides more biomass, which can be used to generate energy. Each neighborhood employs its own unique array of landscape types, from neighborhood parks, recreation and sports areas, skate parks, forest knolls, and an overlook mound to English gardens, formal squares, muses, and a wide variety of water treatments, with bioswales in the middle or down the edges of streets. Each neighborhood has developed its own unique landscape response to its surroundings: Bo01's treatment of the water's edge overlooking the Öresund Sound has become a defining city amenity; Hammarby Sjöstad's continuous access to a richly varied landscape treatment of the lake edge defines the neighborhood; Kronsberg's shaded allée gives definition to and prospect at the edge of the neighborhood overlooking the rural landscape; and Vauban's access to the west-side creek becomes both a prelude and access to the neighboring rural landscape.

The landscape treatment is not limited to the ground plane. Green facades shade the east and west faces of many Baugruppen buildings in Vauban; multiple green surfaces enrich the gardens, courts, and backyards of Bo01; and green roofs cover 50 percent of the buildings in Vauban, insulating, reducing runoff, and modifying the climate. While still emergent in their applications, these neighborhoods point to the idea of the urban landscape as a living three-dimensional framework delivering a full range of eco-services and cobenefits.

In many ways, the radical transformation of the urban landscape was a necessary design response to the simple but powerful requirement, in Bo01 and Hammarby Sjöstad, that every unit have access to public green space within 300 meters, or the requirement in Bo01 that the total surface area of every project have a green space factor of 0.5 (see the case study). The resulting landscape designs are precursors to what has become known as "landscape urbanism,"[7] which was just being formulated at the time. These neighborhoods confirm how the urban landscape can completely change the sensory experience of the city, having a favorable effect not only on energy, CO_2 emissions, and climate but also, even more important, on health and well-being.

1/2 mile radius walking distance

Figure 6.9. Comparative plan for Bo01. *(Drawing by Natalia Echeverri.)*

Bo01

AREA:
54 acres, 22 hectares

POPULATION (projected):	2,352
NUMBER OF UNITS:	1,567

DENSITY (gross):
29 dwelling units/acre,
71 dwelling units/hectare

PARKING RATIO:	0.5

COVERAGE:

Buildings	21%
Roads and parking	9%
Green space	32%
Water	28%

JOBS: (within one-half mile)	6,505
HOUSING (units):	2,352
JOBS/HOUSING RATIO:	275%

1/2 mile radius walking distance

Figure 6.10. Comparative plan for Hammarby Sjöstad. *(Drawing by Natalia Echeverri.)*

Hammarby Sjöstad

AREA:
494 acres, 200 hectares

POPULATION (projected):	25,000
NUMBER OF UNITS:	11,000

DENSITY (gross):
22 dwelling units/acre,
54 dwelling units/hectare

PARKING RATIO:	0.7
COVERAGE: Buildings	15%

Roads and parking 8%
Green space 45%
Water 22%

RESIDENTIAL:	1,080,000 m²
COMMERCIAL:	200,000 m²
JOBS: (within one-half mile)	5,193
HOUSING (units):	11,000
JOBS/HOUSING RATIO:	47%

Kronsberg

AREA:
172 acres, 70 hectares

POPULATION (projected):	6,600
NUMBER OF UNITS:	3,000

DENSITY (gross):
18 dwelling units/acre,
42 dwelling units/hectare

PARKING RATIO:	0.8
COVERAGE: Buildings	18%

Roads and parking 16%
Green space 64%
Water 2%

RESIDENTIAL:	240,000 m²
COMMERCIAL:	23,000 m²
JOBS: (within one-half mile)	2,000
HOUSING (units):	3,000
JOBS/HOUSING RATIO:	67%

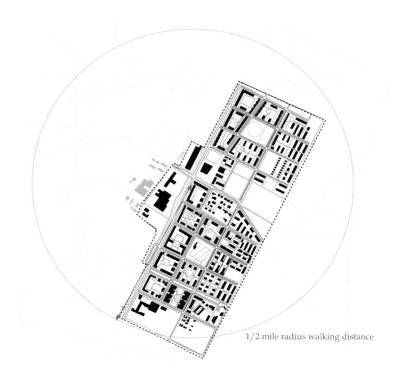

1/2 mile radius walking distance

Figure 6.11. Comparative plan for Kronsberg. *(Drawing by Natalia Echeverri.)*

Vauban

AREA:
84 acres, 34 hectares

POPULATION (projected):	5,000–6,000

DENSITY (gross):
21 dwelling units/acre,
53 dwelling units/hectare

PARKING RATIO: 0.2

COVERAGE: Buildings	19%
Roads and parking	11%
Green space	68%
Water	2%
RESIDENTIAL:	179,800 m²
COMMERCIAL:	40,800 m²
JOBS:	600
HOUSING (units):	1,793
JOBS/HOUSING RATIO:	33%

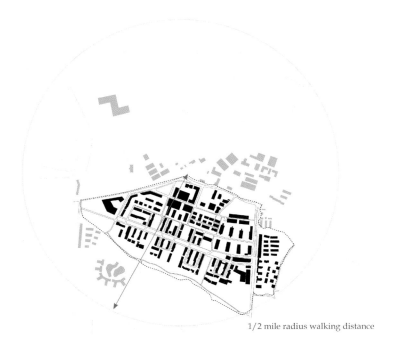

1/2 mile radius walking distance

Figure 6.12. Comparative plan for Vauban. *(Drawing by Natalia Echeverri.)*

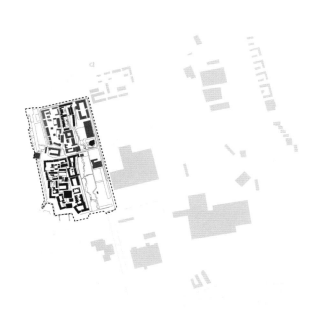

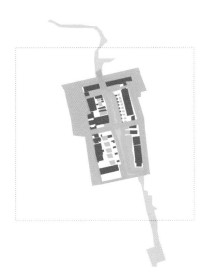

Figure 6.13a. Block plan A data for B001. Block area 10,004 m²; 81 units; density 34 units/acre; building coverage 2,488 m² (25 percent); roads and parking 1,100 m² (11 percent); paths 1,443 m² (15 percent); green space 4,923 m² (49 percent). *(Drawing by Nancy Nam; calculations by Harrison Fraker.)*

Figure 6.13. Block plan locations for B001. *(Drawing by Nancy Nam.)*

Figure 6.13b. Block plan B data for B001. Block area 3,600 m²; 388 units; density 436 units/ acre; building coverage 748 m² (20 percent); roads and parking 108 m² (3 percent); paths 2,027 m² (56 percent); green space 720 m² (20 percent). *(Drawing by Nancy Nam; calculations by Harrison Fraker.)*

Figure 6.13c. Block plan C data for B001. Block area 48,995 m²; 714 units; density 63 units/acre; building coverage 21,583 m² (44 percent); roads and parking 1,469 m² (3 percent); paths 17,398 m² (35 percent); green space 9,014 m² (18 percent). *(Drawing by Nancy Nam; calculations by Harrison Fraker.)*

Figure 6.14. Block plan locations for Hammarby Sjöstad. *(Drawing by Nancy Nam.)*

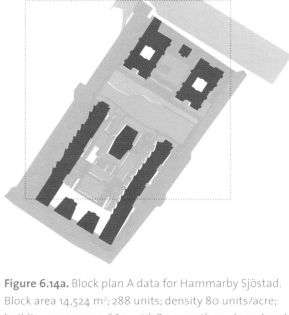

Figure 6.14a. Block plan A data for Hammarby Sjöstad. Block area 14,524 m²; 288 units; density 80 units/acre; building coverage 5,660 m² (38 percent); roads and parking 580 m² (4 percent); paths 2,387 m² (16 percent); green space 6,277 m² (42 percent). *(Drawing by Nancy Nam; calculations by Harrison Fraker.)*

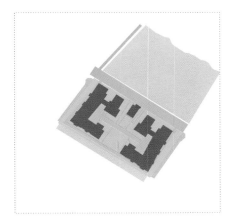

Figure 6.14b. Block plan B data for Hammarby Sjöstad. Block area 3,321 m²; 101 units; density 123 units/acre; building coverage 2,031 m² (61 percent); roads and parking 66 m² (2 percent); paths 228 m² (6 percent); green space 1,062 m² (31 percent). *(Drawing by Nancy Nam; calculations by Harrison Fraker.)*

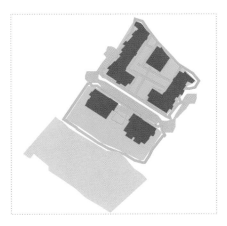

Figure 6.14c. Block plan C data for Hammarby Sjöstad. Block area 4,226 m²; 111 units; density 106 units/acre; building coverage 2,127 m² (50 percent); roads and parks 211 m² (5 percent); paths 487 m² (11 percent); green space 1,412 m² (34 percent). *(Drawing by Nancy Nam; calculations by Harrison Fraker.)*

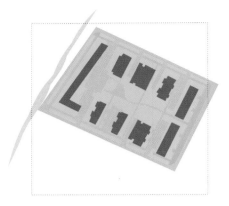

Figure 6.15a. Block plan A data for Kronsberg. Block area 15,261 m²; 388 units; density 102 units/acre; building coverage 4,276 m² (28 percent); roads and parking 4,253 m² (27 percent); paths 2,325 m² (15 percent); green space 4,407 m² (28 percent). *(Drawing by Nancy Nam; calculations by Harrison Fraker.)*

Figure 6.15. Block plan locations for Kronsberg. *(Drawing by Nancy Nam.)*

Figure 6.15b. Block plan B data for Kronsberg. Block area 7,139 m²; 64 units; density 36 units/acre; building coverage 2,308 m² (33 percent); roads and parking 428 m² (6 percent); paths 289 m² (5 percent); green space 3,443 m² (56 percent). *(Drawing by Nancy Nam; calculations by Harrison Fraker.)*

Figure 6.15c. Block plan C data for Kronsberg. Block area 10,000 m²; 245 units; density 99 units/acre; building coverage 4,596 m² (45 percent); roads and parking 493 m² (5 percent); paths 805 m² (8 percent); green space 4,297 m² (42 percent). *(Drawing by Nancy Nam; calculations by Harrison Fraker.)*

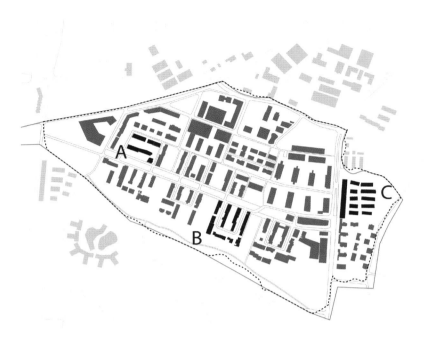

Figure 6.16. Block plan locations for Vauban. *(Drawing by Nancy Nam.)*

Figure 6.16a. Block plan A data for Vauban. Block area 7,296 m²; 120 units; density 67 units/acre; building coverage 2,151 m² (28 percent); roads and parking 362 m² (4 percent); paths 1,077 m² (14 percent); green space 3,868 m² (53 percent). *(Drawing by Nancy Nam; calculations by Harrison Fraker.)*

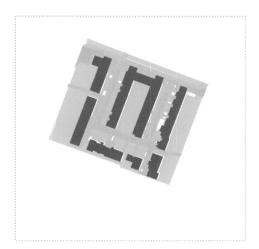

Figure 6.16b. Block plan B data for Vauban. Block area 12,308 m²; 396 units; density 130 units/acre; building coverage 7,429 m² (48 percent); roads and parking 1,786 m² (14 percent); paths 930 m² (8 percent); green space 3,692 m² (30 percent). *(Drawing by Nancy Nam; calculations by Harrison Fraker.)*

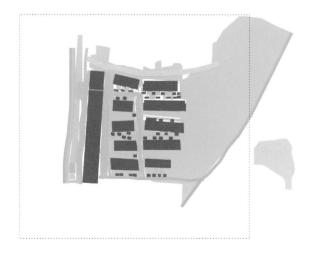

Figure 6.16c. Block plan C data for Vauban. Block area 10,226 m²; 267 units; density 106 units/acre; building coverage 5,407 m² (52 percent); roads and parking 1,329 m² (13 percent); paths 532 m² (5 percent); green space 3,119 m² (30 percent). *(Drawing by Nancy Nam; calculations by Harrison Fraker.)*

Figure 6.17. Section drawing of B001. *(Drawing by Brian Chambers.)*

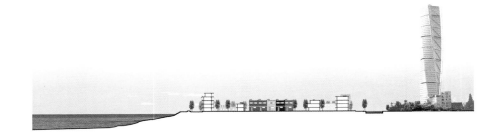

Figure 6.18. Section drawing of Hammarby Sjöstad. *(Drawing by Mahammad Momin.)*

Figure 6.19. Section drawing of Kronsberg. *(Drawing by Deepak Sohane.)*

Figure 6.20. Section drawing of Vauban. *(Drawing by Mahammad Momin.)*

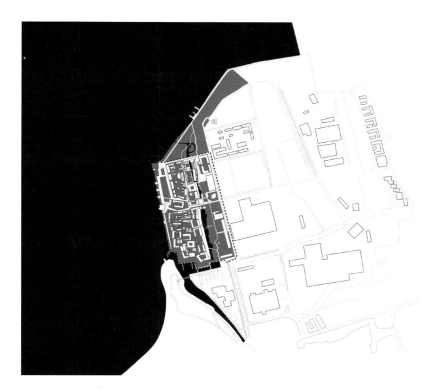

Figure 6.21. Green space plan for B001. *(Drawing by Mahammad Momin.)*

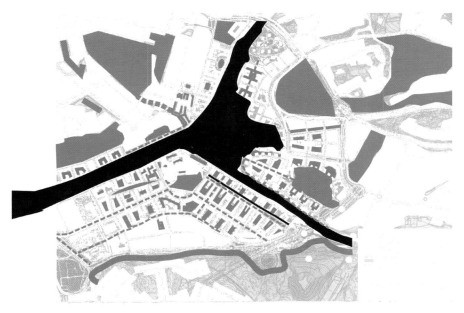

Figure 6.22. Green space plan for Hammarby Sjöstad. *(Drawing by Ariel Utz.)*

Figure 6.23. Green space plan for Krons-berg. *(Drawing by Mahammad Momin.)*

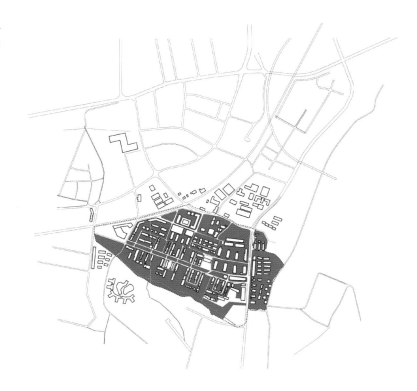

Figure 6.24. Green space plan for Vauban. *(Drawing by Mahammad Momin.)*

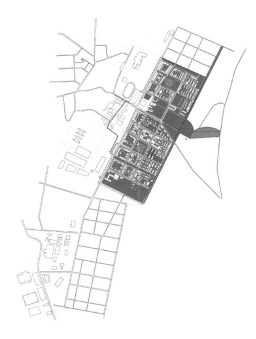

The health benefits of contact with nature have long been the subject of serious yet limited research. The prestigious Oxford Journals publication *Health Promotion International* published a multiauthored, peer-reviewed article in 2005 titled "Healthy Nature Healthy People: 'Contact with Nature' as an Upstream Health Promotion Intervention for Populations,"[8] which summarized the empirical, theoretical, and anecdotal evidence drawn from a literature search. The survey led the authors to state, "Empirical, theoretical and anecdotal evidence demonstrates [that] contact with nature positively impacts blood pressure, cholesterol, outlook on life and stress reduction," which adds up to improved health and well-being. Their findings were so convincing that the researchers called for "contact with nature" as a health strategy and for "public parks to be considered a fundamental health resource."[9] The researchers go so far as to say, "The individual and community benefits arising from contact with nature include biological, mental, social, environmental and economic outcomes. Nature can be seen therefore as an under-utilized public resource in terms of human health and well-being, with the use of parks and natural areas offering a potential gold mine for population health promotion."[10]

Whether or not the planners of these neighborhoods were aware of this body of research, intuitively the residents have recognized the expanded presence of the urban landscape as a hidden potential, a quality that makes these neighborhoods different and desirable. They may not recognize the subtle energy benefits or know of the health benefits, but they can *sense* the difference. It is the urban landscape in all four neighborhoods that delivers the distinctive identity, the "styling"—the special quality alluded to in the Chrysler ad—that makes sustainability a delight worth building. For people in the neighborhoods, it is not necessary to understand the expanded role of the urban landscape in whole-systems design; the design quality is enough.

Energy

Energy systems can be explained in two parts: the "demand" side, which is the sum of all the energy loads, and the "supply" side, which is how the energy is delivered to all the loads.

Demand Reduction

There is general agreement that to achieve a high percentage of energy supply from renewable energy sources, aggressive building energy efficiency measures to help reduce demand are a requisite first step. In other words, low energy demand equals high renewable supply. Of course, this principle is contradicted when there is an abundant local renewable resource or a combination thereof, as demonstrated in B001. Even though it reports the highest energy demand in the units measured, it is the only neighborhood with a 100

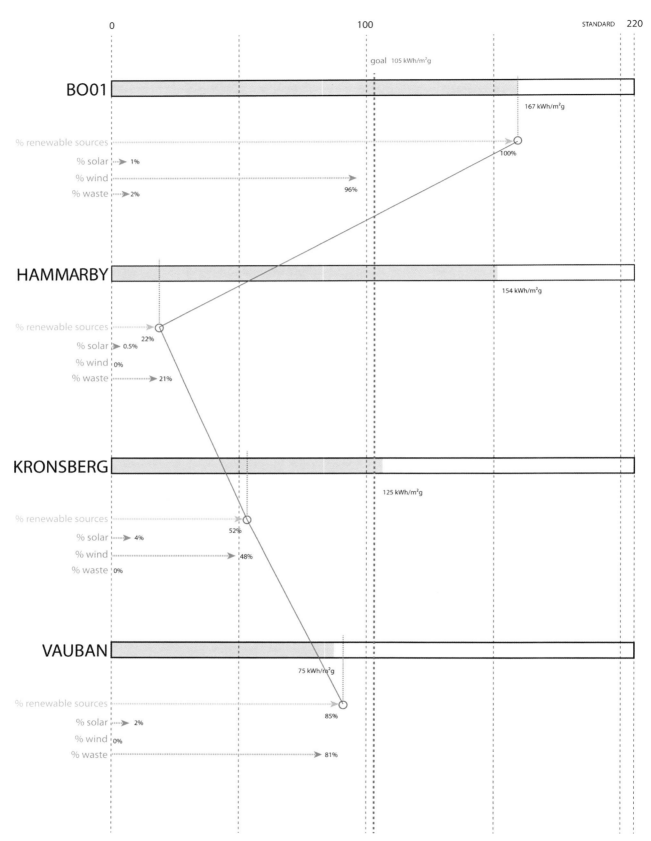

Figure 6.25. Comparative percentages of renewable energy supply. *(Diagram by Nancy Nam.)*

percent renewable supply, thanks to the robust combination of wind power and the groundwater-source heat pump.

In spite of this contradiction, low demand does make it much easier to supply a high percentage of energy from on-site renewables. The case studies provide the first real benchmarks, real performance data, in how much energy demand reduction is necessary to attain a high percentage of renewable supply. As can be seen with Vauban, which has the lowest energy demand, the combination of solar photovoltaics and a waste-to-energy cogeneration plant burning wood chips comes very close to 100 percent renewable.

On the building energy efficiency side of the equation, good insulation, high-quality windows, and low air infiltration resulting from good-quality construction are well-established first steps. Vauban demonstrates that climate-responsive architecture using passive solar power, natural ventilation, and both fixed and movable seasonal green shading design strategies is also necessary to achieve the lowest demand targets (see the zero-energy and plus-energy Baugruppen discussed in chapter 5). Vauban performed better than its targets, 65 kWh/m²/y, 55 kWh/m²/y, and 15 kWh/m²/y (passive house), by having the owners directly engaged in the design and building process, ensuring quality construction and efficient resident behavior. Kronsberg met its heating target of 55 kWh/m²/y by training contractors, providing detailed prescriptive standards and careful inspections, by conducting a blower door test before issuing an occupancy certificate, and by providing extensive resident education. Boo1 and Hammarby Sjöstad did not meet their heating targets of 65 kWh/m²/y, which was attributed in large part to flaws in construction, excessive glazing, orientation of buildings, and user behavior.

Energy efficiency in the use of electricity did not receive the same attention as that in heating (perhaps because the neighborhoods are located in cold climates with approximately 6,000 heating degree days). The three neighborhoods with data on electricity usage went over their targets: Boo1, 49 versus 38 kWh/m²/y; Hammarby Sjöstad, 46 versus 35 kWh/m²/y; and Kronsberg, 30 versus 22 kWh/m²/y (data were not available for Vauban).

Electricity usage on the demand side of the equation remains an important target for efficiency breakthroughs. While higher-efficiency lights (LEDs), appliances, and computers hold technical promise for reducing demand, user behavior is just as critical. Kronsberg, the best performer, had the most extensive program to help influence user behavior, including economic subsidies for energy-efficient lightbulbs and appliances and extensive resident education. Nonetheless, Kronsberg reported that only a small percentage of residents took advantage of these incentives, which is why they did not meet their target.

Remote sensor networks and the concept of real-time feedback on performance, like the dashboard concept from the Prius, show great promise for further reductions in actual usage through more intelligent human behavior.

While three of the four case studies went over their targets for total energy demand, it should be noted that their average measured total consumption (approximately 125 kWh/m²/y) was approximately half the standard at the time and remains more than half the US average at present for similar climate zones. Certainly a 50 percent reduction in measured energy demand is significant, but even more important is the performance of the more energy-efficient outliers, the passive houses (Kronsberg, 15 kWh/m²/y), the passive apartment buildings (zero energy in Vauban) and the plus-energy development (Vauban).

Their performance demonstrates that heating energy targets of 15–25 kWh/m²/y in a cold climate (6,000 heating degree days) are feasible. When this is combined with a more efficient but feasible electric demand target of 20–25 kWh/m²/y, total energy consumption in the range of 40–50 kWh/m²/y (including cooking and hot water) is reasonable and cost-effective. As an indicator, the Swedish standard today is 45 kWh/m²/y.[11] Energy demand at half the current measured performance of these four case studies makes it much more feasible to supply most, if not all, energy from local renewables.

Renewable Supply

All four case studies have a combination of renewable energy supplies at the neighborhood scale:

- B001: wind and geothermal (ground- and seawater heat pump plus solar)
- Hammarby Sjöstad: three types of waste-to-energy systems, including combustible waste cogeneration plus solar (limited) systems
- Kronsberg: wind and solar (limited) plus a gas-fed cogenerator
- Vauban: solar and waste-to-energy (wood chips) cogeneration

Three of the four use cogeneration to supply both electricity and district hot water (combined heat and power, or CHP).

The integrated hybrid combination of systems is the secret "wizardry under the hood" that produces the high percentage of renewable supply (like the Prius's gas and electric power system, with energy and recovery from the braking system):

- B001: 100 percent renewable supply. A 2-megawatt (MW) wind machine provides all electricity for both the 1,000-plus units of housing and the ground- and seawater heat pump, which delivers all heating and cooling (with limited solar assist), even though the measured energy consumption was higher than targeted.

- Vauban: 80–90 percent renewable supply (in some areas, more than 15 percent renewable). The cogeneration plant powered by wood chips supplies 100 percent of the district heating demand and 60 percent of the electric demand. The 1,200 m² of photovoltaics supply 15 percent of the electric demand (or 4 percent of the total energy demand). This leaves approximately 25 percent of the electric demand, or 10 percent of the total energy demand, supplied by gas.

- Kronsberg: 52 percent renewable supply. The cogeneration plant supplies all of the district heating demand, and two 2 MW wind machines supply approximately 10 percent of the electric demand. In this hybrid combination of wind and cogeneration, the gas acts as the primary supply for heating and as the backup for electricity.

- Hammarby Sjöstad: 22 percent renewable supply. With negligible solar and no wind or geothermal power, Hammarby Sjöstad has optimized waste-to-energy systems, using combustible waste as the fuel source in a cogeneration plant, biogas from sludge for cooking, and heat recovery from treated sewage for heating.

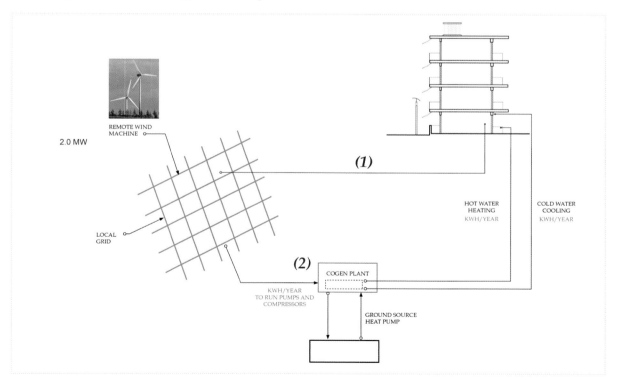

Figure 6.26. Performance data for B001. The goal for total energy consumption was 105 kWh/m²/y. The measured consumption was 167 kWh/m²/y. The energy sources are 100 percent renewable (1 percent solar, 99 percent wind, 0 percent waste). *(Drawing by Natalia Echeverri. Data source: Formas [Swedish Research Council for Environment, Agricultural Sciences and Spatial Planning].)*

Figure 6.27. Performance data for Hammarby Sjöstad. The goal for total energy consumption was 105 kWh/m²/y. The measured consumption was 154 kWh/m²/y. The energy sources are 22 percent renewable (0.5 percent solar, 0 percent wind, 21 percent waste). *(Drawing by Natalia Echeverri. Data source: GlashusEtt, City of Stockholm.)*

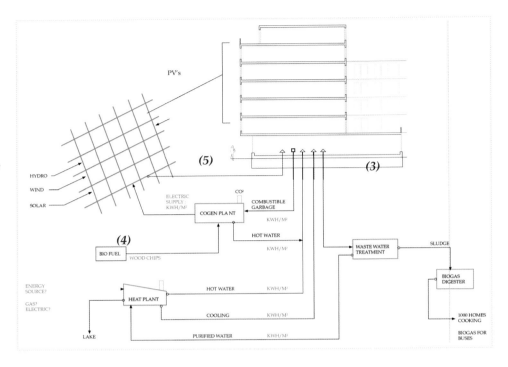

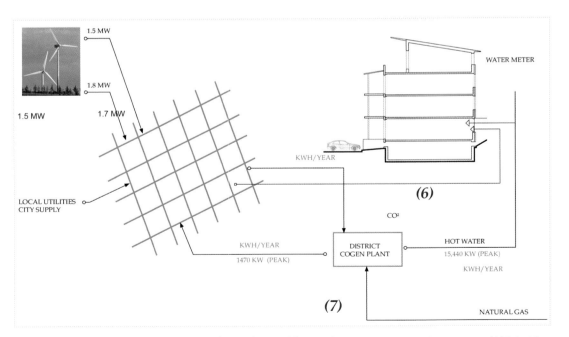

Figure 6.28. Performance data for Kronsberg. The goal for total energy consumption was 105 kWh/m²/y. The measured consumption was 125 kWh/m²/y. The energy sources are 52 percent renewable (4 percent solar, 48 percent wind, 0 percent waste). *(Drawing by Natalia Echeverri. Data source: Rumming, Hannover Kronsberg Handbook.)*

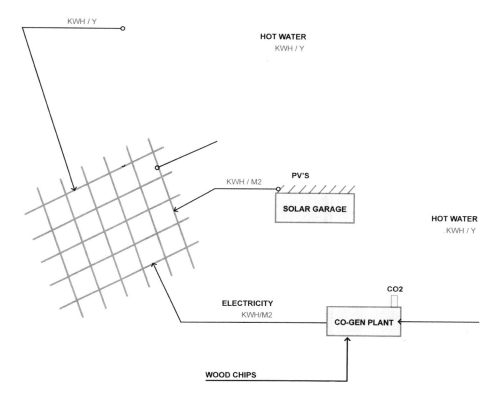

Figure 6.29. Performance data for Vauban. The goal for total energy consumption was 105 kWh/m²/y, and the reported consumption was 75 kWh/m²/y. The energy sources were 85 percent renewable (4 percent solar, 0 percent wind, 81 percent waste [wood chips].) *(Drawing by Natalia Echeverri. Data source: Hannes Linck, "Quartier Vauban: A Guided Tour" [Freiburg: District Association Vauban, 2009], 19.)*

Together, the four neighborhoods demonstrate all the effective means by which a significant percentage of energy can be supplied from renewable sources. Paradoxically, the neighborhood with the lowest percentage of renewable energy supply (Hammarby Sjöstad, 22 percent) may hold the biggest secret for filling the gap in renewable energy supply that cannot be met by wind, solar, or geothermal power. By not throwing the waste away but capturing its energy potential, it demonstrates the value of waste as a fourth source of renewable energy supply. Vauban also demonstrates the value of waste as energy with the burning of wood chips in its cogeneration plant. In addition, the small pilot biodigester project, which captures biogas from sludge and food waste for use in cooking, demonstrates the energy value of organic waste flows. Since waste flows are generated continuously by neighborhoods and cities, they can be rethought of as a first source of renewable energy supply. All forms of combustible waste can be a primary fuel source for cogeneration, and biogas digested from sludge, organic food waste, and green waste can be an additional fuel source for cogeneration and cooking. When waste is reconceived as a renewable energy source, it suddenly becomes a positive resource for cities rather than a significant cost burden for its removal and dumping.

Together, the four case studies point to a promising model for how neighborhoods can approach zero to plus energy in operation and close to zero in CO_2 emissions. The equation is simple. First, using a full array of building efficiency strategies and climate-responsive building design, lower the total energy demand to 40–50 kWh/m²/y (as demonstrated in the case studies). At such a level of energy demand, the energy generated from the local waste flows (approximately 30 kWh/m²/y for residential areas) is almost sufficient to supply the demand. It takes only a small amount of wind, solar, or geothermal energy (if available) to reach a 100 percent renewable energy supply. An integrated hybrid combination of waste-to-energy systems, wind power, and solar power creates the opportunity to optimize the size and cost of each system and also to balance use and the timing of each renewable source. In this manner, the neighborhood is powered by a combination of its best available natural and waste capital; it becomes its own micro-utility. Such an integrated system presents a new technical and business model for utilities.

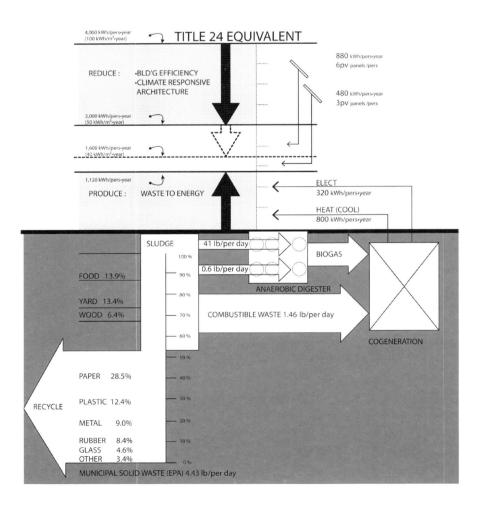

Figure 6.30. Reduce/produce diagram (efficiency and waste-to-energy plus solar). *(Diagram by Nancy Nam.)*

Water

Water conservation has been pursued in all four neighborhoods by encouraging the use of water-conserving toilets and fixtures, buttressed by extensive resident education and information on the value of water conservation. Little hard data have been reported on actual water usage, but it can be assumed to be well below averages for urban water usage in both Sweden and Germany (below 200 liters per person per day, or less than 50 gallons per person per day). Rainwater capture and reuse has not been widely applied. There are limited applications for toilet flushing (Vauban) and limited applications for landscape irrigation (Vauban and Hammarby Sjöstad).

Storm-water treatment and retention are major features of the urban landscape design in all four neighborhoods. Open dry swales along the streets in Kronsberg and Vauban clean and slow storm-water runoff to natural levels. Linear retention ponds in Hammarby Sjöstad and Bo01 clean and hold storm-water runoff before delivering it to the lake or sound, respectively. When it rains the systems come alive, animating the streets and park areas with the sounds and flow of water. The urban landscape displays one of its suppressed functions, that of recovering and absorbing rainwater rather than carrying it away as quickly as possible in pipes. These systems enrich the sensory experience of each neighborhood's public space.

Waste

There are many forms of urban waste. The three major flows are discussed below.

Solid Waste

All four neighborhoods have extensive provisions for solid waste recycling. Source separation is provided for glass, metals (cans), newspaper, and plastics at drop-off and pickup stations located conveniently around the neighborhoods. Hammarby Sjöstad has installed a vacuum chute system at the building scale and at neighborhood locations in order to consolidate recycling collections to a single pickup location, limiting the CO_2 emissions and pollution of traditional garbage collection. Combustible waste is collected and used as a fuel source in city waste-to-energy cogeneration in both Hammarby Sjöstad and Bo01. The energy generated from the system is not taken into account in the energy equation in Bo01, but it is a major factor in Hammarby Sjöstad.

Wastewater (Sewage)

In Hammarby Sjöstad, sludge in the wastewater is captured at the municipal treatment plant and converted into biogas for cooking and for use in the city buses. The sludge from Bo01 is also digested in the Malmö city biodigester, but like the combustible waste in B001 it is not taken into account in the energy balance equation of the neighborhood.

Organic Waste (Food Garbage)

As explained in the case studies, the organic food waste in Hammarby Sjöstad and Kronsberg is composted. By contrast, B001 tried to capture organic food waste from the neighborhood in two different pilot projects but failed to achieve sufficient purity in the waste stream to pursue its digestion. On the other hand, Vauban succeeded in combining the sludge and food waste in a digester to generate biogas at one of the Baugruppen. As described above, Hammarby Sjöstad demonstrates most clearly the value of the waste flows (combustible waste and sludge) in generating renewable energy. In spite of problems at B001 in capturing the organic food wastes in sufficient purity for anaerobic digestion, the successes of the pilot project at Vauban (and other digester projects around the globe) demonstrate that organic food waste, sludge, and green waste can add to the renewable energy captured from waste flows. Many cities in Sweden, Denmark, and other Scandinavian countries have recognized this and have developed the technology and tradition of capturing it.

The analysis of Hammarby Sjöstad's system in its case study gives a clear benchmark of the amount of energy that can be captured from neighborhood waste streams (30 kWh per person per year) and shows that it can potentially contribute 20–50 percent of energy supply.

What is clear from examining the integrated system performance of all four neighborhoods is that 100 percent renewable, zero-carbon operation is a reasonable goal. It is achieved by the integration of systems by capturing potential sources of energy across systems that is lost under the current practice of keeping each system isolated. It is also clear that there are many opportunities for even greater whole-systems integration—especially in capturing the potential energy in organic waste streams (food, sludge, and green waste), which were only piloted in the case studies. This is the simplest form of "closing the circle," wherein one system's waste is another system's resource. As with any paradigm shift in thinking, the biggest challenge comes not just in designing new technology systems but also in transforming the institutions that are invested in the structure of current practices.

Social Agenda

All four neighborhoods share fundamental underlying characteristics that contributed to their social sustainability. To begin, none of the neighborhoods is a single-use bedroom community or an isolated public housing project. They are all mixed-use and, to some degree, mixed-income neighborhoods.

Both Kronsberg and Vauban have succeeded in providing a large proportion (over 80 percent) of the housing as affordable. While Bo01 and Hammarby Sjöstad have demonstrated the feasibility of achieving low-carbon operation with middle- to upper-middle-income housing, Kronsberg and Vauban have demonstrated that it is feasible while providing a large proportion of affordable housing.

Provision for convenience shopping, schools, and a full array of social and recreational services, all within convenient walking distance, increases the chances for informal social interaction, for neighbors getting to know one another while conducting daily routines. Increased biking and walking, frequent use of public transit, and convenient access to public parks add to these chances for informal exchanges. Beyond convenience and shopping, a full array of social services, including schools, is equally important. Healthcare facilities, arts and community centers, senior services, community rooms, and local libraries all provide ways for residents to connect directly with other community members around shared interests. All of these build a sense of belonging to something larger than the residents' private lives and are keys to social health and well-being.

In all four cases, elements of the development process have played a major role in promoting social sustainability. Major public education efforts about sustainable living—during the development process, continuing during early occupation, and ongoing to this day—have created a sense of belonging to something new and special. The organizations sponsoring these efforts have been located on-site, providing a focus for residents' participation. In Bo01 it was through a series of city initiatives, including (1) a lecture series; (2) *folkbildning*, the teaching of subjects concerning a sustainable society; (3) Klimat-X, a program for schoolchildren; and (4) a project that addressed the question "How should we live?" emanating from the Association for Civic Education in Europe. In Hammarby Sjöstad, it was the information and activities hosted by the GlashusEtt facility on-site. In Kronsberg, the city formed the Kronsberg Environmental Liaison Agency (KUKA) to take the lead in promoting the community's ecological development through public relations, guided tours, information, skill building, and training in ecological construction for contractors, and public education for residents of the neighborhood. In Vauban, Forum Vauban organized and promoted resident participation in the design process, and the Baugruppen self-building process engaged residents directly in the design and construction of their homes. It is the existence of these efforts in the development process, and their evolution into ongoing neighborhood institutions supporting multiple activities, that has helped to create the continued social sustainability of the neighborhoods.

It is well understood in the social sciences that next to connecting with loved ones, family, and friends, belonging to a supportive social network is the key to a happier, healthier life. As cited earlier, the spatial organization, material qualities, and sensory richness of a neighborhood can promote a sense of something special, but the social milieu, neighborhood organizations, and recurring social events are equally important in creating a sense of community. These case studies demonstrate that building a neighborhood with specific goals for sustainability, and engaging the residents in the process of achieving these goals, can be a concrete step in building a sense of community. This is not a case of a developer trying to tack a brand name or an arbitrary theme onto a neighborhood. It is a case in which the process makes the neighborhood real and meaningful in people's everyday lives. It is the residents' deeper feeling that they are recognized players in the game. In the end, this is a testimony to "the powerful effect of human agency,"[12] which will sustain the neighborhoods, will operate and maintain the systems. Without the care, engagement, and active participation of the residents, the potential for approaching both an enriched and a low-carbon urban future is severely limited.

Resilience

None of the neighborhoods was planned or designed with resilience in mind. All were designed with mitigation—the reduction of CO_2 emissions—as an important goal. The only nod to climate adaptation was the fact that the ground level in Boo1 was raised to accommodate projected sea level rise. Nonetheless, the four neighborhoods point to strategies for achieving resilience with simple adjustments in how the systems are organized and operated together.

Two of the case-study communities (Boo1 and Hammarby Sjöstad) supply the hot water generated from their power plants (heat pump in Boo1, cogeneration in Hammarby Sjöstad) to the citywide district heating system and then to the units. On the other hand, in Kronsberg and Vauban the hot water produced in cogeneration plants feeds a local district heating system, making each independent of any interruptions in the citywide system, with the obvious benefit of greater resilience in heating.

In all four neighborhoods, the electric energy generated from local renewables (wind in Boo1 and Kronsberg, solar in Vauban, waste in Hammarby Sjöstad) is supplied to the citywide electric grid and then to the units, which are metered normally. This does not have to be the case. The local renewables could supply a local "smart grid" that in turn supplies the units and is also linked to the utility grid on a virtual annual net energy basis (see the discussion of West Village, Davis, California, in the following chapter), providing energy backup. This is a different model for electric utilities. Rather than a large, citywide electric grid supplying individual housing units, it is a network of self-supplying neighborhood (or district) "smart grids" with the regional utility grid as the overall framework and backup. As a concept, it provides an intermediate scale. When it is combined with local cogeneration, it provides incremental and distributed resilience because local cogeneration can absorb the intermittency of local wind and solar supply. Similarly to local district hot-water heating, the neighborhood microgrid can be protected from any interruptions in the regional or citywide electric grid.

Obviously, reconceiving how the electric grid is organized, constructed, and operated raises many questions and issues to be evaluated, not the least of which is who owns, operates, and maintains the network of distributed neighborhood microgrids. While such a change in our electric utility structure may seem radical, many micro-utility grids already exist, for example, on both corporate and university campuses. The benefits of such systems seem promising because the intermediate microgrid with cogeneration integrates renewable supply while potentially protecting the regional grid from its intermittence. It is important to note that local cogeneration provides resilience in both directions—it supplies balance and backup to local neighborhood renewables, but it also can be designed to provide additional backup to the regional grid. The concept of neighborhood-scale electric micro-utilities has the potential to become a critical means of integrating renewables while creating much greater resilience for the whole system.

A similar approach can be applied to both water and waste. While all of the communities in the case studies clean and retain storm water before returning it to the environment, none of them collects it for reuse. Natural and hybrid engineered systems exist that make it feasible to treat both storm water and wastewater on-site, "tailored" for reuse, greatly reducing the demand for water supply. The pilot project at Vauban demonstrates that both organic garbage and sludge can be collected on-site and digested to create biogas for local energy supply. Thus, local water and waste can be integrated into the whole-systems design of neighborhoods, contributing their resource to creation of additional local resilience.

While none of the case-study communities took resilience into account, it is clear that, as first-generation efforts at integrated whole-systems design, the inherent potential in their systems points to promising opportunities at the neighborhood scale for creating much greater resilience.

7. A Road Map for the United States and Beyond

The form of cities in the United States is a complex and eclectic tapestry of multiple city-building eras laid down over the past three and a half centuries. Most cities began as port cities at strategic locations along the nation's waterways because water transport was the fastest, most efficient means of moving people and goods. As trade, commerce, and populations grew, the cities went through numerous periods of expansion, shaped in large part by new developments in transportation technology.[1] In the beginning, cities were relatively compact and dense, clustered around port activities, with city boundaries defined by the limits of foot, horse, and carriage travel. They were generally surrounded by farmland, with the region linked by horse and horse-drawn wagon and coach. With the advent of the railroad-building era in the early to mid-nineteenth century, commerce, trade, and early forms of industry expanded not only around the ports but also along rail lines, rail yards, and depots. Rail transport also initiated the first phase of suburban expansion by the wealthy seeking to escape the teeming, crowded city cores. This era was followed by almost eight decades of growth, largely built around the streetcar, initially the horse-drawn streetcar (1852) and eventually the electric streetcar (1890–1930). Almost every major city has extensive neighborhoods that are remnants of streetcar development.[2]

Streetcar development was (and still is) characterized by a fine-grain pattern of streets and blocks usually oriented on the north–south, east–west cardinal points of the compass. The streetcar lines were distributed along larger streets and boulevards so that residential units were within a five- to ten-minute walk. Mixed-use commercial development grew up along the major streetcar routes or around intersections where stops were located, usually at half-mile intervals. The blocks were subdivided into small lots (fifty by one hundred feet), providing single-family homes at densities ranging from six to twelve units per acre. The densities provided the ridership necessary to make the streetcars profitable and affordable.[3]

The relationships between the cities and real estate developers varied greatly. In some cases, the developers built and operated the streetcar system because providing access was the only way to sell homes. In other cases, the city built and operated the system (with developer subsidy) in order to attract builders and residents. Some cities went far beyond building the basic infrastructure of streets, utilities, and public transit in order to entice people to move there. Using creative public-private partnerships, cities built park networks, sometimes converting poorly drained land into parks with lakes and streams (e.g., the Grand Rounds, Minneapolis–St. Paul; the Emerald Necklace, Boston). In addition, they zoned to enable neighborhood schools and churches, all in order to provide access to the amenities that mattered for potential new homeowners. During this era, the industrial metropolis was at its most efficient. It created the means by which all citizens gained access to jobs, housing, schools, conveniences, and amenities for everyday life.[4]

In the early twentieth century, the introduction of the automobile had a major impact on this urban fabric. The automobile provided Americans with long-awaited access to personal mass transit, offering the freedom to travel whenever and wherever they wanted to go. In the early stages, up to the 1930s, the impact was relatively leisurely. In rural areas, the car and truck provided much-needed access to regional service centers. In the cities, the car was used for weekend recreation—indeed, many of the early roads were landscaped parkways along scenic routes (Merritt Parkway, Connecticut; Lake Shore Drive, Chicago). But the car also provided access to suburban land beyond the reach of the streetcar and in the spaces between commuter rail corridors. Developers were drawn away from the cities and rail corridors to the cheaper land. The suburban developers no longer needed to build or subsidize streetcars to attract home buyers. This signaled the end of the streetcar era and the beginning of suburban sprawl.

The explosion in suburban development that followed World War II is a familiar story. It has lasted for six decades and remains the dominant mode of development even today. It was driven by the availability of cheap land in large parcels at the periphery, new single-use zoning laws, and the desire among a burgeoning postwar population to achieve the American dream of owning a home, all subsidized by a full range of government policies at all levels providing low-interest loans and income tax deductions on mortgage interest, obliging lenders to invest in home building and in financing road construction. This era has been dubbed the "freeway era,"[5] enabled by the Federal-Aid Highway Act of 1956, which financed the building of limited-access freeways in, around, through, and between cities. It soon reshaped every part of the city and its metropolitan region—turning its structure inside out.

As the freeway system matured, it provided relatively easy access to almost any location on the network, allowing the deconcentration of urban functions into freestanding single-use developments. Real estate developers, corporations, industries, manufacturers, and retailers took advantage of this opportunity, building a sprawling suburban landscape of shopping centers, strip malls, office parks, auto malls, medical centers, suburban housing tracts, and truck-based office and warehouse parks near highway intersections around every major city. In this regional landscape you no longer had to live close to your work—you could live in one place, work in another, and shop in a third, but the car was no longer a luxury or a recreational vehicle. It was a necessity.

By the 1970s to the 1990s, depending on the city, all the goods and services (the gross domestic product) provided in the outlying suburban areas were equal to those of the central city and its central business district. Soon the sprawl encompassed vast megaregions, gobbling up neighboring cities and creating suburban subcenters, all competing for real estate development and its sales tax base. The effect on the original compact industrial metropolis was profound. Large areas of the industrial waterfronts, with their warehousing and manufacturing, were rendered obsolete and abandoned, having lost in the competition with cheaper single-story, truck-based suburban operations. Large areas zoned for industry and warehousing along rail corridors or close to ports suffered a similar fate. At the same time, as jobs moved out, low-income neighborhoods suffered the further loss of jobs, creating even greater poverty and crime. Those parts of the city that had gone through an earlier phase of "urban renewal" in the 1960s—the so-called projects—became even more "blighted."

Of course, at the height of suburban sprawl, counterforces began to emerge that made development back in central cities more attractive. Traffic congestion resulting from sprawl increased on the freeways in almost every major city, to the point, in some cases, where the average speed at rush hour dropped to fifteen miles per hour. Dramatic increases in commute times (up to two hours each way) made the suburban lifestyle much less attractive. Even more dramatic changes in population demographics from the 1950s and 1960s meant that the single family (married couple with children) no longer made up the majority of the population. Single adults, professional couples without children, retirees, emigrants, and others sought the convenience of an urban lifestyle. As a result, parts of many cities have been regenerating over the past thirty years with new start-ups, loft living, and new medium-density housing, resulting in a vibrant urban lifestyle including restaurants, commercial services, cultural facilities, and urban recreational activities.

The successive phases of suburban development have experienced a similar cycle of obsolescence and abandonment to newer models of retail, commercial, office, and housing real estate development "products." The result has been the creation of megaregions with pockets of vital new development at the very same time as the creation of large areas of abandonment and urban decay. It is quite common to have some areas that exhibit the qualities of "shrinking cities"[6] and some areas with dramatic urban growth. This is a vast urban landscape with tremendous challenges, but it is also one with great opportunities for new sustainable development, depending on the particular history and geography of each city.

The question becomes, Are there areas and development opportunities that are particularly well suited to applying the lessons learned from the European case studies? The answer is yes, but it will take a new way of thinking and a major change in the development process. Cities will have to take much more of a leadership role. The city must return to being a more proactive developer, the way it performed in the earlier streetcar city building era.

Urban Landscapes of Opportunity

The paradox of the US city-building process, especially suburban sprawl, is that the resulting pockets of abandonment and underdevelopment are now potential opportunities for sustainable neighborhood development, within both the core cities and the multiple phases of suburban sprawl. Three of the four case studies (Boo1, abandoned shipbuilding and manufacturing; Hammarby Sjöstad, obsolete industrial manufacturing site; Vauban, former military barracks) seized this opportunity, and similar conditions exist throughout the United States.

Three of the four European case studies are examples of new development on reclaimed and repurposed industrial land, and one (Kronsberg) is new development on a greenfield site. While the US metropolitan landscape affords many similar opportunities, large portions of American cities (50 percent of the urban land) are built out. The question remains whether any of the integrated whole-systems concepts from the case studies, in part or in whole, have retrofit potential for US cities. Even though the common assumption is that whole-systems integration is possible only with new development, many of the lessons learned from the European examples have promising retrofit potential for making American cities both more resilient and more sustainable, while also creating a healthier and enriched urban life. This is possible because American cities, like most cities, are constantly in flux. They illustrate a process of physical and functional obsolescence and abandonment as well as a vigorous process of renewal. It can be argued that one of the greatest assets of American cities is that they are so unfinished. In fact, more than 50 percent of all construction in the United States involves renovation, repair, and maintenance. While continuous maintenance has always been the case with buildings (it is "how buildings learn"[7]), deferred maintenance has become a major challenge for urban infrastructure. The need to respond to this challenge presents the opportunity to remake American cities using a new paradigm employing the principles of whole-systems thinking.

Large areas of our cities' waterfronts remain abandoned, with empty industrial, manufacturing, and warehousing zones, where current land use and zoning regulations no longer make economic sense. The same is true for many similar land use designations along rail corridors. Many metropolitan regions have multiple military base closings, with their large parcels of land given over to cities. Earlier projects of urban renewal are up for renovation and redevelopment. Many of the boulevards of the first ring of streetcar suburbs are run down and ripe for redevelopment at higher density. The suburbs offer a long list of large parcels of potential development opportunities, including the following:[8]

- Failed shopping malls and strip developments
- Large corporate manufacturing campuses where much of the operation has been outsourced
- Planned unit developments of low density with large amounts of open space available for infill development at higher densities

During the stages of suburban growth, many cities built regional transit systems to alleviate congestion on the freeways, but the model was based on a suburban park-and-ride concept similar to that of earlier commuter rail corridors. The stations are surrounded by vast areas of parking and open space, which could be rezoned for much higher-density, mixed-use transit-oriented development. Many cities have taken advantage of these opportunities to build higher-density developments, but the cities (with a few exceptions) have not seized the opportunity to rethink their development process, to realize the potential of a more integrated, whole-systems, sustainable development model.

Because all of the infrastructure systems already exist in various configurations, one of the challenges and opportunities is to find the most appropriate places to engage the systems in capturing hidden or unrealized potentials. Even though many of the potentials involve crossing boundaries, it is useful to explore the potentials system by system.

Transportation and Land Use Strategies

The European case studies clearly confirm one of the well-known principles of sustainable development: that easily accessible, high-quality, and frequent public transportation is an essential first step not only to lower the carbon footprint for transportation in cities but also to improve the livability of neighborhoods. Fortunately, the principle has become widely accepted in the United States and is being actively promoted by the US Environmental Protection Agency under a broader set of principles labeled "smart growth."[9] In an effort to provide more mobility options, cities around the country have been creating new and exclusive bike routes and lanes, improving walking amenities, improving bus service—frequency, quality, rates, and information—building light-rail systems (thirty-five new systems in the past twenty years),[10] providing bus rapid transit with exclusive signal-prioritized lanes, and encouraging car sharing. These improvements have occurred in hundreds of cities around the country, from Atlanta to Phoenix, Buffalo to Minneapolis, Salt Lake City to Denver, San Diego to Los Angeles to San Francisco to Portland to Seattle. The change in transit behavior, the split between transit modes for daily trips, is measurable. While none of the results compares with 80 percent for pedestrians, bikes, and public transit as in Hammarby Sjöstad and Vauban, in some US cities bike trips have increased to over 22 percent of total daily commutes, walking to over 15 percent, and public transit to 40 percent of commuter trips.[11] While these are isolated cases, the impact on the carbon footprint and livability of individual neighborhoods is significant. Even though travel within the United States is still dominated by the car (over 80 percent of daily commutes), the examples of pedestrian- and bike-friendly transit-oriented development have maintained or increased their value during the shock of the housing bubble.

This principle of increasing mobility options in the "smart growth" menu has its antecedents. The concept was initially described as transit-oriented development, wherein transportation organizes and fosters development. And of course it was the model for streetcar neighborhoods. It has received considerable research attention in the transportation planning fields over the past twenty-five to thirty years.[12] There are many variables in what makes transit-oriented development successful, some related to characteristics of the transit system itself and others related to the urban design, land use, and demographics characteristic of the physical and social context.[13] The most important include the following:

System

1. Safety and security
2. Cost (and ease of purchase)
3. Time of travel (especially versus the car)
4. Frequency of headways
5. Connectivity to desired destinations
6. Reliability and performance of service
7. Ease and length of access time (usually measured in walking distance or time)
8. Real-time information on arrivals and departures

Context

1. Density of housing units within a half-mile radius of stops (varies by system type)
2. Density of jobs within a quarter-mile radius of stops (varies by system type)
3. Quality and interest provided in the pedestrian environment
4. Tolls and parking charges for car access to destinations
5. Level of congestion on freeways and streets at the time of travel
6. Mobility options at destinations
7. Access to conveniences and services

Obviously, the characteristics for success vary by transit system type and the urban fabric around stops. A vast body of data is emerging from hundreds of transit-oriented development systems around the country, pointing to measures of success.[14] While the data analyses are ongoing, some rules of thumb are emerging.

Time and Cost

1. If the cost of transit is equal to the cost of parking, gas, and tolls and the time is predictable and equivalent to that of car travel (even slightly longer), it will increase ridership and the value of the catchment neighborhood (assuming convenient access and reasonable frequency of service).

2. If the use of public transit can avoid the cost of owning a second car, it will increase ridership and the value of the catchment neighborhood.

3. Transit users are recognizing the higher quality of time spent on public transit as compared with driving time because of digital communications and the ability to read or even daydream.

Land Use, Density, Accessibility

It is generally acknowledged that a fine-grain pattern of streets and blocks in neighborhoods around transit stops increases walkability and access (see writings by Michael Southworth, Robert Cervero, Patrick Condon, and Peter Calthorpe). When augmented by dedicated bike lanes and pedestrian short-cuts and alternative routes through a park network, access is even better. Assuming this kind of street pattern and urban fabric around stops, table 7.1 summarizes the mix of jobs and housing densities at different radii from stops to ensure sufficient ridership. (This also assumes that the time, cost, and connectivity characteristics have been met.)

With a complex set of variables, it is difficult to narrow the predictions of success down to a few rules of thumb,[15, 16] but efforts are ongoing to create such a tool kit of criteria for US cities. What is so promising about US cities and their metropolitan landscapes is that they are replete with large areas (literally hundreds of thousands of acres) ripe for transportation and land use ret-

Table 7.1. Minimum Densities for Jobs and Housing One-Fourth and One-Half Mile, Respectively, from Transit Stops

	Jobs at One-Fourth Mile	**Net Housing Density at One-Half Mile**
Bus	30 jobs/acre	12–16 units/acre
Bus rapid transit	30 jobs/acre	16–20 units/acre
Light-rail transit	50 jobs/acre	20–40 units/acre
Heavy-rail rapid transit (subway)	50+ jobs/acre	30+ units/acre

rofits to organize and foster growth. The old streetcar neighborhoods already have the fine-grain pattern of streets and blocks, the "bones" that provide convenient pedestrian access to the old streetcar avenues and boulevards. In those cities where bus service has been improved or light-rail installed along old trolley lines, with modest increases in zoning densities and height restrictions, the neighborhoods are seeing a revival of investment in new businesses and new mixed-use development projects and the renewal and upgrading of housing properties (see development along Portland's east–west avenues as an example). The same is true of partially abandoned and underutilized industrial corridors where new light-rail transit and rezoning for mixed-use housing has spurred significant new development (see San Francisco's Third Street Light Rail Project).

In many cases around the country, cities are seeking to change the park-and-ride land use concept around heavy-rail stops to "live and ride." The small town of Orinda in Contra Costa County, California, for example, has a Bay Area Rapid Transit (BART) station, which has divided the city for almost fifty years. A citizens' group has developed a plan to add a high-density, mixed-use, pedestrian-friendly housing development on the parking areas around the station. The plan has the added benefit of stitching the downtown back together. The potential value of this kind of retrofit is best illustrated by what happened to land values around Metro stops in the Washington, DC, region. Land values around park-and-ride stations in the outlying counties lost up to 40 percent in value, while the land values around higher-density, walkable neighborhoods closer to the city actually increased in value during the financial crisis beginning in 2008. Add to these opportunities the reintroduction of water transit (high-speed ferries and taxis) as a way to promote development on old industrial waterfronts (see Oakland and South San Francisco) and vast areas exist where new development does not have to depend on the car as the only means of transit. While the potentials vary by city, multiple studies have shown that 50–100 percent of the projected growth of a metropolitan region can be accommodated by infilling on underdeveloped urban land with these kinds of transit-oriented developments. Studies of Melbourne have shown that the city's population can be doubled on just 7.5 percent of the urban area using "strategic residential intensification" along the existing tram and bus networks and including underutilized grayfield sites with a combination of three- or four-story development and seven-story blocks similar to those in Barcelona.[17]

Seizing these opportunities is one of the most important first steps in making US cities more resilient, healthier, and more sustainable. Many policy recommendations call for converting the fuel sources for vehicle travel to biofuels and electricity as part of a critical path to a low-carbon future.[18] Yet giving Americans a positive opportunity to use their cars less, not to need a second car or even any car at all, has immediate and direct cobenefits: less sprawl and loss of agricultural land, improved air quality and health, and lower energy consumption and carbon emissions, not to mention improvements in freedom of choice and quality of life. Retrofitting US cities with "green" transit-oriented, mixed-use infill projects and neighborhoods along transit corridors is the most promising first step in a US road map to sustainability.

Environmentally Responsive Building

The movement to improve building energy efficiency in the United States goes back forty years, to the early 1970s. Strategies for improving insulation values and the performance of windows, incorporation of passive solar technology, careful use of daylighting and natural ventilation, and increased efficiency of lighting and appliances, along with better heating, ventilation, and air-conditioning management and controls, are all recognized as the most cost-effective means for reducing energy demand and consumption.[19] This effort has been backed by considerable research carried out by universities and national laboratories, and its implementation has been supported by government subsidies and utility rebates. It has achieved considerable success. Most noteworthy is the so-called Art Rosenfeld effect, which kept electricity consumption in California from 1975 to the 2000s at a flat rate through energy efficiency strategies even as population increased.

Efforts continue with subsidies and rebates for solar photovoltaic installations on both residential and commercial buildings and the installation of

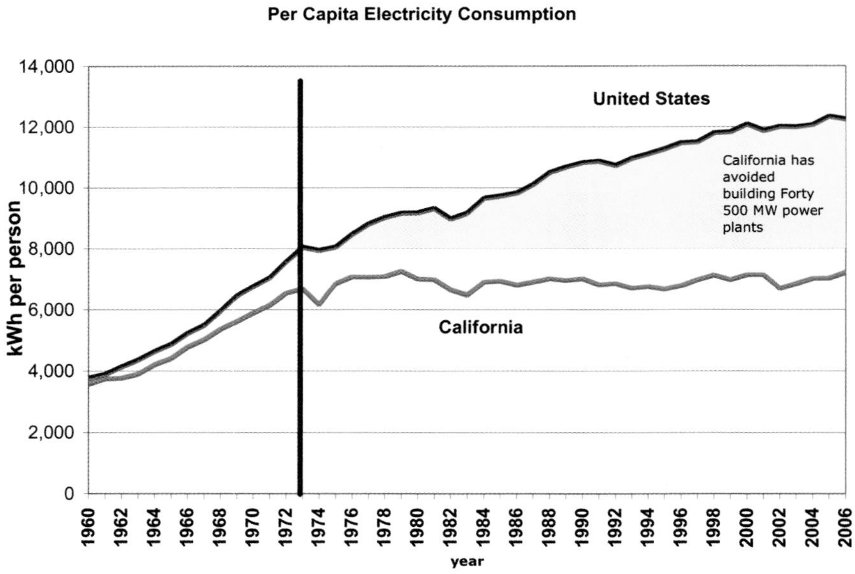

Per Capita Electricity Consumption

Figure 7.1. Art Rosenfeld effect.
(Source: California Energy Commission.)

new "smart" meters to give users real-time feedback on performance. There is an extensive literature on how to accomplish energy efficiency, including Web sites and utility-sponsored and private energy audits that evaluate options. These strategies not only are especially effective in new construction but also are applicable and effective as retrofits. In his 2030 Challenge, Edward Mazria points out that over the next twenty to thirty years the United States will renovate and repair up to 50 percent of its building stock. He has argued in US Senate testimony that setting goals to reduce carbon-based energy consumption in buildings to zero by 2030 is feasible and cost-effective.[20] He presents a detailed plan mandating performance standards that are 30 percent, 50 percent, 75 percent, and 100 percent below current codes in six-year increments as a way to reach carbon neutrality by 2030. Mazria proposes that federal low-interest loans be granted to buildings that meet the standards as an incentive for both renovation and new construction.

The details of the 2030 Challenge demonstrate that a wide and deep deployment of energy efficiency and renewable energy at the building scale can be an effective means of reducing carbon emissions. The European case studies confirm this fundamental principle. On the other hand, they demonstrate that renewable energy supply at the neighborhood scale (not the building scale) can be an effective whole-systems means of getting to zero carbon without having to rely on the building scale alone.

So what are the neighborhood-scale energy supply retrofit potentials implied in the case studies? There are three: (1) waste-to-energy biogas generation using sludge, organic food waste, and green waste; (2) neighborhood- and block-scale cogeneration using biofuels and combustible waste; and (3) solar photovoltaic and wind retrofits on public lands (parks, freeways, streets, parking lots) or on leased private lands, such as farms.

Waste-to-Energy Systems

An examination of US municipal solid waste flows shows that only approximately 3 percent of organic food waste is composted; the rest goes to landfills.[21] This waste flow (34.76 million tons per year) represents a large potential energy resource. Currently, many municipal sewage treatment plants capture sludge and convert it to biogas through anaerobic digestion and use the gas on-site to power the facility. If the anaerobic digester facilities could be expanded to accommodate the collection and processing of organic food waste, the additional biogas generated could turn sewage treatment plants into power plants. The biogas could be added to the existing natural gas distribution network, or it could power high-efficiency Stirling engines to provide peak electricity to the electric grid. Even though the amount of energy is small (approximately 2 percent) compared with total US consumption, it is energy currently going to waste. It is enough energy to power 3–4 million houses or to provide the cooking load for 20–25 percent of all homes in the United States.[22] If the organic food waste is deposited in landfills, the methane escapes eventually as a greenhouse gas even more potent than carbon dioxide (CO_2). By contrast, capturing the energy in food waste yields a triple dividend—it captures currently wasted energy, produces less greenhouse gas emissions, and reduces trucking to landfills.

Collecting organic food waste and delivering it to an expanded anaerobic digester at a centralized municipal sewage treatment plant takes advantage of existing citywide systems and has the advantage of aggregating waste at the city scale. On the other hand, there can be advantages if the strategy is implemented at a neighborhood scale. The waste from a mixed-use infill project of 5,000 units of housing will produce ten tons of organic food waste per day, enough to justify a small anaerobic digester. If the biogas produced is used to power a waste-to-energy cogeneration plant, the effective output from the biogas is almost doubled because the cogeneration plant produces both heat and electricity. It is feasible to supplement the anaerobic digester with sludge collected from sewage settling tanks or pumping stations in the neighborhood and to expand the fuel source for the cogeneration plant to include dry combustible waste such as yard waste and construction waste. This integrated hybrid waste-to-energy system is comparable to the "wizardry under the hood" of the Prius. The system produces both heat and electricity closest to the demand, reducing line losses, and it captures the potential energy in three waste flows (organic garbage, sludge, and yard waste), reducing the cost of waste disposal. For both new construction and retrofit projects, waste-to-energy strategies provide a promising and underrealized potential for making US cities more sustainable. Why waste the waste?

Cogeneration

Cogeneration is recognized as one of the most efficient means of delivering energy because it produces both electricity and heat from a single fuel source. It is a mature, cost-effective technology. The case studies demonstrate the effective use of renewable fuel sources such as wood chips (Vauban), making the system 100 percent renewable. Biogas can also be used as the fuel source, although this was not specifically demonstrated in the case studies. Wind and solar photovoltaics, in conjunction with cogeneration, can be used as an effective means to cover a portion of the electric load, as demonstrated in Kronsberg.

Distributed cogeneration plants provide an effective retrofit strategy for large institutions such as college campuses, business parks, infill projects, and corporate campuses, or even large single buildings, by increasing the efficiency of the fuel source. They become even more effective in lowering the carbon footprint of cities when powered by renewable sources from the waste streams or when coupled with a renewable supply such as wind or solar power. Cogeneration plants can also take advantage of new sources of natural gas made possible by hydraulic fracturing, or "fracking," as a cost-effective backup fuel source, but only if the negative environmental effects can be avoided. Even better, they may be designed to run on new biofuels, made possible by recent exciting breakthroughs in bioengineering. Rather than building new large power plants, which are increasingly hard to get approved, adding local cogeneration plants can diversify the grid, making the system more resilient and reliable. Transitioning to a more distributed and diversified power grid using cogeneration offers a great potential benefit to cities and represents a promising policy direction.

Wind and Solar Power

Wind machines and solar photovoltaic arrays are the most publicly recognized symbols of renewable energy. The location of wind farms in remote regions with high average annual wind speeds, such as the Altamont Pass and other locales in California, is generally accepted as a necessary public good. Similarly, locating large solar arrays in remote deserts has also become accepted. The location of these renewable technologies within the metropolitan landscape, closer to demand, has been more problematic. Solar arrays on buildings have become more acceptable because they are seen as an appropriate private choice and, for some, a public good. The location of wind machines within municipal boundaries in the United States has not been generally accepted. Local citizens' and environmental groups have objected to their noise, the danger they pose to birds, and the risk of blade failure. By comparison, northern European and Scandinavian countries (locations of the case studies) have embraced the deployment of wind machines throughout the metropolitan landscape, taking advantage of optimal localized conditions. The machines are located on public lands, and sites are also leased from farmers and private landowners. Their presence has been widely accepted as a public good and their operation seen as a graceful way in which humans can work with nature. For some they are even poetic, making awareness of the wind more immediate and alive.

Whether wind machines have a chance of being widely deployed in the US metropolitan landscape is an open question fraught with complicated political and social issues. It pits the "not in my backyard" mentality against perception of them as a common good. It is paradoxical that cities and residents accept the presence of power plants (some in very conspicuous locations, with

Figure 7.2. View of wind farm. *(Photograph by Argonne National Laboratory.)*

Figure 7.3. View of solar farm. *(Photograph by Sunpower Inc.)*

tall stacks) as an unwanted necessity and yet utilities and cities are almost unwilling to entertain the location of wind machines at potentially optimal sites within their municipal boundaries. If this attitude were to change over time with successful demonstration applications, the deployment of wind machines within metropolitan regions would be a mature, cost-effective retrofit strategy.

The application of solar photovoltaics as a retrofit strategy in cities is equally intriguing yet has different opportunities and challenges. Slowly, through federal and state subsidies (usually rebates for a portion of capital costs), reduction in manufacturing costs, and utility buyback agreements for locally generated power, the application of solar photovoltaics on residential and commercial buildings is gaining acceptance and penetration into the market. There are two basic models for financing the installations. In one, the solar array is installed and maintained by a solar company at no cost to the property owner. The costs are paid by the owners (who also realize the profit) through a monthly leasing arrangement, like a monthly bill, which is slightly less than the savings on their energy bill. In effect, owners are getting a guaranteed fixed price for their energy that is less than they previously paid. In the second model, the owners purchase the system from the solar company, receive the rebate directly, and pay for the cost of the system through savings in their energy bill. Usually the payback is in seven to eight years, so the owner profits directly from the savings over the remaining twelve- to fourteen-year life of the system. The purpose of the government subsidies is to help create a larger demand and market for solar photovoltaics to help drive down the cost. While the cost has been dropping,[23] the market is still not big enough to create a step change in costs through new investments in technical and manufacturing innovation. Because the subsidies are focused primarily on the private sector, which is currently undergoing an economic slowdown with much uncertainty, the market has not grown sufficiently.

If the secret to the wide application of solar photovoltaics is to bring the cost down by creating a larger market, then one of the models from the case studies (B001) suggests a promising strategy.[24] It involves cities and utilities collaborating to install photovoltaics on both public and private buildings as well as in public and private open spaces.

The concept is simple—use the roofs (where available) and south-facing facades (where appropriate) of public buildings, lease the same from private

Figure 7.4. View of wind machine at Budweiser plant in Fairfield, California. *(Photograph by Harrison Fraker.)*

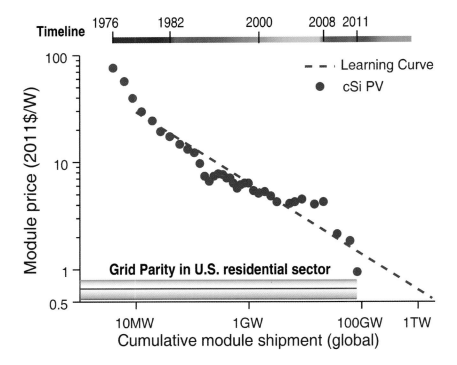

Figure 7.5. Solar photovoltaic cost reductions graph. *(Diagram by Harrison Fraker. Photovoltaic module data from Michael Liebreich [Bloomberg New Energy Finance Summit 2012 keynote presentation, March 20, 2012]. US residential electricity data from US Energy Information Administration, Electric Power Monthly, September 2011, http://www.eia.gov/electricity /monthly/.)*

building owners, and, where there is appropriate solar access, use the public open space of cities to provide a vast potential three-dimensional framework for the application of solar photovoltaics. The utilities could make large purchases of photovoltaics, which they would install and maintain using the most appropriate locations in the framework as part of their power supply system. The installations could take place over time, with successful pilot projects leading to wider deployment. Similarly to the system at Bo01, building owners would not have to worry about owning and operating systems. Because all buildings and public spaces do not have equal solar access, making installations feed the city grid, not just those buildings with solar access, benefits the city as a whole. This strategy uses the financial capacity and purchasing power of the utilities to create the kind of market that would drive down the cost of photovoltaics. It turns the surfaces of the city into a potential source for power generation and overcomes the transmission challenge of remote locations in the desert.

Even without the utilities' leadership or initiative, but with their cooperation, neighborhood solar power, or "community solar," as it is called, is starting to happen through private initiative. At least two innovative business models, one devised by Colorado's Clean Energy Collective and the other by Mosaic in Oakland, California, are capturing the benefit of solar power generation at the

Figure 7.6. View of photovoltaics on a roof, Ontario, Canada. *(Photograph by Sunpower Inc.)*

Figure 7.7. View of photovoltaics on a facade, Monte Rosa, Switzerland. *(Photograph by Sunpower Inc.)*

neighborhood scale. Both models allow individuals to "buy into" a neighborhood solar installation. In the case of Colorado, individuals receive a straight dollar credit on their utility bill based on the proportion of the neighborhood array they have purchased. The array is technically owned by the collective, which sells the tax credits and discounts the price to consumers accordingly. The collective sells the power to the utility as if it were operating a small power plant, and it has developed software to credit the consumer's utility bill directly. In the case of Mosaic, it is a kind of solar finance company. Consumers can buy shares in the community solar company and receive a 4–8 percent rate of return on their investment with which to offset their utility bills.[25]

While widespread utility installations and private sector "community solar" may appear to be radical proposals, their application can have multiple community benefits. There are many aesthetically successful design examples of photovoltaics being integrated into the roofs and facades of buildings, not to mention photovoltaic arrays used to shade large parking lots and as pergolas to create shaded pedestrian routes. In these applications the solar arrays are not only collecting energy; they are also improving the microclimate of cities for the benefit of city dwellers. The solar retrofit of buildings and cities is in its infancy. Its potential depends on innovative business models, creative policy makers, and imaginative designers to use photovoltaics to improve the experience in the public realm.

Figure 7.8. View of photovoltaics over a parking structure. *(Photograph by Sunpower Inc.)*

Green Infrastructure Strategies

Urban infrastructure in the United States faces serious challenges. Multiple studies estimate that our water supply systems lose considerable amounts of water from leaks, that collapsing pipes and breakdowns in treatment plants have become more frequent, and that the system has serious deferred maintenance challenges.[26] There is considerable concern about the adequacy of water supply sources, especially with climate change. In many regions there are long, expensive supply systems (dams, aqueducts, reservoirs, large pipes, etc.), which need continued maintenance and consume considerable energy (primarily for pumping) in delivery. When the energy demand of horizontal distribution is combined with pumping demand from groundwater sources, the energy consumption is significant. Each year, the moving of water in California consumes 19 percent of the state's electricity, 30 percent of cities' natural gas, and 88 billion gallons of diesel fuel.

Storm-water systems are equally challenged. In most US cities, storm-water systems, culverts, pipes, and holding ponds are too small to deal with the increasingly severe storms created by climate change. The resulting increase in local flooding and water damage is both a public and a private financial burden.

Municipal sewer systems have similar problems—leaks, sewer line failure, undersizing—and most of the centralized sewage treatment facilities are

Figure 7.9. California's water infrastructure. *(Photograph by Ian Kluft.)*

over thirty years old and in need of major maintenance overhaul. The cost to replace and repair the existing systems is estimated in the hundreds of billions of dollars.

Fortunately, the challenge has been recognized by the international water industry. Multiple workshops have been conducted over the past three years exploring exciting alternatives to the existing "big pipe, use once, throughput" model. A consensus is building around new models of distributed, decentralized systems that work with nature to do the work of centralized engineered systems.[27] This consensus does not discard the existing systems of water treatment, which are generally considered one of the twentieth century's greatest public health accomplishments. The concept envisions networks of decentralized natural systems with repurposed and at times hybridized central systems. Together the engineered and green networks mimic natural systems, in which water recycles and supports life at a local scale in what is described as "fit for purpose" water. The concept is to restore the "water commons."[28]

In this model, the urban landscape plays a key role providing many eco-services, replacing or enhancing existing engineered infrastructure. The urban landscape can engage and serve at least a dozen major functional areas:

1. Microclimate: expands comfort zone, tempers "heat island" effect
2. Air quality: filters pollutants, absorbs carbon
3. Storm water: treats, detains, and stores storm water for possible reuse
4. Wastewater: treats and stores wastewater for possible reuse
5. Food: provides urban agriculture
6. Energy: creates biogas fuel
7. Aesthetics: enhances design quality and sensory experience
8. Health: improves health and well-being
9. Recreation: creates shared activity and recreational space
10. Community: enhances community gatherings—large and small, quiet and active
11. Habitat: creates habitat for flora and fauna
12. Access: provides streets, sidewalks, boulevards, alleys, and pedestrian and bike paths—all systems of movement and access

It is clear that the urban landscapes in the case-study neighborhoods provide many of these functions. Indeed, the eco-functions delivered and their design qualities are among the important unexpected discoveries, and they point to the role that the urban landscape can play in retrofitting our cities to be more sustainable and livable. In the sections that follow, retrofit strategies are described by functional area.

Microclimate

One of the most promising and cost-effective roles that the urban landscape can play is improving the local microclimate. This is especially true in the hot climate zones across the United States that experience significant heat island effects. The air temperature and mean radiant temperature for surfaces in these cities can be as much as 4°F–10°F warmer than in surrounding suburbs. A coordinated strategy of carefully designed shade trees (or planted trellises) over sidewalks and parking, green facades on the lower floors of buildings, and lighter-colored, permeable paving has been shown to lower heat island temperatures by 4°F–8°F in a careful simulation study for areas of Phoenix conducted at Arizona State University by Harvey Bryan.[29] One of the most encouraging findings of the study showed that the cost of the retrofit measures could be paid for by the savings in air-conditioning costs by the adjacent building owners in two to three years. Yet the most positive effect is the improved comfort for pedestrians, which increases the potential of pedestrian street traffic. This produces cobenefits to shop owners, and it can create a greater sense of community and identity to parts of the city while increasing the sales tax base.

An additional cause of the heat island effect is the color and heat absorption of urban roofs. Studies conducted at Lawrence Berkeley National Laboratory by Art Rosenfeld have shown that retrofitting urban roofs with white, heat-reflecting materials or with green (living) roofs can reduce the heat island effect by 5°F–10°F.[30] Rosenfeld has argued that retrofitting cities with white or green roofs is one of the most cost-effective strategies for combatting global warming: white roofs reflect the sun's rays directly back into space, and green roofs convert more of the the sun's energy into growing plant material and less into heat. Rosenfeld's research group points out that 1,000 square feet of white roof replacing gray offsets the emissions of 10 metric tons of CO_2. If all eligible urban flat roofs were retrofitted with "cool roofs," the offset emissions would be equivalent to 24 billion metric tons of CO_2, or the output of 500 medium-sized coal-fired power plants![31]

Together, these studies suggest that the urban landscape should be thought of as three-dimensional, including not just the surface of the ground but also the walls and roofs of buildings and at least a forty-foot volume of public space above the ground. The idea of a three-dimensional urban green infrastructure was implied in Bo01's simple requirement that 50 percent of all project surfaces be green. It is one of the most promising retrofit strategies for cities.

Air Quality

Another important benefit of greening our cities is the beneficial effect on air quality. Trees, bushes, and hedgerows can filter pollutants from the air and shield pedestrians and residents from elevated pollution levels along high-traffic streets and highways. This strategy is employed most extensively in China, where dense hedge and tree rows (as many as twenty deep) are planted along freeways and major arterials. Besides filtering pollutants and restricting their dispersion, the trees absorb CO_2 emitted from vehicles, acting as a natural form of carbon sequestration. This strategy reconceives the public space of transportation not as just for vehicles but also as an opportunity for the landscape to deliver valuable eco-services.

At a deeper level, it suggests that the urban landscape provides an opportunity to create, in appropriate areas, a virtual "urban forest" with significant carbon sequestration. Joe McBride at the University of California, Berkeley, has studied and quantified the carbon sequestration of different urban tree types in different global cities over the life of the tree.[32] While is it clear that we cannot plant our way out of our CO_2 emission problems, the role of urban trees—the urban forest and its contribution to carbon sequestration—should not be dismissed.

Figure 7.10. View of storm-water planters, SW 12th and Montgomery Streets, Portland, Oregon. *(Photograph by Environmental Services, City of Portland.)*

Storm Water and Wastewater

There are many compelling examples of how to use the urban landscape to treat both storm water and wastewater. The most common are "green streets," which use bioswales to clean and detain storm water before releasing it to the environment (groundwater) or to the storm-water drainage system. More comprehensive citywide systems of storm-water treatment have been proposed for green boulevards in Chicago (Martin Felsen and Sarah Dunn's UrbanLab)[33] and for residual underused public land in San Francisco (Nicholas de Monchaux and Benjamin Golder's Local Code). These proposals include other eco-services related to improving the microclimate and creating enhanced public space for community activities.

Cleaning and retention of storm water before its return to the environment can be accomplished in many urban spaces other than streets. Parking lots can be redesigned to provide similar services (see Stephen Luoni's proposal for University of Arkansas parking lots, figure 7.17); public parks can also be redesigned and green alleyways created. All four case studies in this book demonstrate the positive design potential of these strategies, although each differs in its response to local context.

Figure 7.11. View of green street curb extension, SE Clay Street, Portland, Oregon. *(Photograph by Environmental Services, City of Portland.)*

Figure 7.12. Map showing Chicago water boulevards. *(Source: UrbanLab, Martin Felsen.)*

Figure 7.13. Artist's rendition of Chicago water boulevards. *(Source: UrbanLab, Martin Felsen.)*

The model for storm-water treatment need not be limited to cleaning, retaining, and returning it to the environment, even though recharging the groundwater and reducing the load on existing storm-water systems is a benefit to both the infrastructure and natural environments. Cleaning, capturing, and reusing storm water in the appropriate "fit for purpose" provides an important additional water source for cities. It is an ancient model. For 800 years, the drinking water in Venice was supplied by rainwater: the courtyards were designed to filter and store the water in giant underground cisterns, and the water was drawn up from a well in the middle.

The potential for storm-water and wastewater harvesting and reuse has been recognized by the US National Research Council, which stated that "municipal waste water reuse offers the potential to significantly increase the nation's total water supply."[34] The strategies can be applied at the regional, neighborhood, and even urban block and building scales.

At the neighborhood scale, storm water can be channeled in street bioswales, collected, cleaned, and stored as water features in neighborhood parks. It can then be reused in landscape irrigation, fire protection, and even a gray water system for toilet flushing. A similar strategy can be applied to sewage treatment. The sludge can be removed at pumping stations (or new retrofit treatment stations), and the remaining effluent can be cleaned using a hybrid combination of engineered systems (membrane bioreactors) or "living machines" with a sequence of "finishing" wetlands. Finally, the water can be stored for reuse, for both irrigation and toilet flushing or in water features. These natural storm-water and wastewater retrofit strategies at the neighborhood scale avoid the cost of rebuilding the existing "pipe, treat, and discard" throughput system.

At the urban block scale, natural storm-water and wastewater treatment strategies also have intriguing potentials, but they require more careful integrated whole-systems design thinking. The advantage of the block scale is its relative compactness and its autonomy: the systems do not have to cross legal boundaries. It is easier to collect the various waste flows—storm water, sludge, sewage effluent, and organic garbage—to process them and return the treated water and energy generated to the sources of demand. The challenge is finding space for the various systems: an area for natural storm-water treatment and sewage treatment, space for an anaerobic digester and a cogeneration plant. The layout and block design and the building types need to be engaged to meet the challenge. Borrowing block types from the case studies can be instructive. The courtyards in the perimeter blocks of both Hammarby Sjöstad and Kronsberg are big enough to accommodate a Living Machine® installation to clean the flow of sewage and storm water generated by the units. An even more intriguing, climate-responsive concept is provided by the microclimate environmental filter in Kronsberg. The linear atrium created between the housing units is large enough to accommodate a Living Machine that can treat all the units' wastewater and storm water in a similar fashion. The benefit of the microclimate zone is that it is an in-between space, which avoids the problem of freezing in cold climates.

It is not hard to imagine retrofitting the interior courtyards of urban blocks for natural storm-water (and wastewater) treatment in mild climates. It is more difficult to imagine doing so in freezing climates, but the concept of the in-between space, the microclimate zone, holds a clue. Natural wastewater treatment systems, such as the Living Machine, can be housed in greenhouses, where they can grow ornamental plants. They could become a feature in neighborhood parks, in urban block courtyards, and even along some streets. In many cities the space between buildings has been glazed in as a strategy to conserve energy but also to provide additional space and a microclimate, which allows extended use, as does the microclimate block in Kronsberg. The strategy could be expanded to include provisions for natural wastewater treatment as part of a retrofit.

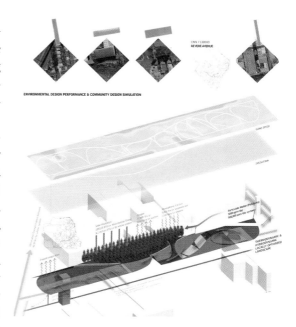

Figure 7.14. Local Code site diagram. *(Source: Nicholas de Monchaux.)*

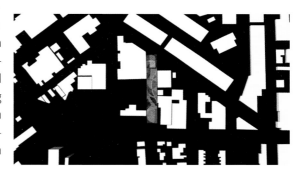

Figure 7.15. Local Code sample site. *(Source: Nicholas de Monchaux.)*

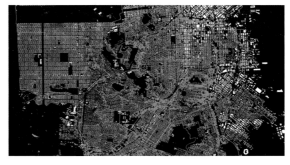

Figure 7.16. Local Code network. *(Source: Nicholas de Monchaux.)*

Figure 7.17. Riparian bands campus hydroscape. *(Source: Stephen Luoni.)*

Figure 7.18. Living Machine® process rendering. *(Source: Worrell Water Technologies, LLC.)*

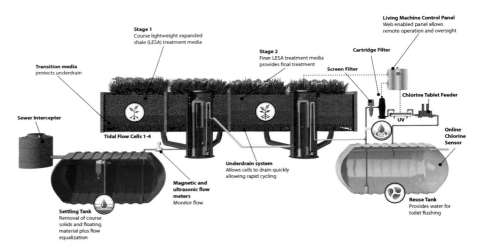

Figure 7.19. Living Machine® greenhouse example. *(Source: Worrell Water Technologies, LLC.)*

While it is easy to continue imagining innovative urban design applications of natural water treatment systems, the science (biochemistry) and the technology of these natural and hybrid systems is complex. They are matched by the complexity of the regulatory environment at the local, state, and national levels that limits their application. Together these challenges are why most applications in the United States have been limited to storm-water treatment and detention, with its release back to the storm-water pipe system or to the natural environment. Understanding the science, health implications, and regulatory constraints is the focus of major research efforts. One of these, Re-inventing the Nation's Urban Water Infrastructure (ReNUWIt), funded by the National Science Foundation's Engineering Research Center Program, includes Stanford University; the University of California, Berkeley; the Colorado School of Mines; and New Mexico State University as partner institutions in a large interdisciplinary team. The goal is to develop a typology of all the potential natural and hybrid urban water treatment systems (both storm-water and wastewater) that evaluates the level of scientific understanding of the processes, effects on human and environmental health, spatial requirements, suitability for different uses, retrofit potential and need, regulatory constraints, and cost implications. The research effort operates on multiple levels: a basic research level, prototype testing, and pilot projects, as well as an assessment of the institutional, process, and cost implications. It is being undertaken in an effort to capture the potential of adding an entirely new natural, distributed urban water treatment system, integrated with our existing centralized engineered infrastructure.

As these systems and their appropriate applications become better understood, they point to a very different concept for the role of the public and semipublic urban landscape in cities, as signaled by the four case studies. It is why the urban landscape has been described as a "fifth infrastructure."[35] Yet beyond the purely eco-service function of the systems, they have been conceived as design features that animate the urban experience. What they offer is a full array of potential cobenefits to the larger public commons. They improve air quality and microclimate; they deliver energy savings and energy production; they avoid costs and add to the resilience of the system. By integrating nature, with both its eco-services and its aesthetic presence, into the city, they create an enriched urban experience. Cities should recognize that it is the design value of these systems—their aesthetic and sensory dimensions, not just their infrastructure service—that will make many retrofit projects acceptable to local neighborhoods.

Food

None of the four case studies has the growing of local food as a major focus of development. Nevertheless, urban agriculture is one of the major functions that the expanded concept of the urban landscape enables. Building desig-

Figure 7.20. Brooklyn Grange, Brooklyn Navy Yards, south end. *(Photograph by Timothy Gonzalez.)*

nated areas for "allotment gardens" in public parks, vacant lots, and vacant industrial spaces and on rooftops and balconies provides the opportunity for growing local food. The concept that local food, or "slow" food, should draw from a fifty-mile-radius "foodshed" has now infiltrated our cities. The explosion of urban agriculture projects in some of our densest cities is not only a tribute to the staying power of the local food movement but also a realization of the potential for urban agriculture in cities. This book is not about the emerging field of urban agriculture, but it does recognize its promising potential as an important urban landscape retrofit strategy. Its by-product, the biomass waste of urban agriculture, points to another function the urban landscape delivers: the biomass potential for energy production.

Energy

The waste-to-energy systems using sludge, organic garbage, and green waste have been discussed earlier from the primary perspective of energy supply systems, not from the perspective of "growing" the fuel source. As the functions of the urban landscape expand, the amount of biomass available as a potential fuel source increases. Already in the United States 57 percent of the 33 million tons of yard trimmings generated each year are either composted or combusted to create electricity and heat.[36] These data demonstrate that many cities recognize green waste as a resource, not waste, and that mature, cost-effective technologies exist for its conversion to energy. Thus, expanding the amount of green waste (yard trimmings) by expanding the eco-services of the urban landscape does not represent a burden on a city's waste stream but is an energy asset. In such a whole-systems scenario, not only does the urban landscape improve the microclimate and air quality, treat storm water and wastewater, and create local food; it is also an energy source, adding further to its economic value.

Aesthetics and Health

Traditionally, the urban landscape is recognized as enhancing community by creating gathering spaces in parks and plazas, providing recreation in the form of sports fields and playgrounds, and providing public access through a comprehensive system of streets, sidewalks, boulevards, alleys, and pedestrian and bike paths—the public movement system of cities. The history of these traditional urban functions and their evolution as urban forms is as old as cities themselves. They are vital elements of the urban landscape, but their traditional forms are not the focus of this discussion. When the eco-functions discussed above are consciously integrated into the design of the urban spaces (both new and retrofitted), they take on a whole new dimension. Their meanings become multilayered. They enrich our senses, transforming our olfactory experience—the smell of cherry blossoms—modifying our auditory environment—the sound of water, the rustle of trees, and the quiet of a grove—and modifying our visual experience—dappled light, shade, and shadow and seasonal color changes. But now these experiences are not just decorative or playful; they are tied to other purposes. All of these experiences are shown to have a positive effect on our health and well-being, so much so that "nature can be seen as an under-utilized public resource in terms of public health and well-being, with the use of parks and nature areas [read urban landscape] offering a potential gold mine for public health promotion."[37]

Thus, the American urban landscape, both new and retrofitted, becomes a critical piece not only in creating more sustainable, low-carbon cities but also in creating cities that are places of delight. It is this expanded role of the urban landscape that can transform the concept of sustainability from a necessity to an object of desire.

Taken as a whole, the potentials described in this book present an extensive agenda of opportunities for city councils, planning departments, and departments of public works in American cities. They could even be conceived and organized into a comprehensive "public works" program similar to the one established in the 1930s, with similar financial benefits to be realized. Many projects are already being undertaken. New transit corridors, more energy-efficient building codes and standards legislating mandatory CO_2 returns, zero to plus energy, climate-responsive buildings, more efficient vehicles, new bike lanes, green streets, green roofs, and urban agriculture are emerging all over the country. These trends are certainly moving in the right direction. Recent reports indicate that CO_2 emissions in the United States have been dropping, but not because of these positive trends. The economic slowdown (less travel and commerce) and the conversion of coal-fired power plants to natural gas (made possible by breakthroughs in fracking technology) are cited as the main causes. By all projections, however, the current reductions in CO_2 emissions are both temporary and insufficient. The challenge remains how to integrate the retrofit opportunities outlined here into a whole-systems approach that can be undertaken incrementally but that also produces the reductions in CO_2 emissions necessary to stabilize the climate. Some, such as Lester Brown, have argued that the only way to change the inertia in our carbon-based system is to put a price on carbon emissions, using either a tax per ton or a cap-and-trade system.[38] In the current political climate it is hard to imagine if and when such a policy shift will be possible on the federal level, even though it is being considered seriously in some states, such as California. In the meantime, the federal government has been active in promoting the concept of sustainable cities. The US Environmental Protection Agency (EPA) has moved from being an "environmental watchdog" to making "sustainability the next level of environmental protection."[39] It has been active in promoting and developing information, education, and research on most of the themes discussed here. Through executive orders, the agency has been working to "conduct [its] environmental, transportation, and energy-related activities under the law in support of [its mission] in an environmentally, economically and fiscally sound, integrated, continuously improving, efficient and sustainable manner." This has led to the Partnership for Sustainable Communities, formed in 2009 by the US Department of Housing and Urban Development (HUD), the US Department of Transportation (DOT), and the EPA.[40]

At the same time, local communities and citizens have been developing their own strategies and measures and sharing best practices, often promoted and coordinated by the International Council for Local Environmental Initiatives (ICLEI—Local Governments for Sustainability) (see the United Nations Urban Environmental Accords).

With all this activity, what perspective and insights do the lessons learned from the European case studies and the first US zero net energy[41] neighborhood (discussed below) bring to the table? There are four major areas, which seem underdeveloped in the efforts to date.

The first is whole-systems integration at the neighborhood scale. With West Village in California being only the first American neighborhood to claim zero net energy, sustainable design at the neighborhood scale in the United States is in its infancy. Its advantages are clear. It affords the opportunity for transportation systems, building systems, infrastructure systems, and the urban landscape to be integrated in a whole-systems design concept.

Its on-site renewables (solar photovoltaics) provide a significant dimension of resilience because the neighborhood could run on its own power even if the regional electric grid went down.

The second is using waste-to-energy systems with cogeneration to capture the potential energy and resources in waste systems. This also demands integrated design thinking across traditionally isolated utility systems. When waste is thought of as a renewable resource with other renewable energy sources (wind, solar, geothermal), it enables more cost-effective system sizing, balancing, flexibility, and resilience.

Third is the more active engagement and expansion of the urban landscape and its eco-services as part of the whole-systems approach, including most especially its role in promoting human health and well-being.

Fourth is the importance of "human agency," not only in the process but also in the engagement of the day-to-day systems operations—participation in the real-time information (as with the Prius), which provides the means to "play the game." When the mutual dependence of these four areas is recognized, it is a game changer for design thinking. We are only just beginning to recognize the multiple synergies possible and only beginning to explore the cost benefits and how to capture them.

Environmental Systems Integration

Currently, American cities have relied on highly centralized and separate public utility companies to deliver a full range of urban services. Energy is provided by large regional power companies that own and operate power plants and build and maintain power and gas lines. Potable water is delivered by water companies drawing on a complex network of water supplies, ranging from rivers and reservoirs to aqueducts, groundwater wells, and desalination plants, most requiring some form of treatment before delivery. Sewage is collected in an elaborate network of sewer lines (including pumping stations) and treated at large centralized treatment plants before being discharged into the environment (rivers, lakes, and oceans). Municipal solid waste is collected by the city and, in most cases, sorted, with partial recycling (recycling 26 percent, composting 8 percent, and combustion with energy recovery 11.7 percent).[42] The remainder is deposited in landfills or dumped in the ocean. Each of these processes is isolated legally and is increasingly expensive, and many have deferred maintenance challenges. One of the fundamental lessons learned from the case studies is that much can be gained by integrating across systems. But the question is, Who can integrate these systems, and how can it be accomplished? In the case studies, the cities were able to bring the utilities together to collaborate on a more integrated approach, but this may not be as easily initiated in the United States, given the fragmented utility structure.

Nonetheless, large global technology and engineering firms (such as Siemens)[43] are recognizing the business potential of delivering comprehensive, integrated micro-utility systems and services for city neighborhoods and districts. With extensive experience in all elements of the technologies and systems—from neighborhood-scale district heating and cooling systems and waste and wastewater treatment to all forms of power generation, including cogeneration—they are uniquely positioned to provide technical integration across systems. With recent developments in information technology involving wireless sensor networks, it is now possible to manage the whole system across the demand and supply chain, from buildings to smart grids to energy supply, including a full menu of renewables. This enables the balancing of supply with demand, but it also allows switching to have demand follow supply when appropriate.[44] In other words, these large global firms can provide the fully integrated whole-systems "wizardry under the hood" that is necessary to achieve low- to no-carbon operation and close to 100 percent renewable generation, with an important increase in resilience.

In order to deliver a distributed, integrated micro-utility concept, these firms are exploring a variety of business models, depending on the development context. In one model, the firm designs, builds, owns, and operates the system, charging customers a fee for all utility services in one comprehensive utility bill. Such a business model would work for private institutions such as campus communities (similar to West Village, discussed below), retirement communities, resort communities, and private developer communities. Call it the private model. In another model, the firm might contract with public utilities to provide all their services and negotiate fees so they fit with the utility rate structure. Call this the public model. It assumes that the firm can design, build, finance, and operate the system for a profit within the utilities' rate structure. This system has creative financing opportunities, but because the fuels are renewable it is not subject to fluctuations in fuel prices and can guarantee the price for utilities over a fixed period. Obviously, there are also many legal and financial complexities, with many alternatives possible, but the potential of one technology firm taking the responsibility and risk and reaping the rewards of integrating across systems is a powerful new means of achieving more sustainable development.

While the ability to deliver low- to no-carbon and close to 100 percent renewable operation requires the appropriate integrated technologies, the role of the users, the role of building design, the urban form, and the design of the urban landscape are just as critical parts of the whole system. This means that global technology firms cannot do it alone. It requires coordination and collaboration among all the key players in the development process. Each with its own motivation can be an important driver in the process. In the

European case studies we have seen, the cities (in some cases with visionary planners) take the lead in demanding innovation and whole-systems integration from the utilities and architect-developer teams. American cities have the legal authority to assume a similar role. Major institutions such as university campuses also have the potential to be major drivers. With their mission of creating new knowledge through basic and applied research, their concern for life-cycle costs of operation, their jurisdiction over a full range of uses, and their self-interest in creating a campus of the highest environmental quality, they are primed to take a leadership role in driving a more integrated and sustainable development process.[45]

Developers themselves are recognizing the economic benefits of delivering more integrated and sustainable projects because the public has become more knowledgeable about the multiple benefits of "green" environments. Unfortunately, there are too many examples of developers using sustainable or green design as a marketing tool and then delivering only the cheapest, most superficial strategies. In spite of these examples of "greenwashing," some developers are starting to realize the full economic potential of integrated whole-systems design.[46] What is emerging is a change in consciousness about the value of integrated, sustainable whole-systems design on the part of all the key players: city officials are recognizing it as part of their responsibility to the public commons, the public good, public health and well-being, and the resilience of their city; institutional clients are seeing it as part of their core mission; utilities are recognizing that integrated distributed micro-utility systems are not only a valuable economic diversification but also an important contribution to the resilience of their overall systems. Developers are recognizing the value of real sustainability to their bottom line; vertically integrated design, engineering, and technology firms (or teams) not only have the tools but also are recognizing the new business potentials of fully integrated systems. This is a changed climate in the public-private landscape of urban development. What is missing in the United States, to return to Lord Nicholas Stern's observation, are the good examples of what these might be and how they might work. Fortunately, examples are starting to emerge in whole or in part. One project is particularly interesting because it incorporates many of the lessons learned from the European case studies but now in a US context.

West Village, Davis, California

The origins of West Village go back to 2003, when the University of California, Davis, was preparing its long-range development plan. Faced with a no-growth policy by the city of Davis and limited local housing opportuni-

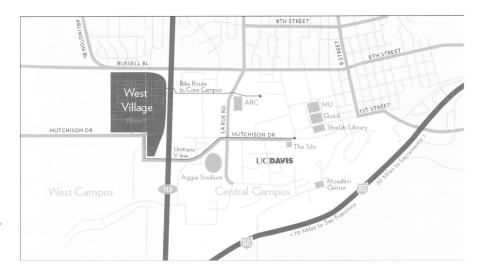

Figure 7.21. Context plan for West Village, Davis, California. *(Source: West Village Community Partnership.)*

ties, UC Davis considered two options for addressing its need for additional student, faculty, and staff housing: (1) maintain the status quo, which would force students, faculty, and staff to commute from long distances (the suburban sprawl model), or (2) create a new campus neighborhood on university land adjacent to the campus connected by bike and bus routes (the smart growth model). Consistent with its long-standing tradition of environmental responsibility, UC Davis chose the latter, and the concept for West Village was born.

From the beginning, the neighborhood was envisioned as a vibrant addition to the campus and city, to include mixed uses, transit options, open space, recreational opportunities, and bikeway connections. It would integrate environmentally sound design practices, drawing on UC Davis faculty expertise, to optimize energy efficiency strategies while generating energy on-site. The initial phase of apartments for students, faculty, and staff (800 beds), 500 square feet of office and retail space, and 20,000 square feet for the Los Rios Community College are currently occupied. Apartments for an additional 1,000 beds are under construction, and planning for 475 single-family homes for purchase is currently under way.

Process and Plan

UC Davis realized from the outset that to accomplish its goals would require a public-private interdisciplinary process. It organized a partnership team including UC Davis (landowner), West Village Community Partnership (developer), Davis Energy Group (energy efficiency consultant), Chevron Energy Solutions (renewable energy integration), Pacific Gas and Electric Company

(PG&E; utility partner), the UC Davis Energy Efficiency Center (faculty advocate and catalyst), and a multidisciplinary advisory committee.

In the beginning, the process involved a long checklist of energy efficiency and renewable energy technologies. It gained focus when the developer decided to create the first zero net energy neighborhood in the United States. This goal motivated the team to examine many design iterations in order to find the most cost-effective balance of reducing energy demand while supplying demand with on-site renewable energy. The research and exploration received considerable outside funding ($7.5 million) from state and federal agencies to support the process. The funds not only supported the analysis of alternatives but also will support ongoing monitoring and research, with the village systems as a living laboratory. The process also involved over thirty community meetings to gain approvals and support. It had many things going for it but also encountered obstacles. Team members said that if they had known how complicated it was going to be, it might have given them pause. Nevertheless, they steadfastly worked to achieve their goals.

Goals

- Zero net energy for the grid on an annual basis
- No higher cost to consumers
- No higher cost to developers
- Deep energy conservation measures
- Multiple integrated renewable resources at a community scale
- Smart grid

Transportation

The plan provides for pedestrian and bicycle traffic and bus transit. The street grid is designed with a comprehensive network of sidewalks and dedicated bike lanes. In addition, informal bike paths meander through some of the apartment courtyards and through one of the north–south boulevards and around the perimeter; all are linked to the central campus by a bike bridge over the freeway. The campus bus system (operated by students) runs north to south to the village square and then on an east–west boulevard such that every unit is within a 5-minute walk of a stop. Bus service will begin with 20-minute headways, which will be increased to every 12 minutes at build-out. Parking is provided primarily on the east perimeter of the site as a buffer to the highway and is shaded by a canopy of photovoltaic panels.

Figure 7.22. Bike and bus transit plan for West Village. *(Source: West Village Community Partnership.)*

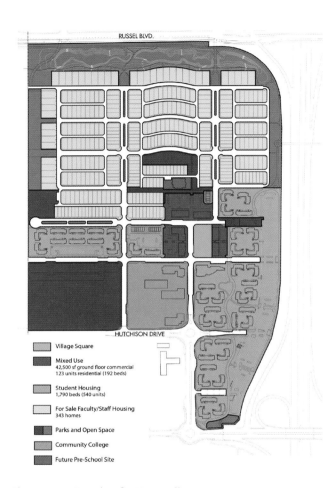

Figure 7.23. Site plan for West Village. *(Source: West Village Community Partnership.)*

Legend:
- Village Square
- Mixed Use — 42,500 sf ground floor commercial; 123 units residential (192 beds)
- Student Housing — 1,790 beds (540 units)
- For Sale Faculty/Staff Housing — 343 homes
- Parks and Open Space
- Community College
- Future Pre-School Site

Urban Form

West Village's urban form is designed to accommodate the following program elements in its final phase:

- Area: 205 acres
- Faculty and staff homes: 475 units
- Student housing: 3,000 beds (1,200 apartments)
- Retail and office space: 45,500 square feet
- Community college: 60,000 square feet
- Gross density: 8 units per acre
- Net density, apartments: 20 units per acre
- Net density, homes: 12 units per acre

The urban form of West Village is a remarkably simple north–south, east–west grid of streets and blocks. The plan centers on a mixed-use village square, which includes the teaching facilities of a local community college, a day care center, a recreational center, and commercial and office space. The village square is located at the intersection of two linear zones of apartment blocks forming an L shape, one stretching north to south and the other running east to west. The square has a village green in the middle that is designed to accommodate a market and social events. A zone for single-family homes is located to the north in a grid of east–west blocks. The single-family zone is linked to the central area by two north–south green boulevards.

Energy

The strategy is simple—reduce energy demand enough to be able to supply the demand by on-site renewables, resulting in zero net energy from the grid. Energy efficiency is accomplished by the following measures:

Building Envelope
- Walls (exterior): 2 x 6 16-inch open cell R-21 batt with 1/2-inch exterior foam. Quality insulation inspection.
- Roof (attic): R-49 blown insulation. Radiant barrier roof sheathing.
- Roofing products: Aged solar reflectance ≥0.2, thermal emittance ≥0.75 (cool roofing products).

- Glazing U-factor, solar heat gain coefficient: Average U-value <0.33, SHGC <0.21.
- Distributed thermal mass: Additional 1/2-inch gypcrete on floors 2 and 3.

Heating, Ventilation, and Air-Conditioning
- Cooling: 12 SEER/12.5 EER heat pump.
- Heating: 8.5 HSPF heat pump.
- Ducts: R-6.0 ducts in conditioned space.
- Fresh air mechanical ventilation: Per ASHRAE 62.2.
- Ceiling fans: In bedrooms.

Water Heating
- Type: central high-performance water heater in each building.

Lighting and Appliances
- High-efficacy lighting: hardwired lighting, fluorescent or LED. Assume 80 percent hardwired lighting. Lighting controls, vacancy sensors.
- Energy Star appliances: Dishwasher, refrigerator, washing machine.
- Cooktop and oven: standard electric.
- Miscellaneous load control: energy usage displays.

Energy efficiency is augmented by climate-responsive building strategies that capture passive solar energy in the winter and employ natural ventilation and external shading in the summer. The result is an estimated reduction in demand versus Title 24 standards of 58 percent on average, from 9,781,500 kWh/y equivalent to 4,067 kWh/y for total energy use in the apartments. For example, in comparison with the European case studies, it is 58 kWh/m²/y versus 140 kWh/m²/y.

Energy for the multifamily housing and mixed-use facilities is supplied by a 4-megawatt installation of photovoltaics with a power purchase agreement between West Village Community Partnership and SunPower. The photovoltaic arrays are located over parking areas and on the roofs of the apartments.

Initially, the photovoltaic system was to be augmented by a biogas digester and microturbine power plant using agricultural

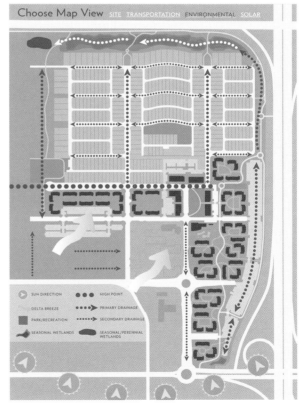

Figure 7.24. Environmental response diagram for West Village. *(Source: West Village Community Partnership.)*

Figure 7.25. View of external shading in West Village. *(Photograph by West Village Community Partnership.)*

Figure 7.26. View of photovoltaic arrays on roofs in West Village. *(Photograph by West Village Community Partnership.)*

Figure 7.27. View of biodigester in West Village. *(Photograph by the University of California, Davis.)*

Figure 7.28. View of storm-water treatment, West Village Square. *(Photograph by West Village Community Partnership.)*

and food waste from the campus. The plant is designed to process twenty-five tons of waste per day. It is estimated that it will generate 32.9 million cubic feet of biogas per year and produce approximately 3 megawatt-hours per year. In the end, it was decided to deliver the electricity to the campus grid, not the neighborhood, in part because the feedstock comes from the campus but also because it is anticipated that the photovoltaic system alone will supply the village demand on an annual basis.

Water

The village site plan incorporates a natural storm-water treatment and retention system in bioswales and retention ponds. The reduction in the capital cost of the storm-water piping system more than covers the cost of the natural system.

Waste

The neighborhood is part of a comprehensive campus recycling system that includes composting of organic waste. Even though it does not capture the potential energy in the food or green waste, it could easily be incorporated in the campus biogas plant in the future, making up for any shortfall in the annual energy supply by photovoltaics.

A US Model

West Village is not only the first US neighborhood to design for zero net energy but also the first US example to employ all of the major lessons learned from the European case studies. Even though no performance data have been reported yet, the strategies are comprehensive and their performance is predictable. In transportation, the pedestrian, bike, and bus systems should reduce car trips by 70–90 percent. The combination of energy efficiency, climate-responsive design, and on-site renewables should be very close to zero carbon operation as predicted. This will most likely be the first US neighborhood to surpass the 80 percent reduction in CO_2 emissions required to stabilize climate change (less than 2 metric tons per year). What is most promising is that this integrated whole-systems approach has been achieved at no net increase in cost to the developer or the residents. In this innovative model, the developer is the financial agent, the third-party intermediary between the utility and the residents. He charges a single utility fee as part of the rent, which is no larger than a typical utility bill. It covers the added cost of energy efficiency measures and climate-responsive designs as well as the purchase agreement with SunPower for photovoltaic electricity. He has a virtual annual net metering agreement with PG&E wherein the utility supplies electricity when needed and buys back electricity when the village produces extra. In this manner, the utility functions as a backup storage system. Accounting is done on a monthly basis and should add up to zero on an annual basis.

The economic model is why columnist Kerry Dolan of *Forbes* magazine wrote, "The most amazing thing about the project? It's not some boondoggle,

Figure 7.29. Aerial view of West Village. *(Photograph by West Village Community Partnership.)*

government-funded utopian experiment." The developer expects to make a profit in the single digits for his investors; as he explains, "It's a market-driven project."[47]

This is also the first US neighborhood to demonstrate the "hidden dimensions": the focus on urban design, the environmental whole-systems wizardry, user engagement with real-time information on energy use, and alternatives to use of the car, which are necessary to make sustainability desirable. The principles are reproducible and could become a new US model. "Made in Davis, California!"

Increasing Opportunities for Low-Carbon Communities: The Role of the Redevelopment Agency

With the renewed urgency in pursuing strategies of both mitigation and adaptation in addressing climate change, as Robert Yaro indicated, we have to rethink all the fundamental systems and processes of city building, operation, and maintenance, including "'hard' infrastructure changes and 'soft' solutions."[48] This means demanding a much more integrated, innovative, and whole-systems approach, bringing the jurisdictionally fragmented city planning agencies, departments, and utilities together to come up with new solutions. This urgency calls attention to the powers of the redevelopment agency, one of the tools cities have to cut across disaggregated and isolated processes and their jurisdictional divides. It gives cities the power to bring the many essential players and constituents to the table, demanding collaboration, cooperation, and innovative whole-systems design. While it has a checkered history, if used creatively it could play a key role in enabling our cities to transition to a low-carbon, more resilient, and environmentally enriched future.

Since the mid-twentieth century, US cities have been granted broad local redevelopment authority by federal law and state enabling legislation. The purpose has been to improve, upgrade, and revitalize areas within cities that have been "blighted" as a result of deterioration, disuse and unproductive conditions, inappropriate zoning, and high vacancy rates. The overall goal has been to improve the cities' health, safety, and welfare—their quality of life and economic vitality. While the enabling legislation varies widely by state, the fundamental tools of a redevelopment agency include the following:

1. The authority to acquire real property
2. The power of eminent domain
3. The authority to develop property
4. The authority to sell property
5. The authority and obligation to relocate persons who have interests in the property acquired

Financing of redevelopment projects has included the sale of tax-exempt bonds and tax increment financing of loans from federal or state governments, and in many cases a portion of up-front planning costs has been absorbed by developers. Cities have been given wide-ranging scope in redevelopment projects as part of the redevelopment process. They include demolition, clearance, and the construction of "real properties which are necessary and convenient or desirable, such as streets, sewers, utilities, parks, site preparation, landscaping, and administrative, community, health, recreational, educational, and welfare facilities." Municipalities have the responsibility for implementing redevelopment plans and projects. This responsibility can be carried out directly or contracted with developers. In short, US cities, through their redevelopment authority, have similar powers, tools, and responsibilities to those exercised by the cities in the four European case studies.

Redevelopment authority in the United States has a mixed history, to the point in some states where redevelopment authority has been repealed.[49] Nonetheless, most cities still have this powerful tool to revitalize and reshape parts of their city.

The role of the city in redevelopment has varied widely around the country, but in general cities have played an enabling role. They identify areas for redevelopment, prepare general plans, including land use and zoning regulations, and either issue requests for proposals from developers or wait for proposals. In some cases, developers come with proposals that require the city to exercise redevelopment authority in order to make projects possible. In this role the city is reactive; it exercises its power by picking and choosing among competing visions by developers. The city provides a general framework of requirements but defers to the developer on issues of market, building types, design, and cost, the assumption being that once the land agreement is reached, the developer bears most of the risk and knows best what the market wants. This model rarely leads to innovation, or it leads to very narrowly framed improvements, because in general developers are very conservative and usually build what they know how to build and what has worked in the past. Clearly, this is neither the model nor the role played by the cities in the case studies. In all four cases, the cities played a major role in leadership, demanding innovation at multiple levels, even shaping the detailed dimensions and requirements of the plan. The question becomes, Can US cities assume such a role?

A careful reading of redevelopment authority law would answer yes, but it will take a very different way of thinking from current practice. Some would argue that cities exercise this kind of leadership through the details of their general plan, zoning requirements, and building codes, in other words, through their rule making. But the planning process is so incremental and disaggregated in its execution that achieving the kind of whole-systems thinking demonstrated in the case studies is extremely difficult. Most likely it will take a visionary city or a visionary developer to come up with a new US model for sustainable development similar to West Village, but the power and authority exist with the city. There is no legal reason why a city cannot designate a redevelopment area where the city becomes the horizontal developer: developing the overall plan; specifying street types, block sizes, land use, density, public transit systems, parks, recreation, and public services; requiring all buildings to meet strict energy efficiency standards; and using its authority to work with utilities to create an integrated, whole-systems approach to energy, water, and waste that is 100 percent renewable. The city can then contract to build the horizontal infrastructure of streets, utilities, parks, and public open space and then sell development sites in small lots to architect-developer teams. Such a process can be funded by the traditional means of tax-free bonds or tax increment financing, but it might also involve the creative involvement of private capital in partnership with the city. In fact, it might be that sustainable neighborhoods can be conceived as start-ups, requiring the investment of venture capital to prod and expand a city's willingness to innovate.

8. Conclusion

The four European case studies and the first American example of a zero net energy neighborhood demonstrate the feasibility of attaining low- to no-carbon and 100 percent renewable energy operations. They illustrate the value added by designing for sustainability at the neighborhood or district scale, in contrast to the building scale or large utility scale. The neighborhood is the in-between scale, the unit so important to city building. It provides not only the conveniences of everyday life but also a sense of identity and belonging. It is so often the neighborhoods that give cities their defining qualities.

The neighborhood scale expands the field of opportunities for integrated whole-systems design thinking. It involves thinking and designing across the multiple flows, scales, and traditional parts of the city as one system. Although none of the case studies was specifically designed for it, the neighborhood scale enables reconceiving its infrastructure as a micro-utility, generating all its energy locally while recycling and reusing its water and waste as a resource. It entails converting the neighborhood electric grid to a quasi-independent "smart grid," which is connected to the electric utility on a virtual annual net metering basis (similar to the arrangement in West Village). This provides greater resilience because the neighborhood can run on its local renewable energy supply if and when central infrastructure services are interrupted. It also means that new development can be incremental and distributed, adding resilience to the citywide system as a whole, one step at a time.

Each subsystem that contributes to this whole-systems approach interacts on multiple levels and across boundaries. By implication, there is no one solution. The case studies create a set of design domains, a framework of issues and considerations to be explored through design. On the other hand, the neighborhoods point to specific baseline metrics (the hidden potential), which are useful in any design exploration.

Process and Plan

The case studies underscore the importance of process as essential in the making of sustainable neighborhoods. The key dimensions in the process include the following:

- *Leadership.* Someone or some agency has to take the lead with the authority to insist on an integrated whole-systems approach to the challenge of achieving low- to no-carbon and 100 percent renewable operation. Leadership means having the vision, the courage of conviction, that it is the right thing to pursue and taking the risk and reaping the reward in the process. The European case studies and the American example demonstrate that leadership can come from the city but also can come from a visionary institution and developer and a visionary urban designer or planner.

- *Interdisciplinary and interagency collaboration.* No one person or agency has all the expertise to get the job done. It involves multiple players—city politicians; multiple city agencies; multiple utilities; design professionals in multiple disciplines, including planning, urban design, architecture, and landscape architecture; and a full complement of engineering disciplines: civil, transportation, energy, water, and waste. The process is complex, requiring a spirit of cooperation and a willingness to invest in the additional expense required. The process itself needs to be carefully planned.

- *Goals.* Setting clear and ambitious goals has been shown to be critical in the process.

- ***Whole-systems technical expertise.*** Whether this comes from the utilities, city departments, private planners, design and engineering consultants, educational institutions, or a collaboration among them all, it is essential in creating whole-systems performance. It means having knowledge and expertise across traditional disciplinary boundaries.

- ***Engagement of homeowners and residents.*** The neighborhoods that have engaged the homeowners and residents in the process from the beginning have been the most successful in achieving their goals. Whether it was educating the residents about the systems, how to use them to "play the game," and why sustainability is important or giving the residents their own cooperative authority to set more aggressive goals, to design and build systems to beat the required targets—either way, the residents' participation in the process has made the difference. It gives them knowledge, ownership, and a stake in the process of creating a more enjoyable and sustainable lifestyle.

When these dimensions are part of the process, it not only increases the chances of creating a sustainable neighborhood that is low to no carbon and 100 percent renewable in operation but also builds a strong sense of community, of belonging to something special, of contributing to the neighborhood's social sustainability.

Transportation and Urban Form

The case studies confirm that the urban form has to be fine-grain, privileging walking, biking, and access to public transit, avoiding total dependence on the private car, as the first step to a lower-carbon, more livable urban future. The specific metrics are similar to those associated with transit-oriented development, or smart growth:

- Transit stops should be within a five-minute walk (one-fourth mile) to jobs and a ten-minute walk (one-half mile) to housing.

- Densities around stops should be at least 12–15 units per acre (small lots with carriage apartments) for bus systems and 20–30 units per acre (townhouses or row houses) for tram or light-rail transit systems.

- Mixed use should include convenience shopping, commercial, live/work, office, and community facilities to provide jobs, to reduce the need for trips outside the neighborhood, and to add resilience.

- The walking environment should optimize the microclimate for comfort and provide interest and convenience.
- Transit headways should be no longer than twelve to fifteen minutes.
- Transit routes should provide connections to desired destinations.

When these metrics are provided, the benefits are multiple: land values within the transit-shed go up, carbon emissions go down as a result of reductions in car trips, and the daily increase in incidental exercise from walking and biking has a dramatic effect in reducing the probability of chronic disease in both children and adults. Most important, freedom of choice in mobility increases livability.

The case studies also demonstrate the robust capacity of the urban perimeter block, as a city building model, to create a richly varied, high-density, mixed-use urban form. The block types can vary in density, coverage, heights, and setbacks, enabling essential climate-responsive building design and also defining an expanded role for the urban landscape in shaping the public realm and delivering eco-services as part of the whole-systems design.

Environmental Systems

The case studies demonstrate that the metrics that enable 100 percent renewable energy supply are simple:

- *Demand reduction.* This is the most important first step. It has been shown that by using a full array of climate-responsive building design strategies (which vary by climate) and energy-efficient appliances, equipment, and lighting with real-time user information and controls, energy demand can be reduced to 40–50 kWh/m²/y cost-effectively in almost all climates. It does require the knowledgeable application of climate-responsive building design wherein the building envelope is conceived as a dynamic environmental filter, capturing assets when available and limiting liabilities. While not absolutely essential, it is assisted by urban block orientations that optimize solar potentials, both passive solar and daylighting (and minimize liabilities), as well as enabling natural ventilation.
- *Renewable supply.* The sources and amounts of renewable energy supply need to be evaluated for each site and can vary widely. All of the case studies use a combination of renewable sources in proportions appropriate to the resources available on their sites. The surprising discovery is that the waste flows—which, unlike wind and solar power, are always available and continuous—can supply a large

percentage of the base demand, up to 50–75 percent, depending on the demand reductions achieved. Capturing the potential energy in the waste flows can be the critical missing link in achieving 100 percent renewable supply. Powering a neighborhood on local renewable energy sources provides an important dimension of resilience that adds an emergency avoided cost value to the systems.

- *Cogeneration.* The case studies confirm the value of using neighborhood or district cogeneration as a central part of the system. It is not absolutely necessary (see Bo01), but it is extremely useful for a simple reason—cogeneration delivers both electricity and heat from a single fuel source. It optimizes the efficiency of energy captured from limited on-site waste flows such as combustible solid waste and biogas from food waste, sludge, and digestible green waste. There are many types and scales of cogeneration (combined heat and power, or CHP) systems, and while the technology is mature and cost-effective at efficiencies of 70–95 percent, technical breakthroughs in both efficiency and cost-effectiveness continue to be developed, even on scales as small as the building scale. The greatest potential of neighborhood-scale cogeneration is its ability to make the neighborhood independent of central utilities for both heating and electricity (at least for as long as its fuel source lasts). This adds a significant measure of resilience to a new neighborhood, but it is also a great retrofit strategy, adding resilience to existing neighborhoods. It becomes even more resilient if its fuel source comes from local waste streams.

- *Waste recovery—"closing the loop."* Once waste is conceived of and used as an energy resource, the way in which it is separated, collected, and processed and the scale and stage in the process at which these steps are performed become important system design considerations. Since the collection and disposal of waste poses a significant cost to cities and is part of residents' daily routines, financial resources and user activities can be redirected to optimize the system, providing the necessary separation and purity of the waste flows. While the experience of capturing waste flows is mixed in one of the case studies (Bo01), the others demonstrate viable systems that are simple and convenient for residents and that are already practiced in many cities around the globe.

When all of these elements and metrics are applied in an integrated systems approach, it is possible to achieve low- to no-carbon and 100 percent renewable operation with much greater resilience than is possible with our current utility models. An added benefit is that the amount of energy required

Figure 8.1. Reduce (maximize efficiency) / produce (waste-to-energy + solar) = zero carbon. *(Diagram by Nancy Nam.)*

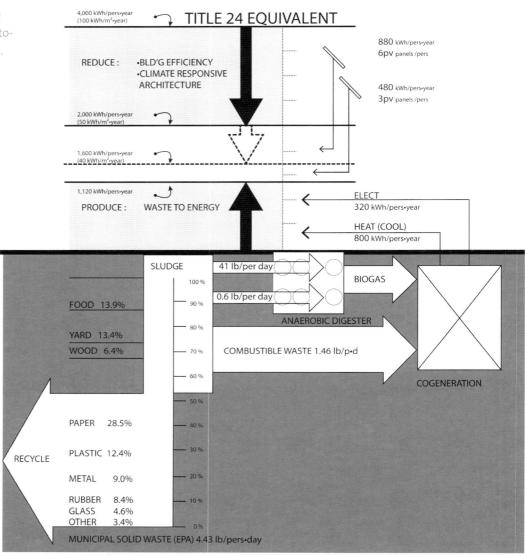

from wind, solar, and geothermal power has been minimized. It also means that the mix, sizing, and cost-effectiveness of these more typical renewables can be optimized for timing and load balancing.

Public Commons

The case studies point to the need for reconceptualizing design of the public commons to include an expanded role of the urban landscape as a three-dimensional green infrastructure, which, in concert with traditional infrastructure, delivers a full range of eco-services and participates in creating an enriched space of public delight. Beyond its customary role of providing all forms of public access, public recreation, social gathering, and aesthetic embellishment, the design of the public commons should address the following potential eco-service dimensions as a part of developing a compelling design identity:

- Microclimate
- Air quality
- Carbon absorption
- Storm-water treatment
- Wastewater treatment
- Biomass production for energy
- Food production
- Habitat creation

When these eco-services are incorporated into the three-dimensional design of public space, it transforms the experience of the traditional city. It replaces a predominantly hardscape infrastructure with one that is dynamic and alive, in which nature in all its sensory presence is reintegrated into the everyday life of the city. The positive effect on health and well-being is measurable; it is supported by research findings indicating that everyday contact with nature "can be seen as an under-utilized public resource in terms of health and well-being."[1]

Figure 8.2. Three-dimensional green infrastructure. *(Drawing by Deepak Sohane.)*

Looking Forward

With the devastation caused by recent severe climate events, a sense of urgency has returned about how to respond to climate change. Fortunately, states such as California have already taken the threat seriously and passed a set of laws that require dramatic reductions in carbon dioxide (CO_2) emissions by 2050.[2] It is generally agreed that an 80–90 percent reduction below 1990 levels is necessary to return our climate to a stable balance, limiting global warming to 2°C (4°F). A large part of the challenge is providing the increase in energy required to supply California's projected growth in population from 37 million to 55 million by 2050, a 48 percent increase. This is where a new model for community development could make a huge impact, but its full potential does not seem to be recognized. A recent study, "California's Energy Future: The View to 2050," conducted by the California Council on Science and Technology (CCST), calls for "aggressive policies, both near and sustained over time, to catalyze and accelerate energy efficiency and electrification,"[3] but it does not specify what these policies should be. The study is primarily a technical assessment of the potential for "energy system portraits" to reduce greenhouse gas emissions. It assumes business as usual in California's existing transportation and land use pattern and its utility structure. The energy system portraits are designed to plug into California's large regional utility model, and they assume energy efficiency at the building scale. This approach is essential to the retrofitting of existing developments and their energy systems. It does identify "behavior change" as part of the measures necessary to reach an 80 percent reduction, but it does not elaborate on what this means. It seems to undervalue the potential effect of new zero-carbon developments at the neighborhood or district scale as an incremental, reproducible, and scalable way to avoid the CO_2 emissions of new development.

Peter Calthorpe challenges the predominantly technological CCST approach in his book *Urbanism in the Age of Climate Change*. He argues that trying to provide a technological fix for the challenge of energy supply without addressing the root causes of increases in energy demand is "absurd." He argues, "Responding to climate change . . . without a more sustainable form of urbanism will be impossible."[4] He calls for a new form of "green" urbanism that is more compact, mixed-use, transit oriented, building energy efficient, water conserving, and infrastructure cost saving (see his scenario impacts) as a way to achieve the necessary reductions.

The Hidden Potential of Sustainable Neighborhoods gives the first detailed account and demonstration of how to achieve what Calthorpe calls the "12 percent solution"[5]—"green" urbanism. The neighborhoods show that reductions in CO_2 emissions to 1.6 tons per person-year are feasible with a whole-systems approach in which the urbanism, the environmental systems wizardry, and the residents combine to deliver the reductions: approximately 50 percent through reductions in vehicle miles traveled and 50 percent through building energy efficiency and use of on-site renewables. They also show that they can be accomplished incrementally as part of a development process, one that does not require a major change in policies (although incentives and laws mandating reductions help). What it requires is a new way of thinking—a whole-systems approach to all the elements and processes of community building. In short, the lessons learned from the European case studies and the first US example present what Buckminster Fuller described as "a new model, which makes the old model obsolete."

The fact that the US metropolitan landscape is replete with land use opportunities to infill new growth and development using these lessons is promising. The process has already begun in many cities but only partially, without the more complete whole-systems approach necessary to get down to the required reductions. West Village, the first US example of a whole-systems zero net energy neighborhood, could signal the beginning of a paradigm shift. Even though it is still under construction, it is the most promising market-driven public-private partnership in which the private developer is making a profit, and it has gone through a US approval process with all the systems that deliver zero net energy still intact.

The most promising potential discovered in the case studies and the US example is that the neighborhoods are wonderful places to live and have the potential to be more resilient. The process of designing for sustainability has created a more environmentally enriched, healthier, and more comfortable, flexible, socially rewarding, and equitable urban existence, which can be made to run on its own locally available resources. Designing for sustainability does not have to compromise any amenities or conveniences; in fact, it increases them. It does not have to be a distasteful medicine necessary to combat climate change. Many of the elements that contribute to system sustainability are not "under the hood"; they are out in the open, adding sensory delight to daily existence. This is especially true of the expanded role of the urban landscape, the three-dimensional green infrastructure and its eco-services. As these differences are recognized, the hidden potential of sustainable neighborhoods will make them objects of desire.

At its core, this book is much more than a prescriptive description of lessons learned. It is about recognizing and recovering our commitment to, and responsibility for, the design of the public commons as an essential component in a whole-systems approach to a healthier, more equitable, environ-

scenarios:
impacts

SINGLE-FAMILY HOMES IN AN AUTO-BASED ENVIRONMENT.
LARGELY MULTIFAMILY HOUSING IN A CITY CONTEXT.

Trend Sprawl   **Simple Urbanism**

Today the average household travels around 24,000 miles, in a Trend future that increases to over 28,000 while a more urban future reduces that number by 43 percent.

VMT PER HOUSEHOLD

28,600 MILES / HOUSEHOLD   16,400 MILES / HOUSEHOLD

Auto fuel consumption is a burden on our economy, the environment, and our security. Reductions can be gained through more efficient vehicles as well as less driving.

FUEL CONSUMPTION

7.7 TRILLION GALLONS   5.7 TRILLION GALLONS

GHG emissions summed here include residential and commercial buildings as well as personal transportation. These sectors represent over 50 percent of our total GHG emissions today.

GHG EMISSIONS

4,800 MMT   3,600 MMT

Over 15 percent of our urban areas now have levels of pollutants exceeding national standards. The resulting health costs and worker absenteeism are damaging in many ways.

AIR POLLUTION

11.6 MILLION TONS   6.6 MILLION TONS

Cost is the sum of household energy and water utilities combined with the expense of owning, maintaining, insuring, and fuel for transportation.

ANNUAL COST PER HOUSEHOLD

$26,600 $18,500

Figure 8.3. Calthorpe scenario impacts—12 percent solution. *(Source: Peter Calthorpe, Urbanism in the Age of Climate Change [Washington, DC: Island Press, 2010].)*

Urbanism provides more places in which people can drive less. This results in lower
fuel demands, less GHG emissions, less freeway construction, and lower air pollution
levels. When combined with more efficient buildings this reduces average household
costs for utilities and transportation significantly. It also results in less time in cars
and the possibility of more time with family and friends.

TREND SPRAWL WITH GREEN TECHNOLOGY & RENEWABLES.

SIMPLE URBANISM WITH TECHNOLOGY & RENEWABLES.

Green Sprawl

Green Urbanism

DIFFERENCE
TREND SPRAWL VS. GREEN URBANISM

28,600 MILES / HOUSEHOLD

16,400 MILES / HOUSEHOLD

12,200 FEWER MILES

5.3 TRILLION GALLONS

4.1 TRILLION GAL.

Equivalent
to more than
50 YEARS OF OIL
imported to the U.S.

1,500 MMT

1,080 LBS

Offset equal to
forest covering
2/3 OF THE U.S.

11.6 MILLION TONS

6.6 MILLION TONS

43% REDUCTION
in auto air pollution

$18,400

$11,500

Savings more than
$15,000 PER HOUSEHOLD IN 2050

the **12%** solution

mentally enriched, and delight-filled urban future. This is an expanded notion of the public commons beyond just the public space of cities, as important as that space has been shown to be. It includes the idea of the public commons as a public good, central to our professional responsibility. The legal basis for licensure of the design professions is based on the role that the built environment plays in public health, safety, and welfare. It can be argued that the whole-systems approach and the hidden potential presented in this book give a foundation on which to fulfill this responsibility more broadly and deeply conceived; and yet they are just a first-generation beginning. The more expansive implications of their design potentials for our future well-being are still to be discovered.

Notes

Chapter 1. Introduction

1. Robert D. Yaro, Regional Plan Association, "Before the Next Storm," November 12, 2012, http://www.rpa .org/2012/11/before-the-next-storm .html (accessed January 7, 2013).

2. Peter Calthorpe, *Urbanism in the Age of Climate Change* (Washington, DC: Island Press, 2010), 8.

3. *Homo ludens* refers to "man the player." The concept is introduced in a book by Johan Huizinga titled *Homo ludens: A Study of the Play-Element in Culture*, first published in 1938.

4. Work of the studio is published in a 2005 report by the Tianjin Urban Planning and Design Institute and the University of California, Berkeley, College of Environmental Design, "Principles and Prototypes—Tianjin Transit-Oriented Development." See also Harrison Fraker, "Unforbidden Cities," *California* 117, no. 5 (September/October 2006): 44–49.

5. The EcoBlock concept is summarized in an August 2007 report by ARUP Americas, Inc., "Qingdao EcoBlock Prototype, Pre-Feasibility Study Report."

6. William J. Clinton Foundation and US Green Building Council, "Clinton Climate Initiative to Demonstrate Model for Sustainable Urban Growth with Projects in Ten Countries on Six Continents," press release, May 18, 2009.

7. Author's notes from a presentation by Lord Nicholas Stern in the closing plenary session of the Copenhagen Climate Change Congress, March 10–12, 2009.

8. Adam Ritchie and Randall Thomas, eds., *Sustainable Urban Design: An Environmental Approach*, 2nd ed. (London: Taylor and Francis, 2009), 3.

Chapter 2. Bo01, Malmö, Sweden

1. Bengt Persson, ed., *Sustainable City of Tomorrow: Bo01—Experiences of a Swedish Housing Exposition* (Stockholm: Formas [Swedish Research Council for Environment, Agricultural Sciences and Spatial Planning], 2005), 9.

2. Ibid., 7.

3. Ibid., 9.

4. Ibid.

5. Ibid.

6. Ibid., 11.

7. Ibid., 12.

8. Ibid., 39.

9. Ibid., 42.

10. Ibid.

11. Ibid., 14.

12. Klas Tham, "Bo01: City of Tomorrow" (unpublished paper, March 2007).

13. Persson, *Sustainable City of Tomorrow*, 51.

14. Ibid., 52.

15. Ibid., 43.

16. Ibid., 45.

17. Ibid., 53.

18. William McDonough and Michael Braungart, *Cradle to Cradle: Remaking the Way We Make Things* (New York: North Point Press, 2002).

19. Persson, *Sustainable City of Tomorrow*, 14.

20. Ibid., 35.

21. Ibid., 39.

22. Ibid.

Chapter 3. Hammarby Sjöstad, Stockholm, Sweden

1. Cas Poldermans, "Sustainable Urban Development: The Case of Hammarby Sjöstad" (Stockholm: Stockholm University, Department of Human Geography, 2006), 11, http://www.hammarbysjostad.se/miljo/pdf/CasPoldermans.pdf.

2. Stockholm City Planning Administration, "Hammarby Sjöstad" (Stockholm: City of Stockholm, 2007), 1.

3. Poldermans, "Sustainable Urban Development," 16.

4. Ibid., 18.

5. Stockholm City Planning Administration, "Neighborhood Planning Quality Guidelines" (Stockholm: City of Stockholm, 2005), 1.

6. Stockholm City Planning Administration, "Hammarby Sjöstad," 3.

7. GlashusEtt, *Hammarby Sjöstad: A Unique Environmental Project in Stockholm* (Stockholm: City of Stockholm, 2007), 11.

8. Poldermans, "Sustainable Urban Development," 25.

9. David Fannon, "Hammarby Sjöstad: Report for Arch 209" (Berkeley: University of California, College of Environmental Design, November 2009).

10. GlashusEtt, *Hammarby Sjöstad*, 8.

11. Ibid., 10.

12. Poldermans, "Sustainable Urban Development," 23.

13. Fannon, "Hammarby Sjöstad: Report."

14. Poldermans, "Sustainable Urban Development," 24.

15. GlashusEtt, *Hammarby Sjöstad*, 17.

16. Fannon, "Hammarby Sjöstad: Report."

17. GlashusEtt, *Hammarby Sjöstad*, 21.

18. Ibid., 18.

19. Ibid., 27.

20. Ibid., 19.

21. Future Communities, "Hammarby Sjöstad, Stockholm, Sweden, 1995 to 2015: Building a 'Green' City Extension," http://www

.futurecommunities.net/case-studies
/hammarby-sjostad-stockholm-
sweden-1995-2015 (accessed December
12, 2012).

22. Ibid.

Chapter 4. Kronsberg, Hannover, Germany

1. Karin Rumming, ed., foreword to *Hannover Kronsberg Handbook: Planning and Realisation* (Leipzig: Jütte Druck, 2004), 4.

2. Inge Schottkowski-Bahre, ed., *Modell Kronsberg: Sustainable Building for the Future* (Leipzig: Jütte Druck, 2000), 9.

3. Rumming, *Hannover Kronsberg Handbook*, 47.

4. Ibid., 48.

5. Ibid., 50.

6. Ibid., 53.

7. Ibid.

8. Ibid.

9. Ibid., 56.

10. Ibid., 23.

11. Ibid., 51.

12. Ibid., 54.

13. Ibid., 120.

14. Ibid.

15. Ibid.

16. Ibid., 122.

17. Ibid., 71.

18. Ibid., 78.

19. Ibid., 82.

20. Ibid., 14.

21. Ibid., 15.

Chapter 5. Vauban, Freiburg, Germany

1. Chris Turner, "Solar Settlement," *Azure*, January 5, 2007, 2.

2. Jan Scheuerer, "Vauban District, Freiburg, Germany" (Perth, Western Australia: Murdoch University, Institute for Social Sustainability, 2009), 1, http://www.vauban.de/info/abstract.html (accessed January 19, 2012).

3. Ibid.

4. Ibid., 2, http://www.vauban.de/info/abstract2.html.

5. Ibid., 1, http://www.vauban.de/info/abstract.html.

6. Ibid.

7. Ibid.

8. Elisabeth Rosenthal, "In German Suburb, Life Goes On without Cars," *New York Times*, May 11, 2009, http://www.nytimes.com/2009/05/12/science/earth/12suburb.html (accessed May 15, 2012).

9. Hannes Linck, *Quartier Vauban: A Guided Tour* (Freiburg: District Association Vauban, 2009), 17.

10. Ibid., 13.

11. Scheuerer, "Vauban District," 4, http://www.vauban.de/info/abstract4.html.

12. Ibid.

13. Linck, *Quartier Vauban*, 19.

14. Scheuerer, "Vauban District," 4, http://www.vauban.de/info/abstract4.html.

15. Linck, *Quartier Vauban*, 41, 43.

Chapter 6. Observations across Neighborhoods

1. William J. Clinton Foundation and US Green Building Council, "Clinton Climate Initiative to Demonstrate Model for Sustainable Urban Growth with Projects in Ten Countries on Six Continents," press release, May 18, 2009.

2. Climate Positive Development Program, within the Sustainable Communities Initiative of the C40 Cities Climate Leadership Group.

3. Interviews by author with Bo01 planner Eva Dahlman, December 2008, Malmö, Sweden, and Hammarby Sjöstad planner Malin Olsson, March 2009, Stockholm, Sweden.

4. Author's calculation.

5. US Centers for Disease Control and Prevention, "How Much Physical Activity Do You Need?," http://www.cdc.gov/physicalactivity/everyone/guidelines/index.html (accessed July 5, 2012).

6. Richard J. Jackson, *Designing Healthy Communities* (companion book to PBS series of the same title) (San Francisco: Jossey-Bass, 2012).

7. Although its antecedents go back to a student's thesis in 1994, "landscape urbanism" is generally recognized as having begun with James Corner (Field Operations) and others at the University of Pennsylvania School of Design. It coalesced at a conference sponsored by the Graham Foundation in 1997 titled "Landscape Urbanism" and has been publicized by Charles Waldheim in The *Landscape Urbanism Reader* (New York: Princeton Architectural Press, 2006).

8. Cecily Maller et al., "Healthy Nature Healthy People: 'Contact with Nature' as an Upstream Health Promotion Intervention for Populations," *Health Promotions International* 21, no. 1 (March 2006): 45–54, http://heapro.oxfordjournals.org/content/21/1/45.full.pdf+html (accessed August 8, 2012).

9. Ibid., 51.

10. Ibid., 52.

11. Reported to the author by the Lund City Planning Office, Lund, Sweden, May 2012.

12. Melanie Dodd, "Overview," in Esther Charlesworth and Rob Adams, eds., *The EcoEdge: Urgent Design Challenges in Building Sustainable Cities* (New York: Routledge, 2011), 10.

Chapter 7. A Road Map for the United States and Beyond

1. Peter Muller, "Transportation and Urban Growth: The Shaping of the American Metropolis," *Focus* 36, no. 2 (Summer 1986): 8–17, http://www.web1.cnre.vt.edu/lsg/Intro/trans.htm (accessed July 20, 2012).

2. Patrick M. Condon, *Seven Rules for Sustainable Communities: Design Strategies for the Post-Carbon World* (Washington, DC: Island Press, 2010), 17–22.

3. Ibid., 18, 19.

4. Muller, "Transportation and Urban Growth."

5. Ibid.

6. For a discussion, refer to "Shrinking Cities," *Planetizen*, http://www .planetizen.com/taxonomy/term/697 (accessed July 14, 2012).

7. Stewart Brand, *How Buildings Learn: What Happens after They're Built* (New York: Viking Press, 1994).

8. For example, see Hacienda Business Park, a planned unit development at the Pleasanton, California, BART station.

9. US Environmental Protection Agency, "Making Smart Growth Happen," http://www.epa.gov/dced /sg_implementation.htm (accessed November 16, 2012).

10. American Public Transportation Association, *2011 Public Transportation Fact Book*, 62nd ed. (Washington, DC: American Public Transportation Association, April 2011), 7, table 1, "Number of Public Transportation Service Systems by Mode," http:// www.apta.com/resources/statistics /Documents/FactBook/APTA_2011 _Fact_Book.pdf (accessed November 12, 2012).

11. Brian McKenzie and Melanie Rapino, *Commuting in the United States: 2009*, American Community Survey Reports ACS-15 (Washington, DC: US Census Bureau, September 2011), http://www .census.govprod/2011pubs/acs-15.pdf (accessed October 13, 2012).

12. Robert Cervero, *The Transit Metropolis: A Global Inquiry* (Washington, DC: Island Press, 1998).

13. Robert T. Dunphy et al., *Developing around Transit: Strategies and Solutions That Work* (Washington, DC: Urban Land Institute, 2004).

14. Reid Ewing and Robert Cervero, "Travel and the Built Environment," *Journal of the American Planning Association* 76, no. 3 (May 2010): 265–94.

15. Robert Cervero and Erick Guerra, "Urban Densities and Transit: A Multi-dimensional Perspective," Working Paper UCB-ITS-VWP-2011-6 (Berkeley: University of California, Institute of Transportation Studies, 2011), http:// www.its.berkeley.edu/publications /UCB/2011/VWP/UCB-ITS-VWP-2011-6 .pdf.

16. Erick Guerra and Robert Cervero, "Cost of a Ride: The Effects of Densities on Fixed-Guideway Transit Ridership and Costs," *Journal of the American Planning Association* 77, no. 3 (Summer 2011): 267–90.

17. Rob Adams, "Reprogramming Cities for Increased Populations and Climate Change," in Esther Charlesworth and Rob Adams, eds., *The EcoEdge: Urgent Design Challenges in Building Sustainable Cities* (New York: Routledge, 2011), 36.

18. California Council on Science and Technology, "California's Energy Future: The View to 2050," Summary Report (Sacramento, CA: California Council on Science and Technology, May 2011). Converting to biofuels, electricity, or both for vehicle fuels is among the first four actions recommended in the report's "Key Findings and Messages" section.

19. Energy efficiency strategies are highlighted by Robert Socolow and Stephen Pacala in the article "Stabilization Wedges: Solving the Climate Problem for the Next Fifty Years with Current Technologies," *Science* 305, no. 5686 (August 13, 2004): 968–72.

20. Edward Mazria, videotaped testimony before the US Senate Committee on Energy and Natural Resources, February 26, 2009, http://architecture2030.org/multimedia/videos (accessed September 16, 2012).

21. US Environmental Protection Agency, "Municipal Solid Waste (MSW) in the United States: Facts and Figures," http://www.epa.gov/osw/nonhaz/municipal/msw99.htm (accessed September 9, 2012).

22. Calculation by author using biogas production and electric generation efficiencies from OnSite Power Systems.

23. See the cost reduction curve for solar photovoltaics in figure 7.5.

24. The photovoltaics on the building in Bo01 are owned and operated by the energy company Sydkraft.

25. For further information, see Paul Rauber, "Solar for All," *Sierra*, January/February 2013.

26. Valerie Nelson, "Achieving the Water Commons: The Role of Decentralised Systems," in *Water Sensitive Cities*, ed. Carol Howe and Cynthia Mitchell (London: IWA Publishing, 2011), 10.

27. Ibid., 15.

28. Ibid., 11, 13.

29. Harvey Bryan and Dan Hoffman, "Comfort/Urban Heat Island Study: Downtown Phoenix Urban Form Project" (Tempe: Arizona State University, 2008).

30. Art Rosenfeld, "White Roofs to Cool Your Building, Your City and (This Is New!) Cool the World" (presentation to Global Superior Energy Performance Partnership [GSEP] Working Group on Cool Roofs and Pavements, Crystal City, VA, September 12, 2011), http://www.globalcoolcities.org/wp-content/uploads/2011/09/Rosenfeld-Presentation.pdf (accessed November 12, 2012).

31. Ibid., 22.

32. Jun Yang et al., "The Urban Forest in Beijing and Its Role in Air Pollution Reduction," *Urban Forestry and Urban Greening* 3, no. 2 (2005): 65–78.

33. Martin Felsen, "Urban Design with Water, USA" (presentation at SUDes Conference "Urban Water, Urban Form," Lund University, Lund, Sweden, September 21, 2011).

34. National Research Council, *Water Reuse: Potential for Expanding the Nation's Water Supply through Reuse of Municipal Wastewater* (Washington, DC: National Academies Press, 2012), http://www.nap.edu/catalog.php?record_id=13303 (accessed October 12, 2012).

35. Vicki Elmer and Harrison Fraker, "Water, Neighborhoods and Urban Design: Micro-utilities and the Fifth Infrastructure," in *Water Sensitive Cities*, ed. Carol Howe and Cynthia

Mitchell (London: IWA Publishing, 2011), 193–207.

36. Environmental Protection Agency, "Municipal Solid Waste."

37. Cecily Maller et al., "Healthy Nature Healthy People: 'Contact with Nature' as an Upstream Health Promotion Intervention for Populations," *Health Promotions International* 21, no. 1 (March 2006): 51, http://heapro .oxfordjournals.org/content/21/1/45 .full.pdf+html (accessed August 8, 2012).

38. Lester R. Brown, *World on the Edge: How to Prevent Environmental and Economic Collapse* (Washington, DC: Earth Policy Institute, 2011).

39. Environmental Protection Agency, "Making Smart Growth Happen."

40. Ibid.

41. Net energy is the sum of the energy taken from and delivered back to the utility on an annual basis.

42. Environmental Protection Agency, "Municipal Solid Waste."

43. Author's discussion with Siemens leadership, Beijing, January 13, 2012.

44. Randy Katz et al., "An Information-Centric Energy Infrastructure: The Berkeley View," *Sustainable Computing: Informatics and Systems* 1, no. 1 (March 2011): 7–22.

45. The first US example of a zero net energy neighborhood (described later in this chapter) is an example of this kind of leadership and collaboration.

46. For a description of these powers, see Local Redevelopment and Housing Law N.J.S. 40A:12A1–63, http://www .state.nj.us/dca/divisions/dlgs /programs.au_docs/40a_12a_1.pdf (accessed September 10, 2012).

47. Kerry A. Dolan, "Largest U.S. 'Zero Net Energy' Community Opens in California at UC Davis," *Forbes*, October 14, 2011, http://www.forbes .com/sites/kerryadolan/2011/10/14 /largest-u-s-zero-net-energy-com munity-opens-in-california-at-uc -davis/2/.

48. Robert D. Yaro, Regional Plan Association, "Before the Next Storm," November 12, 2012, http://www.rpa .org/2012/11/before-the-next-storm .html (accessed January 7, 2013).

49. For an update on Governor Jerry Brown's efforts to repeal California redevelopment law, see Karen Gullo, "California Court Strikes Down Redevelopment Funds Law," *Bloomberg Businessweek*, January 4, 2012, http://www.businessweek.com /news/2012-01-04/california-court -strikes-down-redevelopment-funds -law.html (accessed January 5, 2012).

Chapter 8: Conclusion

1. Cecily Maller et al., "Healthy Nature Healthy People: 'Contact with Nature' as an Upstream Health Promotion Intervention for Populations," *Health Promotions International* 21, no. 1 (March 2006): 52, http://heapro .oxfordjournals.org/content/21/1/45 .full.pdf+html.

2. See California Assembly Bill 32, Global Warming Solutions Act, http://

www.arb.ca.gov/cc/ab32/ab32.htm, and Senate Bill 375, Sustainable Communities, http://www.leginfo .ca.gov/pub/07-08/bill/sen/sb_0351 -0400/sb_375_bill_20080930 _chaptered.pdf.

3. California Council on Science and Technology, "California's Energy Future: The View to 2050," Summary Report (Sacramento: California Council on Science and Technology, May 2011), 3.

4. Peter Calthorpe, *Urbanism in the Age of Climate Change* (Washington, DC: Island Press, 2010), 7.

5. Ibid., plates 20–23.

Index